(ISC)²®

Certified Cloud Security Professional

Official Study Guide

(ISC)²® CCSP®
Certified Cloud Security Professional
Official Study Guide

Ben Malisow

SYBEX®
A Wiley Brand

Acknowledgments

The author would like to thank (ISC)² for making this work possible, and the sublime publishing and editing team at Sybex, including Jim Minatel, Kelly Talbot, Katie Wisor, and Christine O'Connor. This book is dedicated to all the candidates seeking CCSP certification; I hope it helps.

About the Author

Ben Malisow,   CISSP, CISM, CCSP, SSCP, and Security+, is an instructor for (ISC)^2, teaching prep classes for the CISSP, CCSP, and SSCP certifications. He has been in the information technology and information security field for almost 25 years. He wrote the internal IT security policy for DARPA, served as the information system security manager for the FBI's most-classified counterterror intelligence-sharing network, and helped develop the IT security architecture for the Department of Homeland Security's Transportation Security Administration. Ben has taught courses at many schools and universities, including Carnegie Mellon's CERT/SEI, UTSA, the College of Southern Nevada, and grades 6–12 in the public school system in Las Vegas. He is widely published in the field, having written for SecurityFocus.com, *ComputerWorld*, and various other publications as well as several books. You can find his blog at Securityzed.com.

About the Technical Editor

Aaron Kraus began his career as a security auditor for US federal government clients. From there he moved into security risk management for healthcare and financial services, which offered more opportunities to travel, explore, and eat amazing food around the world. He currently works for a cyber risk insurance startup in San Francisco and spends his free time dabbling in cooking, cocktail mixology, and photography.

Contents at a Glance

Contents

Introduction

The Certified Cloud Security Professional (CCSP) certification satisfies the growing demand for trained and qualified cloud security professionals. It is not easy to earn this credential; the exam is extremely difficult, and the endorsement process is lengthy and detailed.

The *CCSP (ISC)² Official Study Guide* offers the cloud professional a solid foundation for taking and passing the Certified Cloud Security Professional (CCSP) exam. However, if you plan on taking the exam to earn the certification, this cannot be stressed enough: **you cannot expect to pass the exam using this book as your sole source.** Please refer to the list of additional recommended reading at the end of this introduction.

(ISC)²

The CCSP exam is governed by (ISC)². (ISC)² is a global not-for-profit organization with four primary mission goals:

- Maintain the Common Body of Knowledge (CBK) for the field of information systems security.
- Provide certification for information systems security professionals and practitioners.
- Conduct certification training and administer the certification exams.
- Oversee the ongoing accreditation of qualified certification candidates through continued education.

A board of directors elected from the ranks of its certified practitioners operates the (ISC)².

(ISC)² supports and provides a wide variety of certifications, including the CISSP, SSCP, CAP, CSSLP, HCISPP, and CCSP. These certifications are designed to verify the knowledge and skills of IT security professionals across all industries. You can obtain more information about the organization and its other certifications by visiting www.isc2.org.

Topical Domains

The CCSP certification covers material from the six topical domains. They are as follows:

- Domain 1: Cloud Concepts, Architecture, and Design
- Domain 2: Cloud Data Security
- Domain 3: Cloud Platform and Infrastructure Security
- Domain 4: Cloud Application Security
- Domain 5: Cloud Security Operations
- Domain 6: Legal, Risk, and Compliance

These domains cover all of the pertinent areas of security related to the cloud. All the material in the certification are vendor- and product-agnostic. Each domain also contains a list of topics and subtopics the CCSP-certified professional is expected to know.

The detailed list of domains/topics of knowledge, experience requirements, exam procedures, and exam domain weights can be found in the CCSP Certification Exam Outline: https://www.isc2.org/-/media/ISC2/Certifications/Exam-Outlines/ CCSP-Exam-Outline.ashx.

Prequalifications

(ISC)^2 has defined the qualifications and requirements you must meet to become a CCSP:

- A minimum of five years of cumulative, paid, full-time information technology experience of which three years must be in information security and one year in one of the six domains of the CCSP examination

- Earning the Cloud Security Alliance's CCSK certificate may be substituted for one year of experience in one of the six domains of the CCSP examination.

- Earning the CISSP credential may be substituted for the entire CCSP experience requirement.

Candidates who do not meet these requirements may still sit for the exam and become an Associate of (ISC)^2. Associates have six years (from passing the exam) to fulfill any remaining experience requirements.

Certified members of (ISC)^2 must also adhere to the (ISC)^2 formal code of ethics, which can be found on the (ISC)^2 website at www.isc2.org/ethics.

Overview of the CCSP Exam

The CCSP exam typically consists of 125 multiple-choice questions covering the six domains of the CCSP CBK, and you must achieve a score of 70 percent or better to pass.

You will have three hours to complete the exam. Twenty-five of the questions will be unscored questions used solely for research purposes. Be sure to answer every question as best you can because you will not know which questions are scored and which are not and you will receive 0 points for unanswered questions. Points are not subtracted for incorrect answers; never leave any question unanswered, even if your answer is a guess.

CCSP Exam Question Types

Most of the questions on the CCSP exam are in the multiple-choice format, with four options and a single correct answer. Some are straightforward, such as asking you to identify a definition. Other questions will ask you to identify an appropriate concept or best practice. Here is one example:

1. Putting sensitive operational information in a database away from the production environment in order to provide higher protection and isolation is called _____.

    A. Randomization

    B. Elasticity

    C. Obfuscation

    D. Tokenization

You must select the one correct or best answer. Sometimes the answer will seem obvious to you, and other times it will be harder to discriminate between two good answers and pick the best. Watch out for general, specific, universal, superset, and subset answer selections. In other cases, none of the answers will seem correct. In these instances, you will want to select the least incorrect answer. There are also questions that are based on theoretical scenarios, where you must answer several questions given a specific situation.

> The correct answer to the question above is option D, tokenization. In a tokenized arrangement, sensitive information is placed in a database away from the production environment, and tokens (representing the stored sensitive information) are stored in a database within the production environment. In order to select the correct answer, the reader has to understand how tokenization works and how that method can be used to isolate sensitive data from the production environment; the question does not mention tokens or tokenization, so it requires complex thought. An easier answer would be "data segregation," but that's not an option. This is not an easy question.

In addition to the standard multiple-choice question format, (ISC)^2 has added a new question format that uses a drag-and-drop approach. For instance, you may see a list of items on one side of the screen that you need to drag and drop onto their appropriate counterparts on the other side of the screen. Other interactive questions may include matching terms with definitions and clicking on specific areas of a chart or graphic. These interactive questions are weighted with a higher point value than the multiple-choice type, so you should pay extra attention when answering them.

Study and Exam Preparation Tips

I recommend planning for at least 30 days of intensive studying for the CCSP exam. I have compiled a list of tips that should help:

- Take one or two evenings to read each chapter thoroughly and work through the review material at the end.

- Think about joining a study group, to share insight and perspective with other candidates.

- Answer all the review questions and take the practice exams on the Sybex website associated with this book (see details on the back cover).

- Complete the written labs from each chapter.

- Before you move on to the next section of work, be sure to review the previous day's study to be sure you are retaining the information.

- Take study breaks but stay on track.

- Put together a study plan.

- Review the (ISC)^2 Exam Outline.

Advice on Taking the Exam

Here are some test-taking tips and general guidelines:

- Answer easy questions first. You can mark all of the questions you are unsure of and go back over them after you have completed the exam.

- Eliminate incorrect answers first.

- Be careful of double negatives in the language of the question.

- Read the questions carefully to ensure you fully understand them.

- *Take your time.* Do not hurry. Rushing leads to test anxiety and loss of focus.

- Take a bathroom break and a breather if you need to, but keep it short. You want to maintain your focus.

- Observe all exam center procedures. Even if you've previously taken an exam at a Pearson Vue center, some have slightly different requirements.

Manage your time. You have three hours to answer 125 questions. That equates to just a bit less than two minutes per question, which in most cases is more than enough time.

Make sure you get plenty of sleep the night before. Be sure to bring any food or drink you think you might need, although they will be stored while you are taking the exam. Also, remember to bring any medications you need to take and alert the staff of any condition that might interfere with your test taking, such as diabetes or heart disease. No test or certification is worth your health.

You may not wear a watch into the test lab. There are timers on the computers and in the testing labs. You must also empty your pockets, with the exception of your locker key and ID.

You must bring at least one picture ID with a signature, such as a driver's license, with you to the testing center, and you should have at least one more form of ID with a signature. Arrive at least 30 minutes early to the testing site to make sure you have everything you need. Bring the registration form that you received from the testing center along with your IDs.

Completing the Certification Process

Once you have successfully completed the CCSP exam, there are a few more things to do before you have earned your new credential. First, transmission of your (ISC)^2 score happens automatically. You will receive instructions on the printed results from your test as you leave the testing center. They will include instructions on how to download your certification form, which will ask you for things such as whether you already have another (ISC)^2 credential (such as the CISSP) and similar questions. Once completed, you will need to sign and submit the form to (ISC)^2 for approval. Usually, you will receive notice of your official certification within three months. Once you are fully certified, you can use the CCSP designation in your signatures and other places of importance, per (ISC)^2 usage guidelines.

Notes on This Book's Organization

This book covers all of the six CCSP Common Body of Knowledge (CBK) domains in sufficient depth to provide you with a basic understanding of the necessary material. The main body of the book is composed of 11 chapters that are arranged as follows:

Chapter 1: Architectural Concepts

Chapter 2: Design Requirements

Chapter 3: Data Classification

Chapter 4: Cloud Data Security

Chapter 5: Security in the Cloud

Chapter 6: Responsibilities in the Cloud

Chapter 7: Cloud Application Security

Chapter 8: Operations Elements

Chapter 9: Operations Management

Chapter 10: Legal and Compliance Part 1

Chapter 11: Legal and Compliance Part 2

Obviously, the book does not follow the order of the domains or the official exam outline. Instead, the chapters of the book are arranged in a way to explain the material in a narrative format that conveys the concepts in a linear manner.

Each chapter includes elements designed to assist you in your studies and to test your knowledge of the material presented in the chapter. It is recommended that you read Chapter 1 first to best orient yourself in the subject matter before moving on to the other chapters.

Please see the table of contents and chapter introductions for more detailed domain topics covered in each chapter.

Elements of This Study Guide

This study guide contains several core elements that will help you prepare for the CCSP exam and the real world beyond it:

Real World Scenarios: The book has several real-world scenarios laid out to help you further assimilate the information by seeing where and under what circumstances certain solutions have worked (or not) in the real world and why.

Summaries: The summary is a quick overview of important points made in the chapter.

Exam Essentials: Exam Essentials highlight topics that could appear on the exam in some form. While the author does not know exactly what will be included on a particular exam, this section reinforces significant concepts that are crucial to understanding the CBK and the test specifications for the CCSP exam.

Written Labs: Each chapter includes written labs that bring together various topics and concepts brought up in the chapter. While this content is designed for classroom use in a college/university, it may aid in your understanding and clarification of the material beyond classroom use as well.

Answers to the Written Labs are in Appendix A.

Chapter Review Questions: Each chapter includes practice questions designed to measure your knowledge of fundamental ideas discussed in the chapter. After you finish each chapter, answer the questions; if some of your answers are incorrect, it is an indication that you need to spend more time studying the corresponding topics. The answers to the practice questions are in Appendix B.

What Is Included with the Additional Study Tools

Beyond all of the information provided in the text, this book comes with a helpful array of additional online study tools. All of the online study tools are available by registering your book at www.wiley.com/go/sybextestprep. You'll need to choose this book from the list of books there, complete the required registration information, including answering the security verification to prove book ownership. After that you will be emailed a pin code. Once you get the code, follow the directions in the email or return to www.wiley.com/go/sybextestprep to set up your account using the code and get access.

The Sybex Test Preparation Software

The test preparation software, made by the experts at Sybex, can help prepare you for the CCSP exam. In this test engine, you will find all the review and assessment questions from the book and additional bonus practice exam questions that are included with the study tools. You can take the assessment test, test yourself by chapter, take the practice exam, or take a randomly generated exam consisting of all the questions.

Glossary of Terms in PDF

Sybex offers a robust glossary of terms in PDF format. This comprehensive glossary includes essential terms you should understand for the CCSP certification exam, in a searchable format.

Bonus Practice Exams

Sybex includes two practice exams; these contain questions meant to survey your understanding of the essential elements of the CCSP CBK. Both tests are 125 questions long, the length of the actual certification exam. The exams are available online at www.wiley.com/go/sybextestprep.

Assessment Test

1. What type of solutions enable enterprises or individuals to store data and computer files on the Internet using a storage service provider rather than keeping the data locally on a physical disk such as a hard drive or tape backup?

   A. Online backups

   B. Cloud backup solutions

   C. Removable hard drives

   D. Masking

2. When using an infrastructure as a service (IaaS) solution, which of the following is not an essential benefit for the customer?

   A. Removing the need to maintain a license library

   B. Metered service

   C. Energy and cooling efficiencies

   D. Transfer of ownership cost

3. _____ focuses on security and encryption to prevent unauthorized copying and limitations on distribution to only those who pay.

   A. Information rights management (IRM)

   B. Masking

   C. Bit splitting

   D. Degaussing

4. Which of the following represents the correct set of four cloud deployment models?

   A. Public, private, joint, and community

   B. Public, private, hybrid, and community

   C. Public, Internet, hybrid, and community

   D. External, private, hybrid, and community

5. What is a special mathematical code that allows encryption hardware/software to encrypt and then decipher a message?

   A. PKI

   B. Key

   C. Public-private

   D. Masking

6. Which of the following lists the correct six components of the STRIDE threat model?

    A. Spoofing, tampering, repudiation, information disclosure, denial of service, and elevation of privilege

    B. Spoofing, tampering, refutation, information disclosure, denial of service, and social engineering elasticity

    C. Spoofing, tampering, repudiation, information disclosure, distributed denial of service, and elevation of privilege

    D. Spoofing, tampering, nonrepudiation, information disclosure, denial of service, and elevation of privilege

7. What is the term that describes the assurance that a specific author actually created and sent a specific item to a specific recipient, and that the message was successfully received?

    A. PKI

    B. DLP

    C. Nonrepudiation

    D. Bit splitting

8. What is the correct term for the process of deliberately destroying the encryption keys used to encrypt data?

    A. Poor key management

    B. PKI

    C. Obfuscation

    D. Crypto-shredding

9. In a federated environment, who is the relying party, and what do they do?

    A. The relying party is the service provider, and they consume the tokens generated by the identity provider.

    B. The relying party is the service provider, and they consume the tokens generated by the customer.

    C. The relying party is the customer, and they consume the tokens generated by the identity provider.

    D. The relying party is the identity provider, and they consume the tokens generated by the service provider.

10. What is the process of replacing sensitive data with unique identification symbols/addresses?

    A. Randomization

    B. Elasticity

    C. Obfuscation

    D. Tokenization

11. Which of the following data storage types are associated or used with platform as a service (PaaS)?

    A. Databases and big data

    B. SaaS application

    C. Tabular

    D. Raw and block

12. What is the term used for software technology that abstracts application software from the underlying operating system on which it is executed?

    A. Partition

    B. Application virtualization

    C. Distributed

    D. SaaS

13. Which of the following represents the US legislation enacted to protect shareholders and the public from enterprise accounting errors and fraudulent practices?

    A. PCI

    B. Gramm-Leach-Bliley Act (GLBA)

    C. Sarbanes–Oxley Act (SOX)

    D. HIPAA

14. Which of the following is a device that can safely store and manage encryption keys and is used in servers, data transmission, and log files?

    A. Private key

    B. Hardware security module (HSM)

    C. Public key

    D. Trusted operating system module (TOS)

15. What is a type of cloud infrastructure that is provisioned for open use by the general public and is owned, managed, and operated by a cloud provider?

    A. Private cloud

    B. Public cloud

    C. Hybrid cloud

    D. Personal cloud

16. When transparent encryption of a database is used, where does the encryption engine reside?

    A. Within the database application itself

    B. At the application using the database

    C. On the instances attached to the volume

    D. In a key management system

17. What is a type of assessment that employs a set of methods, principles, or rules for assessing risk based on nonnumerical categories or levels?

    A. Quantitative assessment

    B. Qualitative assessment

    C. Hybrid assessment

    D. SOC 2

18. Which of the following best describes the *Cloud Security Alliance Cloud Controls Matrix (CSA CCM)*?

    A. A set of regulatory requirements for cloud service providers

    B. A set of software development lifecycle requirements for cloud service providers

    C. A security controls framework that provides mapping/cross relationships with the main industry-accepted security standards, regulations, and controls frameworks

    D. An inventory of cloud service security controls that are arranged into separate security domains

19. When a conflict between parties occurs, which of the following is the primary means of determining the jurisdiction in which the dispute will be heard?

    A. Tort law

    B. Contract

    C. Common law

    D. Criminal law

20. Which one of the following is the *most* important security consideration when selecting a new computer facility?

    A. Local law enforcement response times

    B. Location adjacent to competitor's facilities

    C. Aircraft flight paths

    D. Utility infrastructure

21. Which of the following is *always* safe to use in the disposal of electronic records within a cloud environment?

    A. Physical destruction

    B. Overwriting

    C. Encryption

    D. Degaussing

22. Which of the following does not represent an attack on a network?

    A. Syn flood

    B. Denial of service

    C. Nmap scan

    D. Brute force

23. Which of the following takes advantage of the information developed in the business impact analysis (BIA)?

    A. Calculating ROI

    B. Risk analysis

    C. Calculating TCO

    D. Securing asset acquisitions

24. Which of the following terms best describes a managed service model where software applications are hosted by a vendor or cloud service provider and made available to customers over network resources?

    A. Infrastructure as a service (IaaS)

    B. Public cloud

    C. Software as a service (SaaS)

    D. Private cloud

25. Which of the following is a federal law enacted in the United States to control the way financial institutions deal with private information of individuals?

    A. PCI

    B. ISO/IEC

    C. Gramm-Leach-Bliley Act (GLBA)

    D. Consumer Protection Act

26. The typical function of Secure Sockets Layer (SSL) in securing Wireless Application Protocol (WAP) is to protect transmissions that exist _____

    A. Between the WAP gateway and the wireless endpoint device

    B. Between the web server and the WAP gateway

    C. From the web server to the wireless endpoint device

    D. Between the wireless device and the base station

27. What is an audit standard for service organizations?

    A. SOC 1

    B. SSAE 18

    C. GAAP

    D. SOC 2

28. What is a company that purchases hosting services from a cloud server hosting or cloud computing provider and then resells to its own customers?

    A. Cloud programmer

    B. Cloud broker

    C. Cloud proxy

    D. VAR

29. Which of the following is comparable to grid computing in that it relies on sharing computing resources rather than having local servers or personal devices to handle applications?

  A. Server hosting

  B. Legacy computing

  C. Cloud computing

  D. Intranet

30. What is a set of technologies designed to analyze application source code and binaries for coding and design conditions that are indicative of security vulnerabilities?

  A. Dynamic application security testing (DAST)

  B. Static application security testing (SAST)

  C. Secure coding

  D. OWASP

Answers to Assessment Test

1. **B.** Cloud backup solutions enable enterprises to store their data and computer files on the Internet using a storage service rather than storing data locally on a hard disk or tape backup. This has the added benefit of providing access to data should the primary business location be damaged in some way that prevents accessing or restoring data locally due to damaged infrastructure or equipment. Online backups and removable hard drives are other options but do not by default supply the customer with ubiquitous access. Masking is a technology used to partially conceal sensitive data.

2. **A.** In an IaaS model, the customer must still maintain licenses for operating systems (OSs) and applications used in the cloud environment. In PaaS models, the licensing for OSs is managed by the cloud provider, but the customer is still responsible for application licenses; in SaaS models, the customer does not need to manage a license library.

3. **A.** Information rights management (IRM) (often also referred to as digital rights management, or DRM) is designed to focus on security and encryption as a means of preventing unauthorized copying and limiting distribution of content to only authorized personnel (usually, the purchasers). Masking entails hiding specific fields or data in particular user views in order to limit data exposure in the production environment. Bit splitting is a method of hiding information across multiple geographical boundaries, and degaussing is a method of deleting data permanently from magnetic media.

4. **B.** The only correct answer for this is public, private, hybrid, and community. Joint, Internet, and external are not cloud models.

5. **B.** An encryption key is just that: a key used to encrypt and decrypt information. It is mathematical code that supports either hardware- or software-based encryption, is used to encrypt or decrypt information, and is kept confidential by the parties involved in the communication. PKI is an arrangement for creating and distributing digital certificates. Public-private is the description of the key pairs used in asymmetric encryption (this answer is too specific for the question; option B is preferable). Masking entails hiding specific fields or data in particular user views in order to limit data exposure in the production environment.

6. **A.** The letters in the acronym STRIDE represent spoofing of identity, tampering with data, repudiation, information disclosure, denial of service, and elevation (or escalation) of privilege. The other options are simply mixed up or incorrect versions of the same.

7. **C.** Nonrepudiation means that a party to a transaction cannot deny they took part in that transaction.

8. **D.** The act of crypto-shredding means destroying the key that was used to encrypt the data, thereby making the data very difficult to recover.

9. **A.** The identity provider maintains the identities and generates tokens for known users. The relying party (RP) is the service provider, which consumes tokens. All other answers are incorrect.

10. D. Replacing sensitive data with unique identification symbols is known as tokenization, a way of hiding or concealing sensitive data by representing it with unique identification symbols/addresses. While randomization and obfuscation are also means of concealing information, they are done quite differently.

11. A. PaaS uses databases and big data storage types.

12. B. Application virtualization abstracts application software from the underlying operating system on which it is executed. SaaS is a cloud service model. A partition is an area of memory, usually on a drive. *Distributed* is a modifier usually suggesting multiple machines used for a common purpose.

13. C. The Sarbanes–Oxley Act (SOX) was enacted in response to corporate scandals in the late 1990s/early 2000s. SOX not only forces executives to oversee all accounting practices, it also holds them accountable for fraudulent/deceptive activity. HIPAA is a US law for medical information. PCI is an industry standard for credit/debit cards. GLBA is a US law for the banking and insurance industries.

14. B. A hardware security module (HSM) is a device that can safely store and manage encryption keys. These can be used in servers, workstations, and so on. One common type is called the Trusted Platform Module (TPM) and can be found on enterprise workstations and laptops. There is no such term as a *trusted operating system module*, and public and private keys are used with asymmetric encryption.

15. B. This is the very definition of public cloud computing.

16. A. In transparent encryption, the encryption key for a database is stored in the boot record of the database itself.

17. B. A qualitative assessment is a set of methods or rules for assessing risk based on non-mathematical categories or levels. One that uses mathematical categories or levels is called a quantitative assessment. There is no such thing as a hybrid assessment, and an SOC 2 is an audit report regarding control effectiveness.

18. C. The CCM cross-references many industry standards, laws, and guidelines.

19. B. Contracts between parties can establish the jurisdiction for resolving disputes; this takes primacy in determining jurisdiction (if not specified in the contract, other means will be used). Tort law refers to civil liability suits. Common law refers to laws regarding marriage, and criminal law refers to violations of state or federal criminal code.

20. D. Of the answers given, option D is the most important. It is vital that any data center facility be close to resilient utilities, such as power, water, and connectivity.

21. C. Encryption can always be used in a cloud environment, but physical destruction, overwriting, and degaussing may not be available due to access and physical separation factors.

22. C. All of the rest of these options represent specific network attacks. Nmap is a relatively harmless scanning utility designed for network mapping. Although it can be used to gather information about a network as part of the process of developing an attack, it is not by itself an attack tool.

23. B. Among other things, the BIA gathers asset valuation information that is crucial to risk management analysis and further selection of security controls.

24. C. This is the definition of the software as a service (SaaS) model. Public and private are cloud deployment models, and infrastructure as a service (IaaS) does not provide applications of any type.

25. C. The Gramm-Leach-Bliley Act targets US financial and insurance institutions and requires them to protect account holders' private information. PCI refers to credit card processing requirements, ISO/IEC is a standards organization, and the Consumer Protection Act, while providing oversight for the protection of consumer private information, is limited in scope.

26. C. The purpose of SSL is to encrypt the communication channel between two endpoints. In this example, it is the end user and the server.

27. B. Both SOC 1 and SOC 2 are report formats based on the SSAE 18 standard. While SOC 1 reports on controls for financial reporting, SOC 2 (Types 1 and 2) reports on controls associated with security or privacy.

28. B. The cloud computing broker purchases hosting services and then resells them.

29. C. Cloud computing is built on the model of grid computing, whereby resources can be pooled and shared rather than having local devices do all the compute and storage functions.

30. B. Static application security testing (SAST) is used to review source code and binaries to detect problems before the code is loaded into memory and run.

Suggested Reading

In order to properly prepare for the exam, you should definitely review resources in addition to this book. As a bare minimum, the author suggests the following:

Cloud Security Alliance, Security Guidance v4.0:

> https://cloudsecurityalliance.org/research/guidance

OWASP, Top Ten:

> https://www.owasp.org/index.php/Category:OWASP_Top_Ten_Project

The 2017 version of the OWASP top ten threats is the most recent as of publication of this book, but the versions do not vary widely, and understanding the concepts in any version will do for study purposes.

NIST SP 800-53:

https://nvd.nist.gov/800-53

 NIST SP 800-53, Revision 4 is the most current version as of the publication of this book, but a new version is expected soon.

NIST SP 800-37:

https://csrc.nist.gov/publications/detail/sp/800-37/rev-2/final

The Uptime Institute, Tier Standard: Topology:

https://uptimeinstitute.com/resources/asset/tier-standard-topology

Cloud Security Alliance, Cloud Controls Matrix:

https://cloudsecurityalliance.org/artifacts/cloud-controls-matrix-v1-0/

Cloud Security Alliance Consensus Assessments Initiative Questionnaire:

https://cloudsecurityalliance.org/artifacts/
consensus-assessments-initiative-questionnaire-v3-0-1/

Cloud Security Alliance STAR Level and Scheme Requirements:

https://cloudsecurityalliance.org/artifacts/star-level-and-scheme-
requirements

CCSP Official (ISC)^2 Practice Tests:

https://www.wiley.com/en-us/CCSP+Official+%28ISC%292+Practice+Tests-
p-9781119449225

Chapter

1

Architectural Concepts

THE OBJECTIVE OF THIS CHAPTER IS TO ACQUAINT THE READER WITH THE FOLLOWING CONCEPTS:

✓ **Domain 1: Cloud Concepts, Architecture, and Design**

- 1.1. Understand Cloud Computing Concepts
    - 1.1.1. Cloud Computing Definitions
    - 1.1.2. Cloud Computing Roles
    - 1.1.3. Key Cloud Computing Characteristics
    - 1.1.4. Building Block Technologies
- 1.2. Describe Cloud Reference Architecture
    - 1.2.1. Cloud Computing Activities
    - 1.2.2. Cloud Service Capabilities
    - 1.2.3. Cloud Service Categories
    - 1.2.4. Cloud Deployment Models
    - 1.2.5. Cloud Shared Considerations
    - 1.2.6. Impact of Related Technologies
- 1.4. Understand Design Principles of Secure Cloud Computing
    - 1.4.3. Cost Benefit Analysis
    - 1.4.4. Functional Security Requirements

✓ **Domain 4: Cloud Application Security**

- 4.7. Design Appropriate Identity and Access Management (IAM) Solutions
    - 4.7.5. Cloud Access Security Broker (CASB)

✓ **Domain 5: Cloud Security Operations**

- 5.4. Implement Operational Controls and Standards
    - 5.4.10. Service Level Management

This chapter is the foundation for all the other chapters in this study guide. You may find it useful to review this material before reading other chapters.

The CCSP is not a certification of basic computer skills or training; it is a professional certification for practitioners with some background in the field. (ISC)² expects that those who want to earn this particular certification already have experience in the industry; have been employed in an InfoSec position in some professional capacity; and have a thorough understanding of many basic areas related to computers, security, business, risk, and networking. Many people taking the test already have other certifications that validate their knowledge and experience, such as the CISSP. Therefore, this book will not contain many of the basics that, while testable, you are already expected to know. If you aren't coming from a CISSP background, it would be good to supplement your knowledge with CISSP-focused materials as well.

However, the CCSP Common Body of Knowledge (CBK) contains terminology and concepts that may be expressed in specific ways, to include perspectives and usages that may be unique to the CCSP and different from what you are used to dealing with in your current operations. This chapter is therefore intended as a guide, laying down the foundation for understanding the rest of the material and the CBK as a whole.

Cloud Characteristics

Cloud computing has come to mean many things, but the following characteristics have become part of the generally accepted definition:

- Broad network access
- On-demand self-service
- Resource pooling
- Rapid elasticity
- Measured or "metered" service

These traits are expressed succinctly in the NIST definition of cloud computing.

NIST 800-145 Cloud Computing Definition

The official NIST definition of cloud computing says, "Cloud Computing is a model for enabling ubiquitous, convenient, on-demand network access to a shared pool of configurable computing resources (e.g., networks, servers, storage, applications, and services) that can be rapidly provisioned and released with minimal management effort or service provider interaction."

These characteristics are also similar to how cloud computing is defined in ISO 17788 (www.iso.org/iso/catalogue_detail?csnumber=60544).

You can expect to see mention of each of these throughout this book, the CBK, and the exam.

Broad network access means services are consistently accessible by standard means, such as the use of a web browser to access a Software as a Service (SaaS) application regardless of the user's location or choice of computer OS, browser, and so on. This is generally accomplished with the use of such technologies as advanced routing techniques, load balancers, and multisite hosting, among others.

On-demand self-service refers to the model that allows customers to scale their compute and/or storage needs with little or no intervention from or prior communication with the provider. The services happen in real time.

Resource pooling is the characteristic that allows the cloud provider to meet various demands from customers while remaining financially viable. The cloud provider can make capital investments that greatly exceed what any single customer could provide on their own and can apportion these resources as needed so that the resources are not underutilized (which would mean a wasteful investment) or overtaxed (which would mean a decrease in level of service). This is often referred to as a multitenant environment; multiple customers share the same underlying hardware, software, and networking assets.

Rapid elasticity allows the customer to grow or shrink the IT footprint (number of users, number of machines, size of storage, and so on) as necessary to meet operational needs without excess capacity. In the cloud, this can be done in moments, as opposed to the traditional environment, where acquisition and deployment of resources (or dispensing old resources) can take weeks or months.

Finally, measured or metered service simply means that the customer is charged for only what they use and nothing more. This is much like how a water or power company might charge you each month for the services used (with perhaps a minimum monthly charge for maintaining the connection).

Rest assured—we will be going into more detail regarding all of these concepts in the chapters to come.

Real World Scenario

Online Shopping

Think of retail demand during the pre-holiday crush toward the end of the year. The sheer volume of customers and transactions greatly exceeds all normal operations throughout the rest of the year. When this happens, retailers who offer online shopping can see great benefit from hosting their sales capability in the cloud. The cloud provider can apportion resources necessary to meet this increased demand and will charge for this increased usage at a negotiated rate, but when shopping drops off after the holiday, the retailers will not continue to be charged at the higher rate.

Business Requirements

The IT department is not a profit center; it provides a support function. This is even more accurate to describe the security department. Security activities actually hinder business efficiency (because, generally, the more secure something is, be it a device or a process, the less efficient it will be). This is why the business needs of the organization drive security decisions and not the other way around.

A successful organization will gather as much information about operational business requirements as possible; this information can be used for many purposes, including several functions in the security realm (I'll touch on this throughout the book, but a few examples include the business continuity/disaster recovery effort, the risk management plan, and data categorization). Likewise, the astute security professional needs to understand as much as possible about the operation of the organization. Operational aspects of the organization can help security personnel better perform their tasks no matter what level or role they happen to be assigned to. Consider the following examples:

- A network security administrator has to know what type of traffic to expect based on the business of the organization.

- The intrusion detection analyst has to understand what the organization is doing, how business activities occur, and where (geographically) the business is operating to better understand the nature and intensity of potential external attacks and how to adjust baselines accordingly.

- The security architect has to understand the various needs of the organizational departments to enhance their operation without compromising their security profile.

functional requirements: Those performance aspects of a device, process, or employee that are necessary for the business task to be accomplished. Example: A salesperson in the field must be able to connect to the organization's network remotely.

> **nonfunctional requirements:** Those aspects of a device, process, or employee that are not necessary for accomplishing a business task but are desired or expected. Example: The salesperson's remote connection must be secure.

Many organizations are currently considering moving their network operations to a cloud-based motif. This is not a decision made lightly, and the business requirements must be supported by this transition. There are also different cloud service and delivery models of cloud computing, and an organization must decide which one will optimize success.

Existing State

A true evaluation and understanding of the business processes, assets, and requirements is essential. Failing to properly capture the full extent of the business needs could result in not having an asset or capability in the new environment after migration to the cloud.

At the start of this effort, however, the intent is not to determine what will best fulfill the business requirements but to determine what those requirements are. A full inventory of assets, processes, and requirements is necessary, and there are various methods for collecting this data. Typically, several methods are used jointly as a means to reduce the possibility of missing something.

Here are some possible methods for gathering business requirements:

- Interviewing functional managers
- Interviewing users
- Interviewing senior management
- Surveying customers
- Collecting network traffic
- Inventorying assets
- Collecting financial records
- Collecting insurance records
- Collecting marketing data
- Collecting regulatory mandates

After sufficient data has been collected, a detailed analysis is necessary. This is the point where a business impact analysis (BIA) takes place.

The BIA is an assessment of the priorities given to each asset and process within the organization. A proper analysis should consider the effect (impact) any harm or loss of each asset might mean to the organization overall. During the BIA, special care should be paid to identifying critical paths and single points of failure. You also need to determine the costs of compliance—that is, the legislative and contractual requirements mandated for your organization. Your organization's regulatory restrictions will be based on many variables, including the jurisdictions where your organization operates, the industry the organization is in, the types and locations of your customers, and so on.

Assets can be tangible or intangible. They can include hardware, software, intellectual property, personnel, processes, and so on. An example of tangible assets would be things like routers and servers, whereas intangible assets are generally something you cannot touch, such as software code, expressions of ideas, and business methodologies.

Quantifying Benefits and Opportunity Cost

Once you have a clear picture of what your organization does in terms of lines of business and processes, you can get a better understanding of what benefits the organization might derive from cloud migration as well as the costs associated with the move.

Obviously, the greatest driver pushing organizations toward cloud migration at the moment is perceived cost savings, and that is a significant and reasonable consideration. The next few sections describe some aspects of that consideration.

Reduction in Capital Expenditure

If your organization buys a device for use in its internal environment, the capacity of that device will either be fully utilized or (more likely) not. If the device is used at its fullest capacity, then it's quite likely that the function for which it is needed may experience inefficiencies at some point. Even a small uptick in demand for that device will overload its capacity. However, if the device is not fully utilized, then the organization has paid for something for which it is getting less than full value. The unused or excess capacity goes to waste. In effect, the organization has overpaid for the device unless the organization uses the device to the point where it is dangerously close to overload—you cannot buy just part of a device.

Moreover, tax benefits that can be realized from the purchase of a device have to be accrued over years of operation, as depreciation of that device/asset. With a paid service (such as cloud), an operational expenditure, the entire payment (perhaps monthly or quarterly) is tax deductible as an expense.

In the cloud, however, the organization is only paying for what it uses (regardless of the number of devices, or fractions of devices, necessary to handle the load), and no more. This is the *metered service* aspect described earlier. As a result, the organization does not overpay for these assets. However, cloud providers do have excess capacity available to be apportioned to cloud customers, so your organization is always in a position to experience increased demand (even dramatic, rapid, and significant demand) and not be overwhelmed (this is the *rapid elasticity* aspect described earlier).

One way an organization can use hosted cloud services is to augment internal, private data center capabilities with managed services during times of increased demand. We refer to this as *cloud bursting*. The organization might have data center assets it owns, but it can't handle the increased demand during times of elevated need (crisis situations, heavy holiday shopping periods, and so on), so it rents the additional capacity as needed from an external cloud provider. See Figure 1.1.

FIGURE 1.1 Rapid scalability allows the customer to dictate the volume of resource usage.

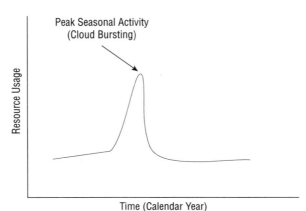

Therefore, with deployment to a cloud environment, the organization realizes cost savings immediately (not paying for unused resources) and avoids a costly risk (the possibility of loss of service due to increased demand).

Reduction in Personnel Costs

For most organizations (other than those that deliver IT services), managing data is not a core competency, much less a profitable line of business. Data management is also a specialized skill, and people with IT experience and training are relatively expensive (compared to employees in other departments). The personnel required to fulfill the needs of an internal IT environment represent a significant and disproportionally large investment for the organization. In moving to the cloud, the organization can largely divest itself of a large percentage, if not a majority, of these personnel.

Reduction in Operational Costs

Maintaining and administering an internal environment takes a great deal of effort and expense. When an organization moves to the cloud, the cost becomes part of the price of the service, as calculated by the cloud provider. Therefore, costs are lumped in with the flat-rate cost of the contract and will not increase in response to enhanced operations (scheduled updates, emergency response activities, and so on).

Transferring Some Regulatory Costs

Some cloud providers may offer holistic, targeted regulatory compliance packages for their customers. For instance, the cloud provider might have a set of controls that can be applied to a given customer's cloud environment to ensure the mandates of Payment Card Industry (PCI) are met. Any customer wanting that package can specify so in a service contract instead of trying to delineate individual controls à la carte. In this manner, the cloud customer can decrease some of the effort and expense they might otherwise incur in trying to come up with a control framework for adhering to the relevant regulations.

> We will go into more detail about service-level agreements, or service contracts, in later chapters.

It is, however, crucial to note here (and I'll repeat it throughout the book) that under current laws, no cloud customer can transfer risk or liability associated with the inadvertent or malicious disclosure of *personally identifiable information (PII)*. This is very, very important to understand: your organization, if it holds PII of any kind, is ultimately responsible for any breaches or releases of that data, even if you are using a cloud service and the breach/release results from negligence or attack on the part of the cloud provider. Legally and financially, in the eyes of the court, your organization is always responsible for any unplanned release of PII.

> PII is a major component of regulatory compliance, whether the regulation comes in the form of statutes or contractual obligation. Protection of PII will be a large part of our security concern in the cloud.

Reduction in Costs for Data Archival/Backup Services

Off-site backups are standard practice for both long-term data archival and disaster recovery purposes. Having a cloud-based service for this purpose is sensible and cost-efficient even if the organization does not conduct its regular operations in the cloud. However, moving operations into the cloud can create an economy of scale when combined with the archiving/backup usage; this can lead to an overall cost savings for the organization. It can enhance the business continuity/disaster recovery (BC/DR) strategy for the organization as well.

Intended Impact

All of these benefits can be enumerated according to dollar value: each potential cost-saving measure can be quantified. Senior management—with input from subject matter experts—needs to balance the potential financial benefits against the risks of operating in the cloud. It is this cost-benefit calculation, driven by business needs but informed by security concerns, that will allow senior management to decide whether a cloud migration of the organization's operational environment makes sense. .

Return on investment (ROI) is a term related to cost-benefit measures. *ROI* is a term used to describe a profitability ratio. It is generally calculated by dividing net profit by net assets.

 A great many risks are associated with cloud migration as well. I will be addressing these in detail throughout this book.

Cloud Evolution, Vernacular, and Models

The arrival of the cloud and its related technology has provided a lot of advantages. To incorporate the cloud and these advantages, it is necessary to understand new terminology and how it relates to the terminology of traditional models. This new technology and its terminology are an integral part of understanding cloud computing service models and cloud computing deployment models.

New Technology, New Options

Fifteen, or even 10, years ago, suggesting that organizations hand off their data and operations to a third party that is geographically distant and run by people that most managers in the organization will never meet would have seemed absurd, especially from a security perspective. The risk would have been seen as insurmountable, and ceding that level of control to an outside vendor would have been daunting. Today, a combination of technological capabilities and contractual trust make cloud computing not only appealing but almost a foregone conclusion, in terms of financial viability.

Several characteristics are emblematic of cloud computing:

- **Elasticity:** Rather than constantly purchasing computers, servers, data storage systems, and other resources and internally maintaining their infrastructure, an organization can contract with a cloud vendor. The cloud provider uses virtualization to flexibly allocate only the needed usage of each resource to the organization, thus holding down costs while maintaining profitability. This also allows users to access their data from diverse platforms and locations, increasing portability, accessibility, and availability.

- **Simplicity:** Proper cloud implementations allow a user to seamlessly use the service without frequently interacting with the cloud service provider.

- **Scalability:** In general, increasing or reducing services can be more easily, quickly, and cost-effectively accomplished than in a non-cloud environment.

The Difference Between a Cloud Customer and a Cloud User

A *cloud customer* is anyone purchasing a cloud service (which could be an individual or a company), whereas a *cloud user* is just someone using cloud services. It could be an employee of a company that is a cloud customer or just a private individual.

For instance, Company A purchases SaaS services from Cloud Provider X. Company A is a cloud customer. All employees of Company A are cloud users, because they're using the cloud services their employer, a cloud customer, has purchased for their usage.

Cloud Computing Service Models

Cloud services are often offered in terms of three general models, based on what the vendor offers and the customer needs and the responsibilities of each according to the service contract. (ISC)² expects you to understand these three models for testing purposes. These models are *infrastructure as a service (IaaS)*, *platform as a service (PaaS)*, and *software as a service (SaaS)*, as shown in Figure 1.2. In the following sections, we'll review each of them in turn.

FIGURE 1.2   Cloud service models

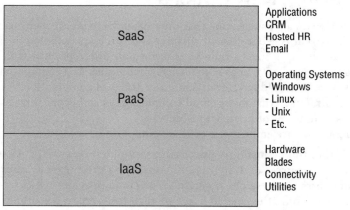

Cloud Service Models

Some vendors and consultants demonstrate a lot of zeal in capitalizing on the popularity of the "cloud" concept and incorporate the word into every term they can think of in order to make their products more appealing. We see a broad proliferation of such labels as networking as a service (NaaS), compliance as a service (CaaS), and data science as a service (DSaaS), but they're mostly just marketing techniques. The only service models you'll need to know for both the exam and your use as a practitioner are IaaS, PaaS, and SaaS.

Infrastructure as a Service (IaaS)

The most basic of cloud service offerings, IaaS allows the customer to install all software, including operating systems (OSs), on hardware housed and connected by the cloud vendor. In this model, the cloud provider has a data center with racks, machines, cables, and utilities and administers all these things. However, all logical resources, such as software, are the responsibility of the customer.

In traditional terms, we might think of this as what used to be considered a "warm site" for BC/DR purposes: the physical space exists, the connectivity exists, and it is available for the customer organization to fill with any type of baseline configuration and populate with any data the customer requires.

IaaS might be optimum for organizations that want enhanced control over the security of their data or are looking to the cloud for a limited purpose, such as BC/DR or archiving. It is usually the least expensive cloud option, in terms of what the customer pays the provider. However, the customer will retain certain capabilities and requirements, such as IT staffing, that may make it difficult to ascertain the true total overall cost.

Platform as a Service (PaaS)

PaaS contains everything included in IaaS with the addition of OSs. The cloud vendor usually offers a selection of OSs so that the customer can use any or all of the available choices. The vendor will be responsible for patching, administering, and updating the OS as necessary, and the customer can install any software they deem useful.

This model is especially useful for customers involved in software development, as the customer can test their software in an isolated environment without risk of damaging production capabilities and determine the viability of the software across a range of OS platforms.

PaaS also includes cloud-based database engines and services as well as "big data"–style services, such as data warehousing and datamining. The provider offers access to the backend engine/functionality, while the customer can create/install various apps/APIs to access the backend.

Software as a Service (SaaS)

SaaS includes everything in IaaS and PaaS with the addition of software programs. The cloud vendor becomes responsible for administering, patching, and updating this software as well. The cloud customer is basically only involved in uploading and processing data on a full production environment hosted by the provider.

There are many examples of SaaS configurations, ranging across a spectrum of functionality. Google Docs, Microsoft's Office 365, and QuickBooks Online are all examples of SaaS products. The provider takes care of all the infrastructure, compute, and storage needs as well as providing the underlying operating systems and the application itself. All of this is completely transparent to the end user, who only sees the application they have purchased/accessed.

Cloud Deployment Models

In addition to viewing cloud offerings in terms of what levels of service are involved, another perspective has to do with ownership. You'll be expected to know the facets of both sets of models.

Public

The public cloud is what we typically think of when discussing cloud providers. The resources (hardware, software, facilities, and staff) are owned and operated by a vendor and sold, leased, or rented to anyone (offered to the public—hence the name). Public clouds are *multitenant* environments; multiple customers will share the underlying resources that are owned and operated by the provider. That means that a customer in a public cloud might be using a virtual machine that actually resides on the same hardware that hosts another virtual machine operated by the customer's direct competitor, and the customer has no way of knowing what other entities are using the same resources.

Examples of public cloud vendors include Rackspace, Microsoft's Azure, and Amazon Web Services (AWS).

Private

A private cloud is typified by resources dedicated to a single customer; no other customers will share the underlying resources (hardware and perhaps software). Therefore, private clouds are *not* multitenant environments.

Private clouds can take various forms. A private cloud might be owned and maintained by the entity that is the sole customer. In other words, an organization might own and operate a data center that serves as the cloud environment for that organization's users. Or a private cloud might be a set of resources (racks, blades, software packages) owned by the single customer but located and maintained at the cloud provider's data center; the cloud provider might offer physical security, some basic administration services, and proper utilities (power, Internet connectivity) for the customer's resources. This is sometimes referred to as a *co-lo* (co-located) environment.

Another private cloud option is for the customer to contract with a cloud provider such that the provider offers exclusive use of specific resources for that customer inside what otherwise would be a public cloud. Basically, the provider carves out a physical and logical section of the overall data center so that the customer will not share any of the resources in that section with any other customers. Obviously, the customer must pay a premium for this type of service (more than what public cloud customers, in a multitenant environment, would pay).

Community

A community cloud features infrastructure and processing owned and operated by (or for) an affinity group; disparate pieces might be owned or controlled by individuals or distinct organizations, but they come together in some fashion to perform joint tasks and functions.

Gaming communities might be considered community clouds. For instance, the PlayStation network involves many different entities coming together to engage in online gaming: Sony hosts the identity and access management (IAM) tasks for the network, a particular game company might host a set of servers that run information rights management (IRM) functions and processing for a specific game, and individual users conduct some of their own processing and storage locally on their own PlayStations. In this type of community cloud, ownership of the underlying technologies (hardware, software, and so on) is spread throughout the various members of the community.

A community cloud can also be provisioned by a third party on behalf of the various members of the community. For instance, a cloud provider might offer a FedRAMP cloud service, for use only by US federal government customers. Any number of federal agencies might subscribe to this cloud service (say, the Department of Agriculture, Health and Human Services, the Department of the Interior, and so on), and they will all use underlying infrastructure that is dedicated strictly for their use. Any customer that is not a US federal agency will not be allowed to use this service as non-governmental entities are not part of this particular community. The cloud provider owns the underlying infrastructure, but it's provisioned and made available solely for the use of the specific community.

Hybrid

A hybrid cloud, of course, contains elements of the other models. For instance, an organization might want to retain some private cloud resources (say, their legacy production environment, which is accessed remotely by their users) but also lease some public cloud space as well (maybe a PaaS function for software development/testing, away from the production environment so that there is much less risk of crashing operational systems).

Cloud Computing Roles and Responsibilities

Various entities are involved in cloud service arrangements:

Cloud Service Provider (CSP), or Cloud Provider or Provider   The vendor offering cloud services. The CSP will own the data center, employ the staff, own and manage the resources (hardware and software), monitor service provision and security, and provide administrative assistance for the customer and the customer's data and processing needs. Examples include Amazon Web Services, Rackspace, and Microsoft's Azure.

Cloud Customer   The organization purchasing, leasing, or renting cloud services.

Cloud Broker   A company that purchases hosting services from a cloud provider who then resells them to its own customers.

Cloud Access Security Broker (CASB)   A third-party entity offering independent identity and access management (IAM) services to CSPs and cloud customers, often as an intermediary. This can take the form of a variety of services, including single sign-on, certificate management, and cryptographic key escrow.

Regulators   The entities that ensure organizations are in compliance with the regulatory framework for which they're responsible. These can be government agencies, certification bodies, or parties to a contract. Regulations include the Health Information Portability and Accountability Act (HIPAA), the Graham-Leach-Bliley Act (GLBA), the Payment Card Industry Data Security Standard (PCI DSS), the International Organization for Standardization (ISO), the Sarbanes–Oxley Act (SOX), and so forth. Regulators include the Federal Trade Commission (FTC), the Securities and Exchange Commission (SEC), and auditors commissioned to review compliance with contracted or asserted standards (such as PCI DSS and ISO), among many others.

Cloud Computing Definitions

Because cloud definitions are at the heart of understanding the following chapters and applying security fundamentals for the Certified Cloud Security Professional (CCSP), I have included some of those definitions here.

Business Requirement   An operational driver for decision-making and input for risk management.

Cloud App (Cloud Application)   The phrase used to describe a software application accessed via the Internet; may include an agent or applet installed locally on the user's device.

Cloud Architect   Subject matter expert for cloud computing infrastructure and deployment.

Cloud Backup   Backing up data to a remote, cloud-based server. As a form of cloud storage, cloud backup data is stored in an accessible form from multiple distributed resources that make up a cloud.

Cloud Computing   The use of computing, storage, and network resources with the capabilities of rapid elasticity, metered service, broad network access, and pooled resources.

Cloud Migration   The process of transitioning all or part of a company's data, applications, and services from on-site premises to the cloud, where the information can be provided over the Internet on an on-demand basis.

Cloud Portability   The ability to move applications and associated data between one cloud provider and another or between legacy and cloud environments.

Cost-Benefit Analysis   This is comparing the potential positive impact (such as profit, efficiency, market share, and so on) of a business decision to the potential negative impact (expense, detriment to production, risk, and so on) and weighing whether the two are equivalent or if the potential positive effect outweighs the potential negative. This is a business decision, not a security decision, and it is best made by managers or business analysts.

However, in order to make an informed decision, the parties involved must be provided sufficient insight and knowledge. In security matters, the CCSP should apprise management of particular risks and benefits of alternatives related to each.

FIPS 140-2   A NIST document that describes the process for accrediting and cryptosystems for use by the US federal government.

Managed Service Provider   An IT service where the customer dictates both the technology and operational procedures, and an external party executes administration and operational support according to a contract. A managed service provider might maintain and administer a data center/network for an organization at that organization's business location, or in the cloud.

Multitenant   Multiple customers using the same public cloud (and often the same hosts, in a virtualized cloud environment).

NIST 800-53   A guidance document with the primary goal of ensuring that appropriate security requirements and controls are applied to all US federal government information in information management systems.

Trusted Cloud Initiative (TCI) Reference Model   The TCI reference model is a guide for cloud providers, allowing them to create a holistic architecture (including the physical facility of the data center, the logical layout of the network, and the processes necessary to utilize both) that cloud customers can purchase and use with comfort and confidence. For more information, visit https://cloudsecurityalliance.org/wp-content/uploads/2011/10/TCI-Reference-Architecture-v1.1.pdf.

Vendor Lock-in   Vendor lock-in occurs in a situation where a customer may be unable to leave, migrate, or transfer to an alternate provider due to technical or nontechnical constraints.

Vendor Lock-out   Vendor lock-out occurs when a customer is unable to recover or access their own data due to the cloud provider going into bankruptcy or otherwise leaving the market.

The successful CCSP candidate will be familiar with each of these terms. I will go into more detail regarding these terms over the course of the book.

Back to Basics

It's also important to remember all the security fundamentals used throughout the industry. For instance, the familiar CIA triad will be mentioned extensively throughout the CBK, the exam, and this book.

- **Confidentiality:** Protecting information from unauthorized access/dissemination
- **Integrity:** Ensuring that information is not subject to unauthorized modification
- **Availability:** Ensuring that authorized users can access the information when they are permitted to do so

Foundational Concepts of Cloud Computing

There are some aspects of cloud computing that are pervasive throughout all discussion of the topic. I'm introducing them here, and you should become familiar with them. These concepts will be included in various discussions throughout the book.

Sensitive Data

Each organization will have its own risk appetite and desire for confidentiality. No matter how each cloud customer makes their own determination for these aspects of their data, the cloud provider must offer some way for the customer to categorize data according to its sensitivity and sufficient controls to ensure these categories are protected accordingly.

Virtualization

Virtualization is one of the technologies that has made cloud services a financially viable business model. Cloud providers can purchase and deploy a sufficient number of host devices for a respective number of customers and users without wasting capacity or letting resources go idle.

In a virtualized environment, a cloud user can access a synthetic computer. To the user, there is no appreciable difference between the virtual machine (VM) and a traditional computer. However, from the provider's perspective, the VM being offered to the user is just a piece of software, not an actual, dedicated piece of hardware being exclusively operated by the user. Indeed, there may be several, or even dozens, of VMs operating on a single host in the cloud space concurrently. When the user logs off or shuts down, the cloud network takes a snapshot of the user's VM, capturing it as a single file that can be stored somewhere else in the cloud until the user next requests access, when the VM can be restored exactly as they left it.

In this way, the cloud provider can offer services to any number of customers and users and not be required to purchase a new hardware device for each new user. This economy of scale allows the cloud provider to offer the same basic IT services that the users expect from traditional networks with much less cost and at an enhanced level of service.

There are many virtualization product vendors, including VMware and Microsoft. There are also a variety of implementation strategies and two fundamental virtualization types (Type 1 and Type 2). These are described in the section "Virtualization" in Chapter 5.

Encryption

As an IT security professional, you should already be familiar with the basic concepts and tools of encryption. However, in terms of cloud services, encryption plays an enhanced role and presents some additional challenges.

Because your cloud data will be in an environment controlled and operated by personnel outside your organization, encryption offers a degree of assurance that nobody without authorization will be able to access your data in a meaningful way. You can encrypt your data before it reaches the cloud and only decrypt it as necessary.

Another concern related to cloud operation is that it necessitates remote access. As with any remote access, there will always be a risk (however great or slight) of interception of data, eavesdropping, and man-in-the-middle attacks. Encryption also assists in alleviating this concern by mitigating this threat to some degree; if data in motion is encrypted, it is that much more difficult to access even if it is intercepted.

Auditing and Compliance

Cloud services pose specific challenges and opportunities for regulatory compliance and auditing.

From a compliance perspective, service providers may be able to offer holistic solutions for organizations under particular regulatory schema. For instance, the cloud provider may have an extant, known, tested control set and procedural outline for creating virtual machines that comply with PCI, HIPAA, or GLBA requirements. This could be extremely appealing to potential customers, as the difficulty and effort expended in trying to stay compliant can now be shifted out of the customer organization and over to the provider.

Conversely, auditing becomes more difficult. Cloud providers are extremely reluctant to allow physical access to their facilities or to share network diagrams and lists of controls; maintaining confidentiality of these things enhances the provider's overall security. However, these are essential elements of an audit. Also, as you'll see in upcoming chapters, it is difficult to determine exactly where (both physically and logically) in the cloud environment a given organization's data is located at any moment or which devices contain a certain customer's data, making auditing even more difficult. Audits will require the cooperation of the cloud provider, and providers have thus far disallowed the requisite level of access for the purpose. Instead, cloud providers often offer an assertion of their own audit success (Service Organization Control [SOC] Type 3 reports, which are discussed in Chapter 6 and Chapter 10). Any organization considering cloud migration should confer with regulators in order to determine if migration will be allowed and/or if additional measures will be required to protect regulated data.

Cloud Service Provider Contracts

The business arrangement between the cloud provider and the cloud customer will usually take the form of a contract, which will include a service-level agreement (SLA). The contract will spell out all the terms of the agreement: what each party is responsible for, what form the services will take, how issues will be resolved, and so on. The SLA will set specific, quantified goals for these services and their provision over a certain timeframe.

For instance, the contract might stipulate that "the Provider will ensure the Customer has constant, uninterrupted access to the Customer's data storage resources." The SLA will then explicitly define the metrics for what "constant, uninterrupted access" will mean: "There will be no interruption of connectivity to data storage longer than three (3) seconds per calendar month." The contract will also state what the penalties are (usually financial) when the cloud provider fails to meet the SLA for a given period: "Customer's monthly fee will be waived for any period following a calendar month in which any service level has not been attained by Provider."

These are obviously rough examples, but they demonstrate the relationship between the contract, the SLA, the cloud provider, and the cloud customer. The book will continually refer to the contract and the SLA based on the relationship explained here.

Related and Emerging Technologies

It is worth mentioning some emerging and related technologies. These technologies are explicitly listed in the (ISC)² Exam Outline, and therefore of concern to the CCSP candidate.

- **Machine learning and artificial intelligence (AI):** Machine learning and AI both refer to the concept of programs and machines being able to acquire, process, correlate, and interpret information and then apply that in various capabilities without needing direct input from users or programmers. A wide variety of IT and cloud products and services claim to have machine learning or AI capabilities. These include firewalls, intrusion detection/prevention systems (IDSs/IPSs), antivirus solutions, and so forth.

- **Blockchain:** Blockchain is an open means of conveying value using encryption techniques and algorithms. It is often referred to as "cryptocurrency." It is basically a transactional ledger, where all participants can view every transaction, thus making it extremely difficult to negatively affect the integrity of past transactions. Blockchain can be perceived as a cloud technology because each record ("block") is distributed among all the participants, regardless of location, type of device, jurisdiction, and so forth in a distributed, or cloud-based, manner.

- **Internet of Things (IoT):** It sometimes seems like every possible product now contains Internet connectivity: household appliances, cameras, toys, vehicles, and so on. This is collectively referred to as the Internet of Things (IoT). The distributed nature of these devices (and their connection to and placement in networks) lends them some cloud characteristics. Perhaps the most salient security aspect of IoT is that devices without proper security can be subverted and used in attacks.

- **Containers:** This term refers to the logical segmentation of memory space in a device, creating two or more abstract areas that cannot interface directly. This is commonly seen in bring your own device (BYOD) environments where employees use their personal devices for work. The containers distinguish two distinct partitions—one for work functions/data and the other for personal functions/data. This gives the employer/data owner additional assurance that the data will not be accidentally or casually lost or stolen.

- **Quantum computing:** This is an emerging technology that could allow IT systems to operate beyond binary math. Instead of using the presence of electrons for calculations (where the electrons exist in one of two states: either present or not present), quantum computing may use subatomic characteristics (electron spin, charm, and so on) to offer computation on an exponentially larger scale. This accelerates the machine's ability to perform calculations/operations dramatically. Such systems are beginning to emerge beyond the theoretical stage, although none are yet commercially available at the time of this writing.

- **Homomorphic encryption:** Homomorphic encryption is a theoretical phenomenon that would allow processing of encrypted material without needing to first decrypt it. If achieved, this could allow cloud customers to upload encrypted data to the cloud and still utilize the data, without ever sharing the encryption keys with the cloud provider, or having to otherwise accomodate decryption as part of the process. This would make the use of cloud environments much more appealing to customers with highly valuable or sensitive data.

Summary

In this chapter, we have examined business requirements, cloud definitions, cloud computing roles and responsibilities, and foundational concepts of cloud computing. This chapter has provided an introductory foundation for these topics. We will explore each of them in more detail as we move ahead.

Exam Essentials

Understand business requirements.   Always bear in mind that all management decisions are driven by business needs, including security and risk decisions. Security and risk should be considered before these decisions are made and may not take precedence over the business and operational requirements of the organization.

Understand cloud terms and definitions.   Make sure you have a clear understanding of the definitions introduced in this chapter. A great deal of the CCSP exam focuses on terms and definitions.

Be able to describe the cloud service models.   It is vitally important that you understand the differences between the three cloud service models—IaaS, PaaS, and SaaS—and the different features associated with each.

Understand cloud deployment models.   It is also important for you to understand the features of each of the four cloud deployment models—public, private, community, and hybrid—as well as their differences.

Be familiar with cloud computing roles and the associated responsibilities. Make sure you know and understand the different roles and the responsibilities of each. We will explore roles in more detail in the chapters that follow.

Written Labs

You can find the answers to the written labs in Appendix A.

1. Go to the CSA website and download the "Security Guidance for Critical Areas of Focus in Cloud Computing," at https://cloudsecurityalliance.org/artifacts/security-guidance-v4/. When you are done, spend some time exploring the site. Review the document on your own.

2. Write down three things you can think of that might be legitimate business drivers for an organization considering cloud migration.

3. List the three cloud computing service models and the advantages and disadvantages of each.

Review Questions

You can find the answers to the review questions in Appendix B.

1. Which of the following is *not* a common cloud service model?
   A. Software as a service (SaaS)
   B. Programming as a service (PaaS)
   C. Infrastructure as a service (IaaS)
   D. Platform as a service (PaaS)

2. All of these technologies have made cloud service viable except _____.
   A. Virtualization
   B. Widely available broadband
   C. Encrypted connectivity
   D. Smart hubs

3. Cloud vendors are held to contractual obligations with specified metrics by _____.
   A. Service-level agreements (SLAs)
   B. Regulations
   C. Law
   D. Discipline

4. _____ drive(s) security decisions.
   A. Customer service responses
   B. Surveys
   C. Business requirements
   D. Public opinion

5. If a cloud customer cannot get access to the cloud provider, this affects what portion of the CIA triad?
   A. Integrity
   B. Authentication
   C. Confidentiality
   D. Availability

6. Cloud access security brokers (CASBs) might offer all the following services except _____.
   A. Single sign-on
   B. Business continuity/disaster recovery/Continuity of Operations (BC/DR/COOP)
   C. Identity and access management (IAM)
   D. Key escrow

7. Encryption can be used in various aspects of cloud computing, including all of these except _____.

    A. Storage

    B. Remote access

    C. Secure sessions

    D. Magnetic swipe cards

8. All of these are reasons an organization may want to consider cloud migration except _____.

    A. Reduced personnel costs

    B. Elimination of risks

    C. Reduced operational expenses

    D. Increased efficiency

9. The generally accepted definition of cloud computing includes all of the following characteristics except _____.

    A. On-demand self-service

    B. Negating the need for backups

    C. Resource pooling

    D. Measured or metered service

10. A gamer is part of the PlayStation Network community cloud. Who owns the PlayStation console in the gamer's home?

    A. Sony

    B. The community as a whole

    C. The company that made the game that the gamer is playing at the time

    D. The gamer

11. The risk that a cloud provider might go out of business and the cloud customer might not be able to recover data is known as _____.

    A. Vendor closure

    B. Vendor lock-out

    C. Vendor lock-in

    D. Vending route

12. All of these are features of cloud computing except _____.

    A. Broad network access

    B. Reversed charging configuration

    C. Rapid scaling

    D. On-demand self-service

13. When a cloud customer uploads personally identifiable information (PII) to a cloud provider, who is ultimately responsible for the security of that PII?

    A. Cloud provider

    B. Regulators

    C. Cloud customer

    D. The individuals who are the subjects of the PII

14. We use which of the following to determine the critical paths, processes, and assets of an organization?

    A. Business requirements

    B. Business impact analysis (BIA)

    C. Risk Management Framework (RMF)

    D. Confidentiality, integrity, availability (CIA) triad

15. If an organization owns all of the hardware and infrastructure of a cloud data center that is used only by members of that organization, which cloud model would this be?

    A. Private

    B. Public

    C. Hybrid

    D. Motive

16. The cloud deployment model that features ownership by a cloud provider, with services offered to anyone who wants to subscribe, is known as _____.

    A. Private

    B. Public

    C. Hybrid

    D. Latent

17. The cloud deployment model that features joint ownership of assets among an affinity group is known as _____.

    A. Private

    B. Public

    C. Hybrid

    D. Community

18. If a cloud customer wants a secure, isolated environment in order to conduct software development and testing, which cloud service model would probably be best?

    A. IaaS

    B. PaaS

    C. SaaS

    D. Hybrid

19. If a cloud customer wants a fully operational environment with very little maintenance or administration necessary, which cloud service model would probably be best?

    A. IaaS

    B. PaaS

    C. SaaS

    D. Hybrid

20. If a cloud customer wants a bare-bones environment in which to replicate their own enterprise for business continuity/disaster recovery (BC/DR) purposes, which cloud service model would probably be best?

    A. IaaS

    B. PaaS

    C. SaaS

    D. Hybrid

Chapter

2

Design Requirements

THE OBJECTIVE OF THIS CHAPTER IS TO ACQUAINT THE READER WITH THE FOLLOWING CONCEPTS:

✓ **Domain 1: Cloud Concepts, Architecture, and Design**

- 1.4. Understand Design Principles of Secure Cloud Computing

  - 1.4.5. Security Considerations for Different Cloud Categories

✓ **Domain 3: Cloud Platform and Infrastructure Security**

- 3.3. Analyze Risks Associated with Cloud Infrastructure

  - 3.3.1. Risk Assessment and Analysis

- 3.5. Plan Disaster Recovery (DR) and Business Continuity (BC)

  - 3.5.1. Risks Related to the Cloud Environment

  - 3.5.2. Business Requirements

I mentioned the asset inventory and BIA in Chapter 1, "Architectural Concepts." It bears repeating: security decisions are driven by business requirements. This is neither new nor unique to the cloud. In this chapter, we will discuss many of the inputs for those security decisions and the business activities we undertake to determine the requirements.

Business Requirements Analysis

Security does not happen in stasis; we need information in order to conduct security activities in a proper and efficient manner. There are certain things we need to know in order to decide how we will handle risks within our organization. These include the following:

- An inventory of all assets
- A valuation of each asset
- A determination of critical paths, processes, and assets
- A clear understanding of risk appetite

Inventory of Assets

To protect our assets, we first have to know what they are. Everything owned or controlled by the organization can be considered an asset, and assets take many different forms. Assets can be tangible items, such as IT hardware, retail inventory, buildings, and vehicles. Assets can also be intangible, such as intellectual property, public perception, and goodwill with business partners and vendors. Personnel can also be considered assets, because of the skills, training, and productivity they provide to the organization.

In order to protect all our assets, we have to know what they are and, to a lesser extent, where they are and what they do. If we lose track of something under our control, it becomes impossible to secure that thing.

Therefore, the first step in creating a good security program would be to perform a thorough, comprehensive inventory. There are many methods and tools for doing so, such as surveys, interviews, audits, and so forth. In performing an IT inventory, we can also incorporate automation into the process, enhancing our capabilities and efficiency.

Valuation of Assets

While we are ascertaining the number, location, and type of assets, we also want to determine the value of each. We need to be able to know which of the assets provide the intrinsic value of our organization and which support this value.

 We need to know the value of the assets we protect so we know how much time, money, and effort to expend to protect them. We do not put a $10 lock on a $5 bicycle.

This is a process known as business impact analysis (BIA). We determine a value for every asset (usually in terms of money, but sometimes according to priority/rank, customer perception, or other measures), what it would cost the organization if we lost that asset (either temporarily or permanently), what it would cost to replace or repair that asset, and any alternate methods for dealing with that loss.

There are various ways to assign cost: we can use the insured value, the replacement cost, or some other method of making that valuation. Usually, we allow the data owners—that is, the individual line-of-business managers responsible for their respective data—to determine the value of the information under their control.

 Usually, the data owner for a given data set is the business manager in charge of that data. This is generally the head of the department that collected or created that data.

There are some risks associated with letting the data owners assign value to their assets. The most significant of these is the tendency of data owners to overvalue assets that belong to them. Ask anyone in the organization which department is the most important, and they will say that it is theirs.

The data owner is also tasked with assigning a category and/or classification to their data, usually when it is created. We will discuss this in Chapter 3, "Data Classification."

Determination of Criticality

Once the inventory and valuation is complete, the BIA effort continues with a determination made by senior management regarding criticality. Criticality denotes those aspects of the organization without which the organization could not operate or exist. These could include tangible assets, intangible assets, specific business processes, data pathways, or even essential personnel.

Real World Scenario

Criticality Examples

Here are some examples of critical aspects in organizations:

- **Tangible Assets:** The organization is a rental car company; cars are critical to its operations—if it has no cars to rent to customers, it can't do business.

- **Intangible Assets:** The organization is a music production firm; music is the intellectual property of the company—if the ownership of the music is compromised (for instance, the copyright is challenged and the company loses ownership, or the encryption protecting the music files is removed and the music can be copied without protection), the company has nothing of value and will not survive.

- **Processes:** The organization is a fast-food restaurant noted for its speed; the process of taking orders, preparing and delivering food, and taking payment is critical to its operations—if the restaurant cannot complete the process for some reason (for instance, the registers fail so that the restaurant cannot accept payment), the restaurant cannot function.

- **Data Paths:** The organization is an international shipping line; matching orders to cargo carriers is critical to its operations. If the company cannot complete its logistical coordination—assigning cargo requests to carriers with sufficient capacity—it cannot provide its services and will not survive.

- **Personnel:** The organization is a surgical provider; the surgeon is critical to the existence of the company—if the surgeon cannot operate, there is no company.

Senior management has the proper perspective for making determinations of criticality. The security professional, however, should have a good understanding of the overall mission and function of the organization, in order to better serve and advise the organization in securing critical elements.

Another function of the BIA process that can support the security effort is the identification of single points of failure (SPOFs). If there is any chokepoint in a process, procedure, or production chain—a place where an entire workflow would halt because of the loss of a single element—that's a SPOF. SPOFs, especially in critical paths, pose a significant risk to the organization and ought be addressed as soon as they are identified. Like critical aspects, SPOFs can be caused by hardware, software, processes, or personnel.

Methods for dealing with SPOFs include the following:

- Adding redundancies so that if the SPOF goes out of service, a replacement is immediately available

- Creating alternative processes to take the place of SPOFs in times of outage

- Cross-training personnel so that they can fill many roles
- Consistently and thoroughly backing up data in a manner from which it can be easily and quickly restored
- Load sharing/balancing for the IT assets

In a cloud environment, customers should expect that the provider has no SPOFs within their facilities and architecture; part of the benefit of moving to the cloud is the ability of cloud providers to offer a robust and resilient service that is not susceptible to failures due to SPOFs. The customer can therefore focus on attenuating any SPOFs on their own side of the operation: accessing and using the data in the cloud. It is important to note that not all SPOFs are part of critical aspects, and not all critical aspects of an organization contain SPOFs.

Quantitative and Qualitative Risk Assessments

Two similar yet different approaches for assessing risk are qualitative risk assessments and quantitative risk assessments. Both methods typically employ a set of methods, principles, or rules for assessing risk. Qualitative risk assessments use nonnumerical categories that are relative in nature, such as high, medium, and low. Quantitative assessments use specific numerical values such as 1, 2, and 3.

Risk Appetite

Again, this is not a new concept, and the use of cloud services does not significantly change anything about it. It bears mentioning here because of the importance of the concept to the overall practice of security and its inclusion in the CCSP Common Body of Knowledge (CBK).

Risk appetite is the level, amount, or type of risk that the organization finds acceptable. This varies wildly from organization to organization, based on innumerable factors both internal and external, and can change over time.

Here's a quick review of some risk fundamentals:

- *Risk* is the likelihood an impact will be realized.
- Risk can be reduced but never eliminated.
- Organizations accept a level of risk that allows operations to continue in a successful manner.
- It is legal and defensible to accept risks higher than the norm, or greater than your competitors, except risks to health and human safety; these risks *must* be addressed to the industry standard or the regulatory scheme to which your organization adheres.

Real World Scenario

Health and Human Safety Risks

An organization cannot accept risks to health and human safety that are beyond industry standards and known best practices; to do so would be unethical, and it would expose the organization to a great deal of liability (which creates its own risk, which must also be considered). There are a few exceptions to this rule; the military is one example, where loss of life and limb are an expected outcome from operations and an acceptable risk.

However, individuals can accept such risks on their own behalf. For instance, commercial fishing has consistently been among the professions with the highest fatality rates in the United States for the past 100 years (in terms of number of hours worked per death), yet there is no shortage of people willing to engage in that industry. For the individual workers, the level of risk is both known and acceptable. From an organizational perspective, however, the relatively high possibility of fatal accidents does not obviate the need for ensuring adherence to industry best practices (perhaps life vests, tether lines, and so forth) and does not remove all liability.

Organizations have four main ways to address risk:

Avoidance   This isn't really a method for handling risk; it means leaving a business opportunity because the risk is simply too high and cannot be compensated for with adequate control mechanisms—a risk that exceeds the organization's appetite.

Acceptance   The opposite of avoidance; the risk falls within the organization's risk appetite, so the organization continues operations without any additional efforts regarding the risk.

Transference   The organization pays someone else to accept the risk, at a lower cost than the potential impact that would result from the risk being realized; this is usually in the form of insurance. This type of risk is often associated with things that have a low probability of occurring but a high impact should they occur.

Mitigation   The organization takes steps to decrease the likelihood or the impact of the risk (and often both); this can take the form of controls/countermeasures and is usually where security practitioners are involved.

Risk is involved in every activity. We can manage risk, attenuate it, even minimize it, but there is always an element of risk in operations. When we choose to mitigate risk by applying countermeasures and controls, the remaining, leftover risk is called *residual risk*. The task of the security program is to reduce residual risk until it falls within the acceptable level of risk according to the organization's risk appetite.

The risk appetite of an organization is set by senior management and is the guide for all risk-management activities in the organization. The security practitioner must have a thorough understanding of the risk appetite of the organization in order to perform their functions properly and efficiently.

Once the business requirements have been determined, and the BIA has been completed, the information acquired can and should be reused throughout many of the organization's security-related efforts. For instance, the BIA results can be utilized in the risk assessment, the selection of specific security controls throughout the environment, and the business continuity/disaster recovery (BC/DR) plans; knowing the critical aspects of the organization and the values of all assets is essential to accomplishing these tasks.

Security Considerations for Different Cloud Categories

In traditional (non-cloud) environments, we had bright-line definitions of the organization's IT perimeter: everything inside the perimeter belonged to the organization, including data, hardware, and risk; everything outside was someone else's problem. We could even point at a specific location, a given cable leaving the facility or campus, and know that it, there, was the place where our control ended and someone else's began. We could armor our defenses at the interface between the internal environment and external factors, building up a demilitarized zone (DMZ).

This is not readily the case with cloud computing. In the cloud motif, our data resides inside an IT environment owned by someone else, riding on a hardware infrastructure that does not belong to us and is largely outside our control. Our users operate programs and machines that we have limited access to and knowledge of. It is therefore difficult to know exactly where the boundaries exist in cloud models, where our risks are, and how far they extend.

In the following sections, I'll apply a notional perspective of cloud computing boundaries. But it is extremely important to remember this: currently, according to most of the world's privacy laws and regulations, the cloud customer *is always ultimately legally liable for any loss of data*. This is true even if the cloud provider demonstrates negligence or malice.

WARNING   The cloud customer can seek restitution if the cloud provider fails in some way, causing damage to the customer. For instance, if the cloud provider hires an administrator who then illegally sells access to data belonging to the cloud customer, the customer can sue the provider for damages. *However, the cloud customer is still legally responsible for all mandates applicable to the loss, such as complying with data breach notification laws in that jurisdiction.* This requirement does not cease just because the cloud customer has outsourced operations to the cloud provider.

So what do these boundaries look like in the different cloud models?

IaaS Considerations

Infrastructure as a service (IaaS) is the cloud model in which the cloud customer has the most responsibility and authority. The provider is responsible for the data center's buildings and land, connectivity and power, and the hardware assets the customer's programs and data will reside on. The customer, however, is in charge of everything from the operating system and up; all software will be installed and administered by the customer, and the customer will supply and manage all the data.

In terms of security, the cloud customer is still losing the degree of authority they would have had in a traditional IT environment. For instance, the customer obviously does not get to select the specific IT assets used in the cloud, so the security of the acquisition process (during which we normally vet vendors and suppliers) must be entrusted to the cloud provider. The cloud customer may also lose some ability to monitor network traffic inside the data center—the cloud provider might not be willing to allow the customer to place monitoring equipment or sensors on the provider's infrastructure and also might refuse to share traffic data they, the provider, have collected themselves.

This makes auditing difficult, which also affects security policy and regulatory compliance. An organization migrating to the cloud will necessarily have to drastically adapt its security policy to reflect the new constraints and will have to find some way to provide the requisite deliverables to appease regulators. This must be negotiated at the outset of migration, and early communication with regulators is highly advisable. For instance, if regulators insist on scheduled audits of the environment where data processing takes place, what form will those audits take if the organization cannot now directly audit network traffic and event logs?

In IaaS, though, the cloud customer may still collect and review event logs from the software, including the OS, which still lends a great deal of insight into the usage and security of the data.

PaaS Considerations

With platform as a service (PaaS), the cloud customer loses still more control of the environment, because the cloud provider is now responsible for installing, maintaining, and administering the OSs as well as the underlying hardware. This will entail further modification of the customer's security policy and additional efforts to ensure regulatory compliance.

The cloud customer still, however, gets to monitor and review software events, since the programs running on the OS will belong to the customer. The responsibilities for updating and maintaining the software will also be the customer's. However, updates and administration of the OS now fall to the provider, which, while posing a loss of control for operational and security purposes on the customer's part, may also represent a cost savings and increase of efficiency.

SaaS Considerations

With software as a service (SaaS), of course, most of the control of the environment is ceded to the provider. The cloud customer will not have ownership of the hardware or the software or the administration of either; the customer only supplies and processes data to and in the system.

For all relevant intents and purposes, the cloud customer, as an organization, has taken the role and responsibilities of what a common user would have in a legacy environment: few administrative rights, few privileged accounts, and very few permissions and responsibilities.

The customer remains liable for all statutory and contractual obligations related to the safeguarding of the data but, in this case, has little control over how that data is protected. The cloud provider is now almost exclusively responsible for all system maintenance, all security countermeasures, and the vast majority of policy (and implementation of that policy) affecting the data.

General Considerations

In all three models, the customer is giving up an essential form of control: physical access to the devices on which the data resides. This is a massive and serious increase of risk and loss of assurance; anyone who can physically access the location of the data can eventually take it, with or without permission.

Can we implement means to reduce the likelihood of breaches as a result of this risk? Of course—and we need to do so, in order to demonstrate due care. Such measures might include ensuring the cloud provider performs strict background checks and continual monitoring of all personnel with access to the data center, extreme physical security measures at the data center location, encryption of data processed and stored in the cloud, assignment of contractual liability to the provider (bearing in mind that legal liability remains with the customer, however), and so forth. It is important to remember, though, that the residual risk of losing physical access always remains, even when controls are utilized or other risk reduction methods are used. The following section will discuss these further.

It is worth noting that there are no defined mandates or uniform solutions ubiquitous throughout the industry; each provider will be different, and each contract will be different, so each set of rights and responsibilities will vary according to what the customer and provider negotiate.

Design Principles for Protecting Sensitive Data

The following sections review some basic secure architectural methods. Bear in mind that this is not an exhaustive list, and these techniques alone will not suffice to protect an organization and its data, but they can serve as a guideline for IT infrastructure controls.

Hardening Devices

In the traditional IT environment, devices in the DMZ (that notional area where the internal network is public-facing and connects with the outside world) were secured as a matter of practice; we knew and understood that these boxes were more likely to suffer intrusion attempts, and we hardened them accordingly.

For the cloud environment, it is probably best to adhere to this same practice, both from the cloud provider side of the equation and as cloud users. It is probably best to treat all resources in a cloud environment as if they are in the DMZ and harden them accordingly. In treating all cloud-related devices as if they are in the DMZ, we are forming good habits and a conceptual way of viewing the cloud.

The cloud provider should ensure that all devices in the data center are secured such that the following conditions are met:

- All guest accounts are removed.

- All unused ports are closed.

- No default passwords remain.

- Strong password policies are in effect.

- Any admin accounts are significantly secured and logged.

- All unnecessary services are disabled.

- Physical access is severely limited and controlled.

- Systems are patched, maintained, and updated according to vendor guidance and industry best practices.

These concepts should not be in any way new to security practitioners, but they continue to have a significant value in the cloud motif.

The cloud customer has a similar and related, but different, list of tasks. Customers must bear in mind the risks related to the way they access the cloud, which often takes the form of a bring your own device (BYOD) environment and always involves remote access. BYOD existed before the current ubiquity of cloud computing, and many of those known security practices can be employed to good effect in our current models.

For instance, cloud customers should ensure that all assets in their BYOD infrastructure that access the cloud should:

- be protected with some form of anti-malware/security software;

- have remote wipe/remote lock capability in the event of loss/theft, with the user granting written permission to the organization to wipe/lock via a signed authorized use policy;

- utilize some form of local encryption;

- be secured with strong access controls (a password, or perhaps a biometric) in a multi-factor configuration;

- have and properly employ VPN solutions for cloud access;

- have some sort of data loss, leak prevention, and protection (DLP) solution installed.

The organization may also want to consider containerization software options for personally owned user devices as a means to isolate their personal data from the organization's information.

It's not only physical devices that need to be hardened—we have to think of virtual devices in the same manner we'd consider their physical counterparts. Because cloud computing relies so heavily on virtualization for load balancing and scalability, it is important to remember that virtual instances will require strong protection both when active (so that data being processed can't be detected by other instances/users) and while stored (as files, because they contain so much material attackers would like to acquire and they are so portable). In terms of configuration, they also have to be hardened in all the same ways we secure physical machines.

Encryption

I've mentioned encryption already, and you can expect to see more references throughout the book; it's impossible to divest modern security practices from various uses of encryption. This is as true in the cloud as it was in the traditional IT environment.

We will cover cloud data security, and the associated encryption mechanisms, in Chapter 4. For the purposes of this specific discussion (basic cloud design requirements), suffice it to say that encryption should be utilized as follows:

- In the cloud data center for:
    - data at rest, which includes long-term storage/archiving/backups, protecting near-term stored files (such as snapshots of virtualized instances), preventing unauthorized access to specific datasets by authorized personnel (for instance, securing fields in databases so that database admins can manage software but not modify/view content);
    - secure sanitization (cryptographic erasure/cryptoshredding)
- In communications between cloud providers and users for:
    - creating secure sessions,
    - ensuring the integrity and confidentiality of data in transit

 Eventually, we'd like to be able to process data in the cloud while it's encrypted, without having to decrypt it, so that it is never exposed, even temporarily, to anyone other than the authorized users. Although this capability is not currently available, ongoing research shows promise. This technology is known as *homomorphic encryption*, and it's worth knowing the term and understanding the possibility, even though it's still in the experimental stages.

Layered Defenses

This is another concept that is not new, but it's one that carries over into the cloud. Also referred to as *defense in depth*, it is the practice of having multiple overlapping means of securing the environment with a variety of methods. These should include a blend of administrative, logical, technical, and physical controls.

From a cloud provider perspective, a layered defense should entail the following:

- Strong personnel controls involving background checks and continual monitoring
- Technological controls such as encryption, event logging, and access control enforcement
- Physical controls related to both the overall campus, the various facilities, the areas within the data center where data is processed and stored, individual racks and particular devices, and portable media entering and leaving the campus
- Governance mechanisms and enforcement, such as strong policies and regular, thorough audits

From a cloud customer perspective, similar efforts should include the following items:

- Training programs for staff and users that include good coverage of security topics
- Contractual enforcement of policy requirements
- Use of encryption and logical isolation mechanisms on BYOD assets
- Strong remote access control methods, perhaps including multifactor authentication

 When considering secure architectures and designs, it is often helpful to refer to existing guidance; there is no reason to rediscover and reinvent every aspect of security for yourself when many publications and tools already exist. Some you might find useful:

- The Cloud Security Alliance Cloud Controls Matrix (https://cloudsecurityalliance.org/group/cloud-controls-matrix/)
- The National Institute of Standards and Technology (NIST)'s Risk Management Framework (SP 800-37) (http://nvlpubs.nist.gov/nistpubs/SpecialPublications/NIST.SP.800-37r1.pdf)
- ISACA's COBIT

Summary

In this chapter, we have gone into some depth discussing how an organization determines its business requirements and critical paths and what that information is used for, in terms of security. We also covered the nominal boundaries of the various cloud service models and the rights and responsibilities related to each, from both the customer and provider perspectives. In addition, we touched on basic cloud architectural and design concepts for protecting sensitive data. In upcoming chapters, we will explore the latter topic in more detail.

Exam Essentials

Know how to determine business requirements. Understand the function and purpose of the business impact analysis and how it enables the organization to ascertain the inventory, value, and criticality of organizational assets.

Be familiar with the boundaries of each of the cloud service models. Know which party is responsible for specific controls in each of the various models. Realize that there is a significant amount of room to negotiate contractual definitions of the responsibilities and rights of both the cloud provider and cloud customer for all of the models.

Understand how cloud architecture and design supports sensitive data security. Be familiar with how hardening devices, encryption, and defense in depth enhances the protection of data in the cloud. Know where to find frameworks, models, and guidance for secure cloud design.

Written Labs

You can find the answers to the written labs in Appendix A.

1. Download FEMA's Business Impact Analysis Worksheet at `https://www.fema.gov/media-library/assets/documents/89526`.

2. Choose a department/function within your organization to use in this exercise; it can be anything you want, whether or not it has to do with IT provision or cloud computing.

3. Choose a hypothetical risk/threat to use in the exercise; this might be a natural disaster, or it could be an attack by malicious actors, or anything else you prefer.

4. Fill out the form using the business function and risk/threat, using information as accurately and realistically as possible.

Review Questions

You can find the answers to the review questions in Appendix B.

1. Gathering business requirements can aid the organization in determining all of these facets of organizational assets except _____.

    A. Full inventory

    B. Usefulness

    C. Value

    D. Criticality

2. The BIA can be used to provide information about all the following elements except _____.

    A. Risk analysis

    B. Secure acquisition

    C. BC/DR planning

    D. Selection of security controls

3. In which cloud service model is the customer required to maintain the OS?

    A. CaaS

    B. SaaS

    C. PaaS

    D. IaaS

4. In which cloud service model is the customer required to maintain and update only the applications?

    A. CaaS

    B. SaaS

    C. PaaS

    D. IaaS

5. In which cloud service model is the customer only responsible for the data?

    A. CaaS

    B. SaaS

    C. PaaS

    D. IaaS

6. The cloud customer and provider negotiate their respective responsibilities and rights regarding the capabilities and data of the cloud service. Where is the eventual agreement codified?

   A. RMF

   B. Contract

   C. MOU

   D. BIA

7. In attempting to provide a layered defense, the security practitioner should convince senior management to include security controls of which type?

   A. Technological

   B. Physical

   C. Administrative

   D. All of the above

8. Which of the following is considered an administrative control?

   A. Access control process

   B. Keystroke logging

   C. Door locks

   D. Biometric authentication

9. Which of the following is considered a technological control?

   A. Firewall software

   B. Fireproof safe

   C. Fire extinguisher

   D. Firing personnel

10. Which of the following is the best example of a physical control?

    A. Carpets

    B. Ceilings

    C. Doors

    D. Fences

11. In a cloud environment, encryption should be used for all the following except
    _____.

    A. Long-term storage of data

    B. Near-term storage of virtualized images

    C. Secure sessions/VPN

    D. Profile formatting

12. The process of hardening a device should include all the following except
_____.

    A. Improve default accounts

    B. Close unused ports

    C. Delete unnecessary services

    D. Strictly control administrator access

13. The process of hardening a device should include which of the following?

    A. Encrypting the OS

    B. Updating and patching the system

    C. Using video cameras

    D. Performing thorough personnel background checks

14. What is an experimental technology that is intended to create the possibility of processing encrypted data without having to decrypt it first?

    A. Homomorphic

    B. Polyinstantiation

    C. Quantum-state

    D. Gastronomic

15. Risk appetite for an organization is determined by which of the following?

    A. Reclusion evaluation

    B. Senior management

    C. Legislative mandates

    D. Contractual agreement

16. What is the risk left over after controls and countermeasures are put in place?

    A. Null

    B. High

    C. Residual

    D. Pertinent

17. All the following are ways of addressing risk except_____.

    A. Acceptance

    B. Reversal

    C. Mitigation

    D. Transfer

18. To protect data on user devices in a BYOD environment, the organization should consider requiring all the following except_____.

    A. DLP agents

    B. Local encryption

    C. Multifactor authentication

    D. Two-person integrity

19. Devices in the cloud data center should be secure against attack. All the following are means of hardening devices except_____.

    A. Using a strong password policy

    B. Removing default passwords

    C. Strictly limiting physical access

    D. Removing all admin accounts

20. Which of the following best describes risk?

    A. Preventable

    B. Everlasting

    C. The likelihood that a threat will exploit a vulnerability

    D. Transient

Chapter 3

Data Classification

THE OBJECTIVE OF THIS CHAPTER IS TO ACQUAINT THE READER WITH THE FOLLOWING CONCEPTS:

Data is an asset. As with all other assets, knowing what data you have, where it is (logically and physically), and its relative value and need for protection is absolutely essential for properly apportioning security resources. In this chapter, we will discuss how data is categorized and classified, why the location of the data matters, intellectual property concepts and practices, and various aspects of data retention and deletion requirements.

Data Inventory and Discovery

In the previous chapter, we discussed the importance of creating an asset inventory; part of that effort will require identifying all the data owned by the organization.

Data Ownership

When we talk about data, we must assign responsibilities according to who has possession and legal ownership of that data. In the cloud computing motif, we tend to assign roles to allocate those responsibilities.

In most cases:

- The *data owner* is the organization that has collected or created the data, in general terms. Within the organization, we often assign a specific data owner as being the individual with rights and responsibilities for that data; this is usually the department head or business unit manager for the office that has created or collected a certain dataset. From a cloud perspective, the cloud customer is usually the data owner. Many international treaties and frameworks refer to the data owner as the *data controller.*

- The *data custodian* is any person or entity that is tasked with the daily maintenance and administration of the data. The custodian also has the role of applying the proper security controls and processes as directed by the data owner. Within an organization, the custodian might be a database administrator.

- *Processing* is anything that can be done to data: copying it, printing it, destroying it, utilizing it. The *data processor* is any organization or person who manipulates, stores, or moves the data on behalf of the data owner. From an international law perspective, the cloud provider is a data processor.

Here are essential points to remember about the rights and responsibilities of data ownership and custody:

- Data processors do not necessarily all have direct relationships with data owners; processors can be third parties, or even further removed down the supply chain.

- Data owners remain legally responsible for all data they own. This is true even if data is compromised by a data processor several times removed from the data owner.

- Ownership, custody, rights, responsibilities, and liability are all relative to the dataset in question and therefore are only specific to that data in that circumstance. For instance, a cloud provider is usually the data processor for a cloud customer's data, but the provider is the data owner for information that the provider collects and creates, such as the provider's own customer list, asset inventory, and billing information.

The Data Lifecycle

The data lifecycle is represented in Figure 3.1.

FIGURE 3.1   Data lifecycle

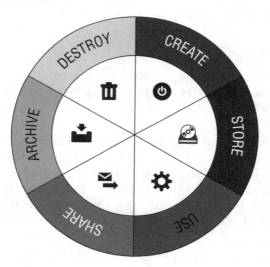

It is important to know the phases of the data lifecycle, in order, both for the CCSP exam and for your understanding of data security concepts. In this section of the chapter, we're mostly concerned with the first phase: Create.

The data owner will be identified in the Create phase. Many data security and management responsibilities require action on the part of the data owner at this point of the lifecycle.

Going with the Flow

In order to apply controls in a sensible way throughout the lifecycle, taking into consideration which aspects are overseen by the cloud customer and which by the provider, it is useful to diagram the way data moves through the various production processes. This can be done with traditional business-oriented flow charts and line diagrams, in order to visually portray the steps in a process, or with more system-oriented data flow diagrams (DFDs). A DFD is extremely useful in systems/software engineering in order to establish functional requirements before selection of the technology takes place; this obviates the likelihood that a choice of platform or component will drive the business process instead of the other way around.

In a cloud-based environment, diagramming allows the cloud customer to determine where specific controls need to be added and which are already supported by the provider (as stated in the contract/terms of service) and can aid in the choice and implementation of controls as well.

Data Categorization

The data owner will be in the best position to understand how the data is going to be used by the organization. This allows the data owner to appropriately categorize the data. The organization can have any number of categories or types of information; these might be clearly defined and reused throughout the organization, or they might be arbitrarily assigned by data owners during the Create phase.

Here are some ways an organization might categorize data:

Regulatory Compliance   Different business activities are governed by different regulations. The organization may want to create categories based on which regulations apply to a specific dataset. This might include the Graham-Leach-Bliley Act (GLBA), Payment Card Industry (PCI), Sarbanes-Oxley (SOX), Health Insurance Portability and Accountability Act (HIPAA), General Data Protection Regulation (GDPR), and/or various other forms of international, national, and local compliance.

Business Function   The organization might want to have specific categories for different uses of data. Perhaps the data is tagged based on its use in billing, marketing, or operations.

Functional Unit   Each department or office might have its own category and keep all data it controls within its own category.

By Project   Some organizations might define datasets by the projects they are associated with as a means of creating discrete, compartmentalized projects.

There is literally no limit to how an organization might categorize data. Whatever motif the organization uses, however, should be adopted and enforced uniformly throughout the organization. Ad hoc categorization is the same as having no categorization at all.

Data Classification

Much like categorization, data classification is the responsibility of the data owner, takes place in the Create phase, and is assigned according to an overall organizational policy based on a specific characteristic of the given dataset. The classification, like the categorization, can take any form defined by the organization and should be uniformly applied.

Types of classification might include the following:

Sensitivity   This is the classification model used by the US military. Data is assigned a classification according to the sensitivity of the data, based on the negative impact an unauthorized disclosure would cause. In models of this kind, classification must be assigned to all data, even in the negative, so material that is not deemed to be sensitive must be assigned the "unclassified" label. We will discuss labeling shortly.

Jurisdiction   The geophysical location of the source or storage point of the data might have significant bearing on how that data is treated and handled. For instance, personally identifiable information (PII) data gathered from citizens of the European Union (EU) is subject to the EU privacy laws, which are much stricter and more comprehensive than privacy laws in the United States.

> Personally identifiable information (PII) is but one of many types of sensitive data. PII is discussed further in many chapters of this book.

Criticality   Data that is deemed critical to organizational survival might be classified in a manner distinct from trivial, basic operational data. As we know from previous chapters, the business impact analysis (BIA) helps us determine which material would be classified this way.

> There are no industry-defined, statutory-mandated definitions for "categorization" versus "classification" of data, except in those areas covered by specific regulations (for instance, the US military uses classification constructs defined by federal law). The terms can often be used interchangeably. For the purposes of discussion in this book, I will try to adhere to this understanding of the terms: data is categorized by its use and classified by a certain trait. Again, this is not an industry standard, and (ISC)² does not create a bright-line distinction between the terms.

Data Mapping

Data between organizations (or sometimes even between departments) must be normalized and translated so that it conforms in a way meaningful to both parties. This is typically referred to as *data mapping*. When used in the context of classification efforts, mapping is necessary so that data that is known as sensitive (and in need of protection) in one system/

organization is recognized as such by the receiving system/organization so that those protections can continue. Without proper mapping efforts, data classified at a specific level might be exposed to undue risk or threats.

Data Labeling

When the data owner creates, categorizes, and classifies the data, the data also needs to be labeled. The label should indicate who the data owner is, usually in terms of the office or role instead of an individual name or identity (because, of course, personnel can change roles with an organization or leave for other organizations). The label should take whatever form is necessary for it to be enduring, understandable, and consistent; for instance, labels on data in hardcopy might be printed headers and footers, whereas labels on electronic files might be embedded in the filename and nomenclature. Labels should be evident and communicate the pertinent concepts without necessarily disclosing the data they describe.

Depending on the needs of the organization and the nature of its operations, labels might include the following kinds of information:

- Date of creation
- Date of scheduled destruction/disposal
- Confidentiality level
- Handling directions
- Dissemination/distribution instructions
- Access limitations
- Source
- Jurisdiction
- Applicable regulation

 Real World Scenario

Labels Work Both Ways

Labels can aid in security efforts by readily indicating the nature of certain information and how it should be handled and protected. For instance, in the US military and federal government, classified data in hardcopy is labeled in a number of ways, including the use of cover sheets. Cover sheets convey only one characteristic of the data: the sensitivity of the material (in military taxonomy, this is called "classification," with a somewhat different meaning than used in this book). Sensitivity is indicated in at least two ways: the title of the class (e.g., Secret, Top Secret) in large, bold letters, and the color of the sheet and markings (blue for Confidential, red for Secret, and so forth). This reminds the user (the person carrying or reading the documents) in a very simple way how to secure the material when it is not in use or is unattended. It also informs anyone else how to react if they come across such material unattended; a manager leaving the office at the end of the workday might do one last walk-through of the workspace, and a red cover sheet left on a desk will immediately catch the eye.

Of course, this also has the same effect for malicious actors; the cover sheet lets someone with ill intent instantly know the potential value of specific material: the pages with the red cover sheet are more valuable than the ones with the blue cover sheet.

Data Discovery Methods

To determine and accurately inventory the data under its control, the organization can employ various tools and techniques. *Data discovery* is a term that can be used to refer to several kinds of tasks: it might mean that the organization is attempting to create an initial inventory of data it owns or that the organization is involved in electronic discovery (*e-discovery*, the legal term for how electronic evidence is collected as part of an investigation or lawsuit; we'll discuss this in more depth in Chapter 11, "Legal and Compliance Part 2"), and it can also mean the modern use of datamining tools to discover trends and relations in the data already in the organization's inventory.

Label-Based Discovery

Obviously, the labels created by data owners in the Create phase of the data lifecycle will greatly aid any data discovery effort. With accurate and sufficient labels, the organization can readily determine what data it controls and what amounts of each kind. This is another reason the habit and process of labeling is so important.

Labels can be especially useful when the discovery effort is undertaken in response to a mandate with a specific purpose, such as a court order or a regulatory demand: if all data related to X is required, and all such data is readily labeled, it is easy to collect and disclose all the appropriate data, and only the appropriate data.

Metadata-Based Discovery

In addition to labels, metadata can be useful for discovery purposes. Colloquially referred to as "data about data," metadata is a listing of traits and characteristics about specific data elements or sets. Metadata is often automatically created at the same time as the data, often by the hardware or software used to create the parent data. For instance, most modern digital cameras create a vast amount of metadata every time a photograph is taken, such as date, time, and location where the photo was shot, make and model of the camera, and so forth; all that metadata is embedded in the picture file and is copied and transferred whenever the image itself is copied or moved.

Data discovery can therefore use metadata in the same way labels might be used; specific fields of the metadata might be scanned for particular terms, and all matching data elements collected for a certain purpose.

Content-Based Discovery

Even without labels or metadata, discovery tools can be used to locate and identify specific kinds of data by delving into the content of datasets. This technique can be as basic as term searches or can use sophisticated pattern-matching technology.

 Content analysis can also be used for more-specific security controls as well as discovery; we will discuss egress monitoring solutions in Chapter 4, "Cloud Data Security."

Data Analytics

Current technological options provide additional options for finding and assigning types to data. In many cases, these modern tools create new data feeds from sets of data that already exist within the environment. These include the following:

Datamining   The term for the family of activities from which the other options on this list derive. This kind of data analysis is an outgrowth of the possibilities offered by regular use of the cloud, also known as "big data." When the organization has collected various data streams and can run queries across these various feeds, the organization can detect and analyze previously unknown trends and patterns that can be extremely useful.

Real-Time Analytics   In some cases, tools can provide datamining functionality concurrently with data creation and use. These tools rely on automation and require efficiency to perform properly.

Agile Business Intelligence   State-of-the-art datamining involves recursive, iterative tools and processes that can detect trends in trends and identify even more oblique patterns in historical and recent data.

Structured vs. Unstructured Data

Data that is sorted according to meaningful, discrete types and attributes, such as data in a database, is said to be *structured*. Unsorted data (such as the content of various emails in a user's Sent folder, which could include discussion of any topic or contain all types of content) is considered *unstructured*. It is typically much easier to perform data discovery actions on structured data because that data is already situated and arranged.

 It's worth your time to understand data analytics options, both for purposes of the exam as well as possible security implications in your organization.

Jurisdictional Requirements

Various legal constructs exist across the globe, and being in the cloud means your organization may be subject to many simultaneously. This can create additional risks for your organization and more complications for you as a security practitioner. It will be your duty to be aware of which laws affect the organization, and you must have a general idea of how to ensure your organization can comply with them all.

Unfortunately, the use of cloud computing comes with some challenges in terms of awareness and compliance with specific jurisdictions. For instance, because of the way resources are dynamically assigned, the cloud user might not know exactly where, in terms of both data centers and geographic locations, the organization's data is physically located at any given moment; the data may cross city limits, state lines, or even national borders as the cloud provider manages virtualized images, stored data, and operational data. (Indeed, depending on the level of automation and data center design, the cloud provider might not even know, moment by moment, which city, state, or country specific data is located in.)

So both for the CCSP exam and for the protection of your organization, you should be familiar with several legal constructs that may significantly affect the data in your charge. The book addresses many of these in some detail in Chapters 10 and 11; I'm simply going to list some of them here, with brief notes, to introduce the concepts.

The United States The United States offers strong protections for intellectual property. There is no singular, overarching federal privacy statute; instead, the United States tends to address privacy with industry-specific legislation (GLBA for banking/insurance, HIPAA for medical care, and so forth) or with contractual obligations (PCI). Many strong, granular data breach notification laws exist that are enforced by states and localities (especially New York and California).

Europe Europe provides good intellectual property protections. It has massive, exhaustive, comprehensive personal privacy protections, including the EU General Data Protection Regulation.

Asia Asia has disparate levels of intellectual property protection. Data privacy protection levels differ greatly by country. With its Act on the Protection of Personal Information, Japan adheres to the EU model, and Singapore does the same. Other countries follow much-reduced guidance. China, for example, has a legal requirement that is the opposite of privacy: all IT traffic and communications in China must be accessible by the Chinese government.

South/Central America South America and Central America have various intellectual property mechanisms. Most countries lack privacy protection frameworks, with the notable exception of Argentina, which with its Personal Data Protection Act is in direct correlation with the EU legislation.

Australia/New Zealand Australia and New Zealand provide strong intellectual property protections and very strong privacy protections, with the Australian Privacy Act mapping directly to the EU statutes.

The EU privacy laws will be a big driver for any organization wanting to do business in or with Europe. For exam purposes, you should be versed in the EU General Data Protection Regulation as well as the mechanisms used in the United States to comply with these laws (known as the Privacy Shield). These are addressed further in Chapters 10 and 11.

Information Rights Management (IRM)

Managing information in accordance with who has rights to it is part of information rights management (IRM). The term DRM is also often used in our industry, sometimes taken to mean "digital rights management" or "data rights management." Other terms used to convey similar meanings include ERM (enterprise rights management") and offshoots such as E-DRM. There is no conclusive international or industry standard defining these terms or how they might be applied in a given process or tool.

Suffice it to say, the concept of "rights management," regardless of the preceding modifier, entails the use of specific controls that act in concert with or in addition to the organization's other access control mechanisms to protect certain types of assets, usually at the file level. For example, an organization might have an overall access control program that requires users to log in to the systems that they use for performing job functions. Beyond that basic access, specific files the users manipulate, such as sensitive financial documents, might have additional protections for "rights management" that prevent the users from deleting, modifying, or copying those files.

For study purposes, bear in mind that the (ISC)² DCO favors the term IRM to discuss this concept. This book will use IRM for this purpose.

Intellectual Property Protections

Intellectual property is that class of valuable belongings that are intangible; literally, assets of the mind. In many countries, there are many legal protections for intellectual property, and you should be familiar with them.

Copyright

The legal protection for expressions of ideas is known as *copyright*. In the United States, copyright is granted to anyone who first creates an expression of an idea. Usually, this involves literary works, films, music, software, and artistic works.

Oddly, copyright does not include titles of works. For instance, while you cannot copy and sell the film *Star Wars*, you could, theoretically, write, produce, and sell a new movie that you call *Star Wars*, as long as it does not cover the same material as the other film with that name. I don't, however, recommend it.

Copyright does not cover ideas, specific words, slogans, recipes, or formulae. Those things can often be secured with other intellectual property protections; we'll discuss them later in this section.

Copyright protects the tangible expression of an idea, not the form of an idea. For instance, copyright protects the content of a book, not the hard-copy version of a book itself; illegal copying of a book's contents would be a copyright infringement, whereas stealing a physical book would be theft. The copyright belongs to the author or whomever the author sells or grants the rights to, not to someone who currently holds the physical copy of the book.

The duration of copyrights vary based on the terms under which they were created, depending on if an individual created the work themselves or if the work was created under contract (a "work-for-hire"). Typically, copyright lasts for either 70 years after the author's death or 120 years after the first publication of a work for hire.

Copyright gives exclusive use of the work to the creator, with some exceptions. The creator is the only entity legally allowed to do the following:

- Perform the work publically.
- Profit from the work.
- Make copies of the work.
- Make derivative works from the original.
- Import or export the work.
- Broadcast the work.
- Sell or otherwise assign these rights.

This discussion goes beyond the scope of the CCSP, but there are exceptions to the exclusivity of copyright:

- **Fair Use:** There is a family of exceptions to copyright exclusivity, known as "fair use." Fair use includes the following scenarios:
    - **Academic Fair Use:** Instructors can make limited copies or presentations of copyrighted works for educational purposes.
    - **Critique:** Portions of the work may be used in critical reviews, discussing or assessing its merit.
    - **News Reporting:** Because an informed populace is essential to a free society, we have waived some intellectual property protections for reporting purposes.
    - **Scholarly Research:** Similar to academic fair use, but among researchers instead of teachers and students.
    - **Satire:** A mocking sendup of the work may be created using a significant portion of the original work.

- **Library Preservation:** Libraries and archives are allowed to make limited numbers of copies of original works in order to preserve the work itself.

- **Personal Backup:** Someone who has legally purchased a licensed work may make a single backup copy for themselves, for use if the original fails. This explicitly includes computer programs.

- **Versions for People with Physical Disabilities:** It is legal to make specialized copies of licensed works for use by someone with a disability.

These exceptions are not unlimited. Anyone using a copyright exception has to consider many subjective factors, including the possible commercial market for the work and the size, scope, and nature of the original work.

The fact that something is copyrighted is often communicated by attaching the copyright symbol to it, sometimes with additional text that emphasizes this fact. See Figure 3.2.

FIGURE 3.2   The copyright symbol

copyright
all rights reserved

 Copyright infringement is usually dealt with as a civil case: the copyright owner has to bring a lawsuit against someone they believe has illegally copied or used their work. However, in some cases, demonstrated willful infringement can be investigated by the government as a criminal matter and often referred to as *piracy*.

Different countries view copyrights in various ways. Although the creator automatically owns the copyright in the United States, in some jurisdictions the copyright belongs to the person who first registers the work in that jurisdiction.

 Real World Scenario

The DMCA

The Digital Millennium Copyright Act (DMCA) is a notorious piece of legislation ostensibly created to provide additional protections to creative works in digital formats. It is generally viewed as both crafted for too specific a purpose and also used in an overly broad manner. It also puts the burden of proof on those accused of copyright infringement and requires presumptive action upon accusation.

The details of how the DMCA came into being might be beyond the scope of the CCSP exam, but they are interesting: The Hollywood film industry was using an electronic encryption mechanism known as CSS—the Content Scramble System—to protect content on DVDs from being illegally copied. A group of people created a program to remove this encryption from DVDs; this program was known as DeCSS. Lobbyists for content producers, under specific direction from the Motion Picture Association of America and eventually with the participation of the Recording Industry Association of America, convinced Congress to pass the DMCA to make DeCSS and programs like it illegal; this would include writing, distributing, and publishing anti-encryption software. The intent was to protect copyrighted material (movies and songs, for the most part) from piracy.

In practice, however, the effect has been quite different. Certain provisions of the DMCA, namely the "takedown notice" process, have been abused as a matter of course. Under the takedown notice clause, any web hosting service must remove content from the Internet if anyone makes the accusation that it is or includes copyrighted material, and that material has to remain off the web until whoever published it can prove either that the material is not copyrighted or that they own the copyright. This has led to a significant use of the takedown notice for frivolous or malicious reasons. This is just one of many unintended consequences of the DMCA.

Trademarks

Unlike copyrights, trademark protection is intended to be applied to specific words and graphics. Trademarks are representations of an organization—its brand. A trademark is meant to protect the esteem and goodwill that an organization has built among the marketplace, especially in public perception.

A trademark can be the name of an organization, a logo, a phrase associated with an organization, even a specific color or sound, or some combination of these.

In order to have a trademark protected by law, it must be registered within a jurisdiction. Commonly, that is the US Patent and Trademark Office (USPTO), the federal entity for registering trademarks. Trademarks registered with the USPTO can use the ® symbol to signify registration. States also offer trademark registration, and trademarks registered with state offices often use the ™ symbol.

Trademarks last into perpetuity, as long as the trademark owner continues to use them for commercial purposes. Trademark infringement is actionable, and trademark owners can sue in court for remedy for infringement.

Patents

The USPTO, as the name indicates, is also responsible for registering patents. Patents are the legal mechanism for protecting intellectual property in the form of inventions, processes, materials, decorations, and plant life. In securing a patent, the patent owner gains exclusivity in the production, sale, and importation of the patented property.

Patents typically last for 20 years from the time of the patent application. There is some provision for extension, since the process of getting a patent can take many months, or even years.

Patent infringement, as with the other intellectual property protections, is cause to sue for relief in federal court.

Globally, prospective patent holders might apply to the World Intellectual Property Office (WIPO) for approval under the Patent Cooperation Treaty, which has 152 signatory member nations. If a patent is approved by the WIPO, the property protected by the patent will be recognized in each of the member countries.

Trade Secrets

Trade secrets are intellectual property that involve many of the same aspects as patented material: processes, formulas, commercial methods, and so forth. They can also include some things that aren't patentable, such as aggregations of information (this might include lists of clients or suppliers, for instance).

Trade secrets are also somewhat like copyrights in the United States, in that protections for them exist upon creation, without any additional requirement for registration.

However, unlike other intellectual property protections, material considered trade secrets must be just that: secret. They cannot be disclosed to the public, and efforts must be made to maintain secrecy in order to keep this legal protection.

Trade secrets are then provided legal protection from illicit acquisition; anyone who tries to acquire trade secrets by theft or misappropriation can be sued in civil court (similar to other forms of intellectual property), but they can also be prosecuted in federal court for this crime.

Trade secret protection does not, however, confer the exclusivity granted by other intellectual property protections. Anyone other than the owner of the trade secret who discovers or invents the same or similar methods, processes, and information through legal means is justified and legally free to use that knowledge to their own benefit. In fact, someone who discovers someone else's trade secret through legitimate means is also free to patent it (assuming there is no existing patent on the same material or concept).

Like a trademark, a trade secret lasts into perpetuity, as long as the owner is still using it in commercial activity.

IRM Tool Traits

IRM can be implemented in enterprises by manufacturers, vendors, or content creators. Usually, material protected by IRM solutions need some form of labeling or metadata associated with the material in order for the IRM tool to function properly.

IRM implementations can vary in technological sophistication and technique. Here are some ways that IRM has been or could be applied:

Rudimentary Reference Checks   The content itself can automatically check for proper usage or ownership. For instance, in many vintage computer games, the game would pause in operation until the player entered some information that could only have been acquired with the purchase of a licensed copy of the game, like a word or a phrase from the manual that shipped with the game.

Online Reference Checks   Microsoft software packages, including Windows operating systems and Office programs, are often locked in the same manner, requiring users to enter a product key at installation; the program would then later check the product key against an online database when the system connected to the Internet.

Local Agent Checks   The user installs a reference tool that checks the protected content against the user's license. Again, gaming engines often work this way, with gamers having to download an agent of Steam or GOG.com when installing any games purchased from those distributors; the agents check the user's system against the online license database to ensure the games are not pirated.

Presence of Licensed Media   Some IRM tools require the presence of licensed media, such as disks, in the system while the content is being used. The IRM engine is on the media, often installed with some cryptographic engine that identifies the unique disk and the licensed content and allowing usage based on that relationship.

Support-Based Licensing   Some IRM implementations are predicated on the need of continual support for content; this is particularly true of production software. Licensed software might be allowed ready access to updates and patches, while the vendor could prevent unlicensed versions from getting this type of support.

IRM implementations usually include adding another layer of access control (beyond what the enterprise employs for its own operational purposes) on files and objects containing protected material. IRM can also be used to implement localized information security policies; specific users or groups of users might have all content they create specially tagged and marked with appropriate access restrictions, for instance.

Employing IRM in the cloud poses some challenges, though. These include the following:

Replication Restrictions   Because IRM often involves preventing unauthorized duplication, and the cloud necessitates creating, closing, and replicating virtualized host instances (including user-specific content stored locally on the virtual host), IRM might interfere with automatic resource allocation processes.

Jurisdictional Conflicts   The cloud extends across boundaries and borders, often in a manner unknown or uncontrolled by the data owner, which can pose problems when intellectual property rights are restricted by locale.

Agent/Enterprise Conflicts   IRM solutions that require local installation of software agents for enforcement purposes might not always function properly in the cloud environment, with virtualization engines, or with the various platforms used in a bring your own device (BYOD) enterprise.

Mapping Identity and Access Management (IAM) and IRM   Because of the extra layer of access control (often involving content-specific access control lists, or ACLs), the IRM IAM processes might conflict or not work properly with the enterprise/cloud IAM. A conflict is even more possible when cloud IAM functions are outsourced to a third party, such as a cloud access security broker (CASB).

API Conflicts   Because the IRM tool is often incorporated into the content, usage of the material might not offer the same level of performance across different applications, such as content readers or media players.

In general terms, IRM should provide the following functions, regardless of type of content or format:

Persistent Protection   The IRM should follow the content it protects, regardless of where that content is located, whether it is a duplicate copy or the original file, or how it is being utilized. This protection should not be easy to circumvent.

Dynamic Policy Control   The IRM tool should allow content creators and data owners to modify ACLs and permissions for the protected data under their control.

Automatic Expiration   Because of the nature of some legal protections of intellectual property (described earlier in this chapter), a significant amount of digital content will not be protected in perpetuity. The IRM protections should cease when the legal protections cease. Conversely, licenses also expire; access and permissions for protected content should likewise expire, no matter where that content exists at the end of the license period.

Continuous Auditing   The IRM should allow for comprehensive monitoring of the content's use and access history.

Replication Restrictions   Much of the purpose of IRM is to restrict illegal or unauthorized duplication of protected content. Therefore, IRM solutions should enforce these restrictions across the many forms of copying that exist, to include screen-scraping, printing, electronic duplication, email attachments, and so on.

Remote Rights Revocation   The owner of the rights to specific intellectual property should have the ability to revoke those rights at any time; this capability might be used as a result of litigation or infringement.

Data Control

The organization also needs to protect data in lifecycle phases other than Create. You will need to make, use, and enforce a set of data management policies and practices that cover topics such as data retention, audit, and disposal. The following sections will address each of those in turn.

Each aspect of data management—retention, audit, and disposal—will need a specific policy addressing it. There is no reason, however, that you cannot include all three policies under one overarching policy, such as a data management policy. Just be sure each area is addressed thoroughly and with sufficient granularity; don't let any individual subpolicy be inferior in quality or comprehensiveness simply because you're aggregating your required governance.

Data Retention

As with all matters involving our profession, the organization's data retention program should start with and be based on a strong, coherent policy. The data retention policy should include the following:

Retention Periods   The retention period is the length of time that the organization should keep data. This usually refers to data that is being archived for long-term storage—that is, data not currently being used in the production environment. The retention period is often expressed in a number of years and is frequently set by regulation or legislation (see the next item). Data retention periods can also be mandated or modified by contractual agreements.

Applicable Regulation   As just mentioned, the retention period can be mandated by statute or contract; the retention policy should refer to all applicable regulatory guidance. This is especially true in cases where there is conflicting regulation; the policy should then also highlight any such disparity, and include mention of senior management's decision for how to approach and resolve this conflict with the policy as an appropriate mechanism. For instance, laws may impose different retention periods for specific kinds of data, and the organization might operate in states with differing mandated periods; the policy should then explicitly explain the conflicting periods as well as the period senior management determined as the solution.

Retention Formats   The policy should contain a description of how the data is actually archived—that is, what type of media it is stored on and any handling specifications particular to the data. For example, some types of data are required by regulation to be kept encrypted while in storage. In these cases, the policy should include a description of the encryption engine, key storage and retrieval procedures, and reference to the applicable regulations.

Data Classification   Highly sensitive or regulated data may entail specific retention periods, by mandate or contract or best practice. The organization can use the classification level of data to determine how long specific datasets or types of data need to be retained. Conversely, the retention period, if mandated, should be considered when the organization crafts the classification policy as a means to describe/create classification levels (e.g., the longer the retention period, the higher the classification).

Archiving and Retrieval Procedures   Having data in storage is useful; stored data can be used to correct production errors, can serve as business continuity and disaster recovery (BC/DR) backups, and can be datamined for business intelligence purposes. But stored data is only useful if it can be retrieved and put back into production in an efficient and cost-effective manner. The policy should mandate the creation of a detailed description of the processes both for sending data into storage and for recovering it. The detailed processes might be included as an attachment to the policy or mentioned by reference to the actual documentation for the processes; the processes might require more frequent updates and editing than the policy and could be kept separate.

Monitoring, Maintenance, and Enforcement   As with all policies in the organization, the policy should list, in detail, how often it will be reviewed and amended, by whom, consequences for failure to adhere to the policy, and which entity within the organization is responsible for enforcement.

> Backups are great; a lot of organizations do regular, thorough backups. However, all too often, these same organizations don't practice recovery from backup, so they are unprepared for those situations where recovery is necessary and recovery efforts are hampered or fail. It is useful, and in some cases required by regulation, to test your organization's recovery from backup in order to ensure this won't happen to you.

Managing data retention in the cloud can be especially tricky; it may be difficult to ensure, for instance, that the cloud provider is not retaining the organization's data beyond the retention period (part of the appeal of the cloud is how good cloud providers are at retaining data, and not losing it; purposefully getting rid of data is a whole other matter). When considering cloud migration, and during negotiations with potential cloud providers, the organization should make a point of ensuring the provider can support the organization's retention policy.

> The data retention policy addresses the activities that take place in the Archive phase of the data lifecycle.

Legal Hold

In some jurisdictions, the concept of a "legal hold" severely affects an organization's data retention and destruction policies because it supercedes them. When an organization is notified that either (a) a law enforcement/regulatory entity is commencing an investigation or (b) a private entity is commencing litigation against the organization, the organization must suspend all relevant data destruction activities until the investigation/lawsuit has been fully resolved. (All "relevant" data destruction activities are those related to the particular case in question. The organization can continue to destroy data/material that is not associated with the particular case.)

This usually takes precedence over any other existing organizational policy, applicable law, contractual agreement, or motivation. For instance, in the United States, this concept is dictated by the Federal Rules of Evidence, which mandates that a legal hold notice has primacy, even over federal laws (such as HIPAA) that would require data to be destroyed at the end of a retention period.

Therefore, a legal hold can be considered a temporary paramount retention period.

Data Audit

As with all other assets, the organization needs to regularly review, inventory, and inspect the usage and condition of the data it owns. Data audit is a powerful tool for these purposes.

As with the other elements of data management, the organization should have a policy for conducting audits of its data. The policy should include detailed descriptions of the following items:

- Audit periods
- Audit scope
- Audit responsibilities (internal and/or external)
- Audit processes and procedures
- Applicable regulations
- Monitoring, maintenance, and enforcement

NOTE   As with all types of audits, the organization should be particularly careful about ensuring that auditors do not report to anyone in the management structure that owns or is affected by the data being audited; conflicts of interest must be avoided for the audits to have validity and utility.

In most organizations and enterprises, audit is predicated on logging. Logging can happen in many forms: event logging, security logging, traffic logging, and so forth. Logs can be generated by applications, OSs, and devices and for general or specific purposes (e.g., devices that collect logs as a byproduct of operations, such as servers, or devices that do logging as their main purpose, such as IDSs [intrusion detection systems] and SIEMs [security information and event monitoring systems]).

Log review and audit is a specialized task for personnel with specific training and experience. Logging is fairly easy; most software and devices in modern enterprises can effectively log anything and everything the organization might want to capture. Reading and analyzing these logs, however, can prove challenging:

Log review and analysis is not often a priority.   Most organizations do not have the wherewithal to dedicate the personnel required to effectively analyze log data. Usually, log review becomes an additional duty for someone tasked to another office (the security department, for instance). And many additional duties do not get accomplished because the personnel assigned to them become task-saturated with their other, regular job tasks.

Log review is mundane and repetitive.   Reviewing logs takes a certain kind of person: someone who can sift through loads of data in order to spot the fractional portion that might vary from the norm. This is not exciting work, and even the best analyst can become lax due to repetition.

Log review requires someone both new to the field and experienced.   This can become a management quandary: the log reviewer must be someone junior enough that they can be assigned to perform log reviews without incurring too much trade-off cost to the organization (that is, other functions they might be performing are not more expensive or valuable than the log reviews), yet the person needs to have sufficient experience and training to perform the activity in a worthwhile manner.

The reviewer needs to have an understanding of the operation.   If the reviewer cannot distinguish between what is authorized activity and what is not, they are not adding security value to the process.

It might serve the organization well for log reviews to only be a part-time function of a specific individual. If a person is only doing log analysis and has no other duties, repetition and boredom might lead to the person missing something in the review that would have otherwise been noticed. However, the person assigned to review logs must perform the task often enough that they recognize baseline activity, and therefore deviations from it; long periods between analysis sessions might lead to the analyst losing institutional knowledge and some atrophy of the skillset.

Logs are like data backups, though: many organizations perform logging; logs are easy to set, acquire, and store. The challenge, then, is to determine how often logs will be reviewed or audited, by whom, the processes for doing so, and so forth. Having the logs is one thing; reviewing the logs you have is something else.

A natural inclination of a security practitioner might be to log everything; people in our field are notoriously loathe to part with data and want to know everything about everything. The problem with doing so? Logging everything creates additional risks and costs. Having so much log data aggregated creates additional vulnerabilities and requires additional protections, and the storage required for logging everything will entail a wholesale duplication of storage systems and space.

Data audit in the cloud can pose some almost insurmountable challenges. The cloud provider may not want to (or, indeed, even be able to, for operational or contractual reasons) disclose log data to the customer for security, liability, or competitive reasons. Therefore, the organization must consider, again, specific audit requirements when opting for cloud migration and include any such specifications in the contract with the cloud provider.

The data audit policy addresses activities that take place in *all* phases of the data lifecycle.

Data Destruction/Disposal

In the traditional environment, where the organization has ownership and control of all the infrastructure, including the data, hardware, and software, data disposal options are direct and straightforward. In the cloud, data disposal is much more difficult and risky.

First, a review of data disposal options in the traditional environment:

Physical Destruction of Media and Hardware   Any hardware or portable media containing the data in question can be destroyed by burning, melting, impact (beating, drilling, grinding, and so forth), or industrial shredding. This is the preferred method of sanitization since the data is physically unrecoverable.

Degaussing   This involves applying strong magnetic fields to the hardware and media where the data resides, effectively making them blank. It does not work with solid-state drives.

Overwriting   Multiple passes of random characters are written to the storage areas (particular disk sectors) where the data resides, with a final pass of all zeroes or ones. This can be extremely time-consuming for large storage areas. This is also not an effective technique for sold-state drives, which are resistant to overwriting.

Crypto-Shredding (Cryptographic Erasure)   This involves encrypting the data with a strong encryption engine and then taking the keys generated in that process, encrypting them with a different encryption engine, and destroying the resulting keys of the second round of encryption.

WARNING   Hardware and media can never be sanitized by simply deleting the data. Deleting, as an operation, does not erase the data; it simply removes the logical pointers to the data for processing purposes.

In the cloud, many of these options are unavailable or not feasible. Because the cloud provider, not the data owner, owns the hardware, physical destruction is usually out of the question. Moreover, because of the difficulty of knowing the actual specific physical locations of the data at any given moment (or historically), it would be next to impossible to determine all the components and media that would need to be destroyed. Likewise, for that same reason, overwriting is not a practical means of sanitizing data in the cloud. Moreover, in a multitenant environment (such as a public cloud), a customer cannot physically destroy or overwrite storage space/media as that would affect other customers' data.

That leaves crypto-shredding as the sole pragmatic option for data disposal in the cloud.

As with the other data management functions, the organization needs to create a policy for data disposal. This policy should include detailed descriptions of the following:

- The process for data disposal
- Applicable regulations
- Clear direction of when data should be destroyed

Of course, we are also concerned with data remanence—that is, any data left over after sanitization and disposal methods have been attempted. If crypto-shredding is performed correctly, there should be no remanence; however, material that is somehow not included in the original encryption (say, a virtual instance that was offline during the encryption process, then added to the cloud environment) might be considered remanence. As in all cryptographic practices, proper implementation is essential for success.

 The data disposal policy addresses activities that take place in the Destroy phase of the data lifecycle.

Summary

In this chapter, we have discussed data management functions within the data lifecycle, including data retention, auditing, and disposal. The various roles, rights, and responsibilities associated with data ownership were described. We also reviewed intellectual property concepts and legal protections for intellectual property as well as IRM solution objectives and functionality. This chapter discussed inventorying data assets and the added value data discovery offers the organization. We touched on some jurisdictional concerns for data, which we will cover in more detail in Chapter 11. For all these topics, we also covered some of the challenges and risks cloud computing poses.

Exam Essentials

Know the different forms of data analytics.   Be familiar with the descriptions of datamining, real-time analytics, and agile business intelligence.

Understand the various roles, rights, and responsibilities related to data ownership.   Know who the data subject, owner, controller, processor, and custodian are. Understand the rights and responsibilities associated with each.

Understand the purpose and method of data categorization/classification.   Know why and how data owners assign categories and classifications to specific datasets under their control.

Be familiar with data discovery methods.   Know how and when data is labeled, and by whom. Also be aware of content-based discovery and the use of metadata in discovery efforts.

Know the data lifecycle.   Know all the phases of the data lifecycle, in order. Know which phases include data labeling, content creation, IRM activities, data disposal, data retention, and data audits.

Be familiar with the various intellectual property protections.   Know the protections for copyrights, trademarks, patents, and trade secrets.

Know what should be included in policies for data retention, audit, and disposal.
Understand essential aspects like terms of *retention* and *disposal*, retention formats, how
regulations dictate these things, and how every policy needs to include details for maintenance, monitoring, and enforcement.

Written Labs

You can find the answers to the written labs in Appendix A.

1. Read the NIST guidelines for cryptographic erasure inNIST SP 800-88 (rev. 1),
    Appendix D: `http://nvlpubs.nist.gov/nistpubs/SpecialPublications/NIST`
    `.SP.800-88r1.pdf`.

2. Select a sample device for lab purposes. Using the sample format shown in 800-88,
    D.1, answer the suitability questions regarding cryptoshredding for the device you have
    selected.

Review Questions

You can find the answers in Appendix B.

1. All of these are methods of data discovery except:
    A. Content-based
    B. User-based
    C. Label-based
    D. Metadata-based

2. Data labels could include all the following except:
    A. Date data was created
    B. Data owner
    C. Data value
    D. Date of scheduled destruction

3. Data labels could include all the following except:
    A. Source
    B. Delivery vendor
    C. Handling restrictions
    D. Jurisdiction

4. Data labels could include all the following except:
    A. Confidentiality level
    B. Distribution limitations
    C. Access restrictions
    D. Multifactor authentication

5. All the following are data analytics modes except:
    A. Real-time analytics
    B. Datamining
    C. Agile business intelligence
    D. Refractory iterations

6. In the cloud, the data owner is usually:
    A. In another jurisdiction
    B. The cloud customer
    C. The cloud provider
    D. The cloud access security broker

7. In the cloud, the data processor is usually:
   A. The party that assigns access rights
   B. The cloud customer
   C. The cloud provider
   D. The cloud access security broker

8. Which of the following is not an acceptable means of sanitizing hardware?
   A. Burning
   B. Deletion
   C. Industrial Shredding
   D. Drilling

9. All policies within the organization should include a section that includes all of the following except:
   A. Policy maintenance
   B. Policy monitoring
   C. Policy enforcement
   D. Policy transference

10. The most pragmatic option for data disposal in the cloud is which of the following?
    A. Melting
    B. Crypto-shredding
    C. Cold fusion
    D. Overwriting

11. What is the intellectual property protection for the tangible expression of a creative idea?
    A. Copyright
    B. Patent
    C. Trademark
    D. Trade secret

12. What is the intellectual property protection for a useful manufacturing innovation?
    A. Copyright
    B. Patent
    C. Trademark
    D. Trade secret

13. What is the intellectual property protection for a very valuable set of sales leads?

   A. Copyright

   B. Patent

   C. Trademark

   D. Trade secret

14. What is the intellectual property protection for a confidential recipe for muffins?

   A. Copyright

   B. Patent

   C. Trademark

   D. Trade secret

15. What is the intellectual property protection for the logo of a new video game?

   A. Copyright

   B. Patent

   C. Trademark

   D. Trade secret

16. What is the aspect of the DMCA that has often been abused and places the burden of proof on the accused?

   A. Toll exemption

   B. Decryption program prohibition

   C. Takedown notice

   D. Puppet plasticity

17. What is the US federal agency that accepts applications for new patents?

   A. USDA

   B. USPTO

   C. OSHA

   D. SEC

18. IRM tools use a variety of methods for enforcement of intellectual property rights. These include all the following except:

   A. Support-based licensing

   B. Local agent enforcement

   C. Dip switch validity

   D. Media-present checks

19. Which of the following does not have a personal privacy law that limits the way all citizens and entities can share personal data?

    A. Japan

    B. Belgium

    C. Argentina

    D. The United States

20. IRM solutions should generally include all the following functions except:

    A. Persistency

    B. Automatic self-destruct

    C. Automatic expiration

    D. Dynamic policy control

Cloud Data Security

THE OBJECTIVE OF THIS CHAPTER IS TO ACQUAINT THE READER WITH THE FOLLOWING CONCEPTS:

✓ **Domain 1: Cloud Concepts, Architecture, and Design**

- 1.3. Understand Security Concepts Relevant to Cloud Computing

  - 1.3.1. Cryptography and Key Management

- 1.4. Understand Design Principles of Secure Cloud Computing

  - 1.4.1. Cloud Secure Data Lifecycle

✓ **Domain 2: Cloud Data Security**

- 2.1. Describe Cloud Data Concepts

  - 2.1.1. Cloud Data Lifecycle Phases

- 2.2. Design and Implement Cloud Data Storage Architectures

  - 2.2.1. Storage Types

  - 2.2.2. Threats to Storage Types

- 2.3. Design and Apply Data Security Technologies and Strategies

  - 2.3.1. Encryption and Key Management

  - 2.3.2. Hashing

  - 2.3.3. Masking

  - 2.3.4. Tokenization

  - 2.3.5. Data Loss Prevention (DLP)

  - 2.3.6. Data Obfuscation

  - 2.3.7. Data De-identification

While cloud technology might be fairly new, the data security fundamentals remain the same: the CIA triad, regulatory constraints, layered defense, and so forth. In this chapter, we will examine the particular security challenges and techniques necessary for making a cloud format both useful and trustworthy.

Cloud Data Lifecycle

Data in the cloud should be perceived, in the general case, to have the same needs and properties as data in the legacy environment. The data lifecycle still has a purpose; only the implementation particulars will change. Figure 4.1 shows the common stages in the data lifecycle.

FIGURE 4.1   Stages of the data lifecycle

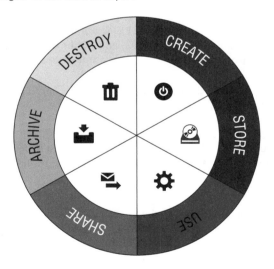

Data will still be created (Create phase)—both in the cloud itself and by remote users. It will be stored, in both the short term (Store phase) and long term (Archive phase), in the cloud. It will be manipulated and modified (Use phase) in the production environment hosted in the cloud. It will be transmitted to other users and made available for collaboration (Share phase) within the cloud; this is one of the significant benefits offered by cloud computing. In addition, we will still have a need to remove data from the production environment and sanitize the media afterward (Destroy phase).

Obviously, the particulars for performing these activities, and doing them in a secure fashion, will evolve to match any new environmental challenges.

In the cloud, each phase of the data lifecycle will require particular protections. Let's review each of the phases in turn and examine some specific control mechanisms we may want to apply in each.

Create

Data will most often be created by users accessing the cloud remotely. Depending on the use case, the data might be created locally by users at their remote workstation and then uploaded to the cloud or it might be created in the cloud data center via remote manipulation of the data residing there.

Data Created Remotely   Data created by the user should be encrypted before uploading to the cloud. We want to protect against obvious vulnerabilities, including man-in-the-middle attacks and insider threat at the cloud data center. The cryptosystem used for this purpose should have a high work factor and be listed on the FIPS 140-2 list of approved crypto solutions. We should also implement good key management practices, which we'll cover later in this chapter.

Sometimes when dealing with keys and managing them, the term *public key infrastructure (PKI)* is used. PKI is a framework of programs, procedures, communication protocols, and public key cryptography that enables a diverse group of individuals to communicate securely.

The connection used to upload the data should also be secure, preferably with an IPsec or TLS (1.2 or higher) VPN solution.

TLS replaces the deprecated SSL standard, but SSL is still utilized in many IT environments, and the practitioner may see both the term *SSL* and the technology used.

Data Created within the Cloud   Likewise, data created within the cloud via remote manipulation should be encrypted upon creation, to obviate unnecessary access or viewing by data center personnel. Again, key management should be performed according to best industry practices, as detailed later in this chapter.

Regardless of where, specifically, the data originates—in the cloud data center via remote access or at the user's location—the Create phase necessitates all the activities described in Chapter 3, "Data Classification": categorization and classification; labeling, tagging, and marking; assigning metadata; and so forth.

Store

From the perspective of the lifecycle diagram, the Store phase takes place right after the Create phase and before the Use and Share phases. This indicates that Store is usually meant to refer to near-term storage (as opposed to the Archive phase, which is obviously long-term storage).

For our purposes, we'll consider the activity in the Store phase to occur almost concurrently with the Create phase—that is, Store will happen as data is created. In that respect, the actions that should occur here have already been described: encryption at rest for mitigating exposure to threats within the cloud service provider and encryption in transit for mitigating exposure to threats while being moved to the cloud data center.

Use

We will need to utilize the same kinds of mechanisms when performing activity in the Use phase as well. Operations in the cloud environment will necessitate remote access, so those connections will all have to be secured, usually with an encrypted tunnel.

Data security in the Use phase will require considering other operational aspects as well. The platforms with which users connect to the cloud have to also be secured; in a BYOD environment, this will entail a holistic approach, since we can never be sure just what devices the users have. Users must be trained to understand the new risks that go along with cloud computing and how they will be expected to use the technology (such as VPN, IRM, and/or DLP agents assigned to them) in a safe manner. Data owners should also be careful to restrict permissions for modifying and processing their data; users should be limited to those functions that they absolutely require in order to perform their assigned tasks. And, as in many circumstances in both the cloud and legacy environments, logging and audit trails are important when data is being manipulated in any fashion.

On the provider side, secure use requires strong protections in the implementation of virtualization; the provider must ensure that data on a virtualized host can't be read or detected by other virtual hosts on that same device. Also, as has been stated several times (and will be repeated throughout the book), the provider will have to implement personnel and administrative controls so that data center personnel can't access any raw customer data.

Share

Although global collaboration is a powerful capability afforded by the cloud, it comes with risks. If users can be anywhere on the planet, so can threats.

Many of the same security controls implemented in prior phases will be useful here: encrypted files and communications, IRM solutions, and so forth. We also have to craft sharing restrictions based on jurisdiction; we may need to limit or prevent data being sent to certain locations in accordance with regulatory mandates. These restrictions can take the form of either export controls or import controls, so the security professional must be familiar with both for all regions where the organization's data might be shared.

Real World Scenario

Export and Import Restrictions

Here are export restrictions you should be familiar with:

- **International Traffic in Arms Regulations, or ITAR (United States):** State Department prohibitions on defense-related exports; can include cryptography systems.

- **Export Administration Regulations, or EAR (United States):** Department of Commerce prohibitions on dual-use items (technologies that could be used for both commercial and military purposes).

And here are import restrictions you should be familiar with:

- **Cryptography (Various):** Many countries have restrictions on importing cryptosystems or material that has been encrypted. When doing business in or with a nation that has crypto restrictions, it is the security professional's responsibility to know and understand these local mandates.

- **The Wassenaar Arrangement:** A group of 41 member countries have agreed to mutually inform each other about conventional military shipments to nonmember countries. Not a treaty, and therefore not legally binding, but may require your organization to notify your government in order to stay in compliance.

Cloud customers should also consider implementing some form of egress monitoring in the Share phase; this will be discussed in the section "Egress Monitoring (DLP)" later in this chapter.

Archive

This is the phase for long-term storage, and we necessarily have to consider this longer timeframe when planning security controls for the data.

Cryptography will be, like most data-related controls, an essential consideration. Key management is of utmost importance, because mismanaged keys can lead to additional exposure or to total loss of the data. If the keys are improperly stored (especially if they are stored alongside the data), there is an increased risk of loss; if keys are stored away from the data but not managed properly and lost, there will be no efficient means to recover the data.

One aspect of cryptography to be aware of is elliptical curve cryptography (ECC). This approach to public key cryptography uses much smaller keys than traditional cryptography to provide the same level of security. ECC uses algebraic elliptical curves that result in much smaller keys that can provide the same level of safety as much larger ones used in traditional key cryptography.

The physical security of the data in long-term storage is also important. In choosing a storage location, we need to weigh risks and benefits for these facets of physical security:

Location   Where is the data being stored? What environmental factors will pose risks in that location (natural disasters, climate, etc.)? What jurisdictional aspects might bear consideration (local and national laws)? How distant is the archive location? Will it be feasible to access the data during contingency operations (for instance, during a natural disaster)? Is it far enough to be safe from events that impact the production environment but close enough for personnel to reach that data during those events?

Format   Is the data being stored on some physical medium such as tape backup or magnetic storage? Is the media highly portable and in need of additional security controls against theft? Will that medium be affected by environmental factors? How long do we expect to retain this data? Will it be in a format still accessible by production hardware when we need it?

Think of all the archaic media formats used to store data in the past, the cost of those formats, and how complicated it would be to find hardware capable of accessing that data today: Jaz disks, Zip disks, Colorado backup tape systems, and so on. Will today's format be outmoded soon, and will we have the hardware necessary to pull that data into a future format?

Staff   Are personnel at the storage location employed by our organization? If not, does the contractor implement a personnel control suite sufficient for our purposes (background checks, reliance checks, monitoring, and so on)?

Procedure   How is data recovered when needed? How is it ported to the archive on a regular basis? How often are we doing full backups (and the frequency of incremental or differential backups)?

Archive phase activities in the cloud will largely be driven by whether we are doing backups in the cloud, whether we are using the same cloud provider for backups and our production environment, or whether we are using a different cloud provider for each. We have to consider all the same factors we would use in the traditional environment but then also determine whether we could impose those same decisions in the cloud environment, on the cloud provider, via contractual means. How will this be monitored? How will it be enforced?

Destroy

We discussed destruction options for the traditional and cloud environments in Chapter 3. As we determined, cryptographic erasure (cryptoshredding) is the only feasible and thorough means currently available for this purpose in the cloud environment.

Cloud Storage Architectures.

There are various ways to store data in the cloud, each with attendant benefits and costs. These ways apply both to larger organizational needs and to personal cloud storage of a single user's data.

Volume Storage: File-Based Storage and Block Storage

With volume storage, the customer is allocated a storage space within the cloud; this storage space is represented as an attached drive to the user's virtual machine. From the customer's perspective, the virtual drive performs very much in the same manner as would a physical drive attached to a tangible device; actual locations and memory addresses are transparent to the user.

Volume storage architecture can take different forms; there is a great deal of discussion among cloud professionals about what type of volume might be preferable: file storage or block storage.

File Storage (also File-Level Storage or File-Based Storage)   The data is stored and displayed just as with a file structure in the traditional environment, as files and folders, with all the same hierarchical and naming functions. File storage architectures have become popular with big data analytical tools and processes.

Block Storage   Whereas file storage has a hierarchy of folders and files, block storage is a blank volume that the customer or user can put anything into. Block storage might allow more flexibility and higher performance, but it requires a greater amount of administration and might entail installation of an OS or other app to store, sort, and retrieve the data. Block storage might be better suited for a volume and purpose that includes data of multiple types and kinds, such as enterprise backup services.

Storage architecture for volumes can include bit splitting and erasure coding, which is basically a means of implementing data protection solutions in the cloud similar to the way RAID arrays protect traditional storage. Volume storage can be offered in any of the cloud service models but is often associated with infrastructure as a service (IaaS).

Object-Based Storage

Object storage is just as it sounds: data is stored as objects, not as files or blocks. Objects include not only the actual production content, but metadata describing the content and object and a unique address identifier for locating that specific object across an entire storage space.

Object storage architectures allow for a significant level of description, including marking, labels, classification, and categorization. This also enhances the opportunity for indexing capabilities, data policy enforcement (such as IRM, described in Chapter 3, and DLP, discussed later in this chapter in the section "Egress Monitoring [DLP]"), and centralization of some data management functions.

Again, any of the cloud service models can include object storage architectures, but object storage is usually associated with IaaS.

Databases

Like their traditional counterparts, databases in the cloud provide some sort of structure for stored data. Data will be arranged according to characteristics and elements in the data itself, including a specific trait required to file the data known as the primary key. In the cloud, the database is usually backend storage in the data center, accessed by users utilizing online apps or APIs through a browser.

Databases can be implemented in any cloud service model, but they are most often configured to work with PaaS and SaaS.

Content Delivery Network (CDN)

A content delivery network (CDN) is a form of data caching, usually near geophysical locations of high use/demand, for copies of data commonly requested by users. Perhaps the best example of why an organization would want to use a CDN is online multimedia streaming services: instead of dragging data from a data center to users at variable distances across a continent, the streaming service provider can place copies of the most requested media near metropolitan areas where those requests are likely to be made, thus improving bandwidth and delivery quality.

Cloud Data Security Foundational Strategies

Just as certain technologies make cloud computing feasible as a whole, certain technologies and practices make data security possible in the cloud and therefore also make cloud computing pragmatic and sensible.

Encryption

It should come as no surprise that cloud computing has a massive dependency on encryption; you have probably noticed how many times, and in how many ways, encryption has been mentioned throughout the book so far.

Encryption will be used to protect data at rest, in transit, and in use. Encryption will be used on the remote user endpoint to create the secure communication connection, within the cloud customer's enterprise environment to protect their own data, and within the data center by the cloud provider to ensure various cloud customers don't accidentally access each other's data.

Realistically, without encryption it would be impossible to use the cloud in any secure fashion.

The book has included some details about encryption implementations already and will continue to do so as we discuss various aspects of cloud computing. In the following sections, we will focus on only two particular topics of encryption in the cloud: key management and an experimental encryption implementation that might create a whole new level of security and trust in the cloud.

Key Management

As we have noted before, how and where encryption keys are stored can affect the overall risk of the data significantly. Here are some things to remember and consider regarding key management for cloud computing:

Level of Protection Encryption keys, which are the mathematical numeric stringcode that allows for encryption and decryption to occur, must be secured at the same level of control, or *higher*, as the data they protect. The sensitivity of the data dictates this level of protection, according to the organization's data security policies. We need to remember that the strength of the cryptosystem is only valid if keys are not disclosed (except for public keys, as part of asymmetric encryption).

 Sometimes databases use transparent encryption, in which the encryption key for the database is stored in the database itself.

 A hardware security module (HSM) is a device that can safely store and manage encryption keys and is used in servers, data transmission, and log files. If implemented properly, it is far stronger than saving and storing keys in software.

Key Recovery For anyone other than a specific user, accessing that user's key should be difficult; however, there are situations in which an organization needs to acquire a user's key without the user's cooperation. This might be because the user was fired from the organization, or died, or lost their key. You need to have the technology and process for getting that key to access that data. Usually, this entails a procedure that involves multiple people, each with access to only a portion of the key.

Key Distribution Issuing keys for a cryptosystem can be difficult and fraught with risk. If the key management process requires a secure connection to initiate the key creation procedure, how do you establish that secure session without a key? Often, passing keys out of band is a preferable, yet cumbersome and expensive, solution. Moreover, keys should never be passed in the clear.

Key Revocation In situations where a user should no longer have access to sensitive material, or where a key has been inadvertently/illicitly disclosed, the organization needs a process for suspending the key or that user's ability to use it.

Key Escrow   In many cases, having copies of keys held by a trusted third party in a secure environment is highly desirable; this can aid in many of the other key management efforts listed in this section.

Outsourcing Key Management   Keys should not be stored with the data they're protecting, and we shouldn't make physical access to keys readily available to anyone who doesn't have authorization and need to know for that data; therefore, in cloud computing, it is preferable to have the keys stored somewhere other than the cloud provider's data center. One solution is for the cloud customer to retain the keys, but that requires an expensive and complicated set of infrastructure and skilled personnel. This would attenuate some of the benefit (in reduced costs) we get from offloading our enterprise to the cloud provider. Another option is using a cloud access security broker (CASB). CASBs are third-party providers that handle IAM and key management services for cloud customers; the cost of using a CASB should be much lower than trying to maintain keys within the organization, and the CASB will have core competencies most cloud customers won't.

 Whether or not a cloud customer chooses to use a CASB or other means of key management, the preferred solution is *not* to store the crypto keys with the cloud provider.

Masking, Obfuscation, Anonymization, and Tokenization

For certain uses in the cloud, we may find it necessary to obscure actual data and instead use a representation of that data. The terms *masking*, *obfuscation*, *anonymization*, and *tokenization* refer to methods to accomplish this.

Here are some examples of reasons you'd want to do this:

Test Environments   New software should be tested in sandboxed environments before being deployed to the production environment. When this type of testing is performed, actual production data should *never* be used within the sandbox. However, in order to determine the actual functionality and performance of the system, it will be necessary to use data that closely approximates the same traits and characteristics of the production data.

Enforcing Least Privilege   We know that the concept of least privilege entails limiting users to permissions and access absolutely necessary to perform their duties. In some cases, that might mean allowing the user access to elements of a data set without revealing its entirety. For instance, a customer service representative might need to access a customer's account information and be shown a screen with that information, but that data might be an abridged version of the customer's total account specifics (such as not showing the customer's full credit card number).

Secure Remote Access   When a customer logs onto a web service, the customer's account might have some data abridged in similar fashion to the least privilege example. The screen might display some of the customer's preferences, but you might not want to display certain elements of the customer's account data, such as payment or personal information, to avoid risks such as hijacked sessions, stolen credentials, or shoulder surfing.

So how are these activities performed? These are some techniques that you can use to obscure data for use in the cloud context:

Randomization   The replacement of the data (or part of the data) with random characters. Usually, and as with most cases of obscuring data, you want to leave the other traits (aside from displaying the actual data) intact: length of the string, character set (whether it was alphabetic or numerical, whether it had special characters, whether there was upper-/lower-case, etc.), and so forth.

Hashing   Using a one-way cryptographic function to create a digest of the original data. Using a hash algorithm to obscure the data gives you the benefit of ensuring it is unrecoverable, and you can also use it as an integrity check later. However, because hashing converts variable-length messages into fixed-length digests, you lose many of the properties of the original data.

Shuffling   Using different entries from within the same data set to represent the data. This has the obvious drawback of using actual production data.

Masking   Hiding the data with useless characters; for example, showing only the last four digits of a Social Security number: XXX-XX-1234. This can be used where the customer service representative or the customer gets authorized access to the account but you want to obscure a portion of the data for additional security.

Nulls   Deleting the raw data from the display before it is represented, or displaying null sets. Obviously, some of the functionality of the data set will be dramatically reduced with this method.

The term *obfuscation* refers to the application of any of these techniques in order to make the data less meaningful, detailed, or readable in order to protect the data or the subject of the data. For instance, I can obfuscate data with masking or by anonymizing it, as will be discussed further in this section.

Obscuring can be done in either static or dynamic configurations. With the static technique, a new (representational) data set is created as a copy from the original data, and only the obscured copy is used. In the dynamic method, data is obscured as it is called, as with the examples I described: the customer service agent or the customer is granted authorized access, but the data is obscured as it is fed to them.

We may also want to add another layer of abstraction to the data to attenuate the possibility that sensitive information may be gleaned from otherwise mundane elements. For instance, even if we're obscuring a person's name in a given data set, if we allow other information, such as age, location, and employer, it may be possible to determine the name without having direct access to that field.

Removing the telltale nonspecific identifiers is called *anonymization* or sometimes *de-identification*. Anonymization can be difficult, because sensitive data must be recognized and marked as sensitive when it is created; if the user inputs the data into open fields (free entry), determining sensitivity might not be simple. Moreover, the mark indicating sensitivity creates metadata that might be valuable to an attacker.

Tokenization is the practice of having two distinct databases: one with the live, actual sensitive data and one with nonrepresentational tokens mapped to each piece of that data.

In this method, the user or program calling the data is authenticated by the token server, which pulls the appropriate token from the token database, then calls the actual data that maps to that token from the real database of production data, and finally presents it to the user or program. Tokenization adds significant overhead to the process but creates an extra degree of security and may relieve the organization's requirement or dependence on encryption (for instance, PCI DSS allows tokenization instead of encryption for sensitive cardholder data). For tokenization to function properly, the token server must have strong authentication protocols. To see how this works a little more clearly, review the following steps, also shown in Figure 4.2:

1. A user creates a piece of data.

2. The data is run through a DLP/discovery tool, as an aid to determine whether the data is sensitive according to the organization's rules (in this example, the data is PII). If the data is deemed sensitive, the data is pushed to the tokenization database.

3. The data is tokenized; the raw data is sent to the PII server, while a token representing the data is stored in the tokenization database. The token represents the raw data as a kind of logical address.

4. Another user requests the data. This user must be stringently authenticated so the systems can determine if the user should be granted access to the data.

5. If the user authenticates correctly, the request is put to the tokenization database.

6. The tokenization database looks up the token of the requested data, then presents that token to the PII database. The raw data is not stored in the tokenization database.

7. The PII database returns the raw data based on the token.

8. The raw data is delivered to the requesting user.

FIGURE 4.2   Basic tokenization architecture

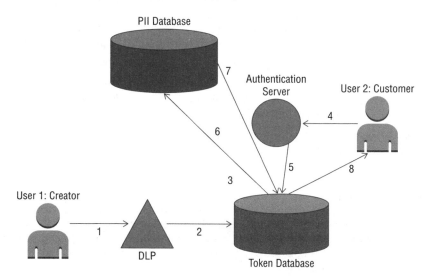

Security Information and Event Management

We use monitoring tools to know how well the systems and security controls in our IT environment are functioning, to detect anomalous activity, and to enforce policy. A large part of the monitoring effort comes in the form of logs: recording activity as it happens, sometimes from specialized devices that only conduct monitoring and other times from operational systems themselves (with their integrated logging functions).

To better collect, manage, analyze, and display log data, a set of tools specifically created for that purpose has become popular. These are known by a variety of terms, since there is no accepted standard. Nomenclature includes security information management, security event management, security information and event management, and permutations of these (including acronyms such as SIM, SEM, and SIEM, pronounced in various ways). We will refer to the entire family of tools inclusively as SIEM.

Goals of SIEM implementation include the following:

Centralize Collection of Log Data   Because logs can be drawn from so many sources (workstations, OSs, servers, network devices, and so on), it can be useful to have a place to aggregate it all for additional processing. If nothing else, this simplifies the activity for the admins and analysts who will be tasked with monitoring the environment. This does create an additional risk; however: having all the log data in one location makes that location an attractive target for attackers, so any SIEM implementation will require additional layers of security controls.

Enhanced Analysis Capabilities   Log analysis is a mundane, repetitive task that requires a special skillset and experience and is not suited for full-time tasking (an analyst who stares at the same data set and data feeds all day, day after day, will become inured to the activity, whereas an analyst who doesn't see the data from the environment often enough won't be as familiar with the baselines and therefore won't recognize anomalous behavior). One way we can offset some of the problems with log analysis is to automate some of the process. SIEM tools should have this capability, in addition to other functions such as advanced trend detection based on large data sets. One thing to remember, however, is that most automated tools will not recognize a particular set of attacks—the "low and slow" style of persistent threats, which may develop over weeks or months and don't have dramatic indicators and therefore may be confused with background attack noise and go undetected by automated analysis.

Dashboarding   Management often doesn't understand IT functions, and understands even less about IT security. SIEMs often offer some graphical output display that is more intuitive and simple for managers to quickly grasp situations within the environment.

Automated Response   Some SIEMs include automated alert and response capabilities that can be programmed to suit your policies and environment.

WARNING   Like logging itself, SIEMs are only useful when someone is actually looking at what they produce; simply having the shiny box that performs security functions is nice, but unless the information it provides is being harvested by someone who knows what they're looking at, the SIEM can be just another bandage in a damaged environment and won't really offer any benefit to the organization.

Egress Monitoring (DLP)

Another set of popular tools are for the purpose of egress monitoring—that is, examining data as it leaves the production environment. These are often called DLP, which can stand for any combination of the terms *data loss*, *leak prevention*, and *protection*. I'm just going to refer to them universally as DLP.

Like SIEM, DLP solutions generally have several major goals:

Additional Security   DLP can be used as another control in the layered defense strategy, one last mechanism designed for mitigating the possibility of inadvertent release or malicious disclosure.

Policy Enforcement   Users can be alerted by the DLP when they are attempting to perform an action that would violate the organization's policy (either accidentally or intentionally).

Enhanced Monitoring   The DLP tool can be set to provide one more log stream to the organization's monitoring suite.

Regulatory Compliance   Specific types and kinds of data can be identified by the DLP solution, and dissemination of that data can be controlled accordingly, in order to better adhere to regulatory mandates.

 DLP solutions can often be linked to IRM tools, allowing extra functionality to the controls on intellectual property.

DLP tools can function in a variety of ways, but the general concept is that data is identified, activity is monitored, and policies are enforced.

The identification task can be automated, manual, or a combination of both. The tool might search the organization's entire storage volumes and production environment to match data against known templates; for instance, the DLP might search for numeric strings nine characters in length in order to detect Social Security numbers. The DLP also might use categorization and classification markings, labels, and metadata assigned by the data owner during the Create phase of the data lifecycle. Or the DLP might use keyword searches for particular information known by the organization to be sensitive for its purposes.

The monitoring task can be implemented at the points of network egress (in traditional systems at the DMZ [demilitarized zone], but in the cloud this would be on all public-facing devices) or on all hosts that process data within the production environment. In the latter case, the DLP solution usually includes local agents installed on user workstations/endpoint devices.

The enforcement mechanism can take many forms. The DLP might be set to alert management or security personnel when a user is conducting an activity that violates policy (say, sending an email attachment that contains data the organization has deemed sensitive). If what we're trying to prevent is more accidental disclosures (as opposed to malicious activity), the DLP might just warn users that the email they're sending contains sensitive data, and confirm that they really intended to send it. Or the DLP might be a bit more draconian and prevent the user from sending the attachment, locking the user out of the account, and notifying management and security. The organization can tailor DLP action to its own needs.

DLP implementation in the cloud comes with related difficulties and costs, though. For one thing, the cloud provider may not allow the cloud customer sufficient access (in terms of both administrative permissions and installation of the requisite systems for implementation) to the data center environment, complicating successful configuration and usage. DLP utilization also incurs significant processing overhead; all that monitoring and functionality comes with a processing cost.

Summary

This chapter addressed the data lifecycle within the cloud environment as well as specific security challenges in each phase. We looked at different data storage architectures that might be implemented in the cloud, and which service model might be best suited for each. We discussed cryptography, including the importance of and difficulties with key management and the possibility of using homomorphic encryption in the future. We discussed why we might want to obscure raw data and only display selected portions during operations, and we talked about various methods for performing this task. We reviewed SIEM solutions, how and why they're implemented, and some risks associated with their use. Finally, we addressed the topic of egress monitoring, how DLP tools work, and specific problems that might be encountered when trying to deploy DLP solutions in the cloud.

Exam Essentials

Understand the risks and security controls associated with each phase of the cloud data lifecycle.   Every phase has its own attendant risks, and those risks are usually associated with a particular set or type of security controls.

Understand how import/export restrictions affect the field of information security. You should be familiar with the ITAR and the EAR and know what the Wassenaar Arrangement is.

Understand the various cloud data storage architectures.   Be able to differentiate between file storage, block storage, databases, and CDN.

Understand how and why encryption is implemented in the cloud.   Know the essential elements of key management; in particular, know that encryption keys are not to be stored alongside the data they were used to encrypt. Know about the emerging technology known as homomorphic encryption and how it might be used in the future to process encrypted data without having to decrypt it first.

Be familiar with the practice of obscuring data.   Know the different techniques of data masking, hiding, anonymization, and tokenization.

Be familiar with SIEM technology.   Understand the purposes of SIEM implementation and the challenges associated with using those solutions.

Understand the importance of egress monitoring.   Be familiar with the goals of DLP solutions, how they are implemented, and what challenges a cloud customer might face trying to implement DLP within the cloud data center.

Written Labs

1. Download and read the ISACA white paper on DLP at www.isaca.org/
    Knowledge-Center/Research/ResearchDeliverables/Pages/
    Data-Leak-Prevention.aspx.
2. In no more than one page, summarize the operational risks listed in Figure 1 of that document.

Review Questions

You can find the answers to the review questions in Appendix B.

1. All of the following are terms used to describe the practice of obscuring original raw data so that only a portion is displayed for operational purposes except_____.

    A. Tokenization

    B. Data discovery

    C. Obfuscation

    D. Masking

2. The goals of SIEM solution implementation include all of the following except _____.

    A. Centralization of log streams

    B. Trend analysis

    C. Dashboarding

    D. Performance enhancement

3. The goals of DLP solution implementation include all of the following except _____.

    A. Policy enforcement

    B. Elasticity

    C. Data discovery

    D. Mitigating loss

4. DLP solutions can aid in deterring loss due to which of the following?

    A. Randomization

    B. Inadvertent disclosure

    C. Natural disaster

    D. Device failure

5. DLP solutions can help deter loss because of which of the following?

    A. Malicious disclosure

    B. Performance issues

    C. Bad policy

    D. Power failure

6. What is the experimental technology that might lead to the possibility of processing encrypted data without having to decrypt it first?

    A. AES

    B. Link encryption

    C. Homomorphic encryption

    D. One-time pads

7. Proper implementation of DLP solutions for successful function requires which of the following?

    A. Accurate data categorization

    B. Physical access limitations

    C. USB connectivity

    D. Physical presence

8. Tokenization requires two distinct _____.

    A. Authentication factors

    B. Databases

    C. Encryption keys

    D. Personnel

9. Data masking can be used to provide all of the following functionality except _____.

    A. Secure remote access

    B. Enforcing least privilege

    C. Testing data in sandboxed environments

    D. Authentication of privileged users

10. DLP can be combined with what other security tools to enhance data controls?

    A. IRM

    B. SIEM

    C. Kerberos

    D. Hypervisors

11. What are the US State Department controls on technology exports known as?

    A. ITAR

    B. EAR

    C. EAL

    D. IRM

12. What are the US Commerce Department controls on technology exports known as?

    A. ITAR

    B. EAR

    C. EAL

    D. IRM

13. Cryptographic keys for encrypted data stored in the cloud should be _____.

    A. At least 128 bits long

    B. Not stored with the cloud provider

    C. Split into groups

    D. Generated with dependencies

14. Best practices for key management include all of the following except _____.

    A. Have key recovery processes

    B. Maintain key security

    C. Pass keys out of band

    D. Ensure multifactor authentication

15. Cryptographic keys should be secured _____.

    A. To a level at least as high as the data they can decrypt

    B. In vaults

    C. By armed guards

    D. With two-person integrity

16. When crafting plans and policies for data archiving, we should consider all of the following except_____.

    A. Archive location

    B. The backup process

    C. The format of the data

    D. Immediacy of the technology

17. What is the correct order of the phases of the data lifecycle?

    A. Create, Store, Use, Archive, Share, Destroy

    B. Create, Store, Use, Share, Archive, Destroy

    C. Create, Use, Store, Share, Archive, Destroy

    D. Create, Archive, Store, Share, Use, Destroy

18. What are third-party providers of IAM functions for the cloud environment?

    A. DLPs

    B. CASBs

    C. SIEMs

    D. AESs

19. What is a cloud storage architecture that manages the data in an arrangement of fields according to characteristics of each data element?

   A. Object-based storage

   B. File-based storage

   C. Database

   D. CDN

20. What is a cloud storage architecture that manages the data in caches of copied content close to locations of high demand?

   A. Object-based storage

   B. File-based storage

   C. Database

   D. CDN

Chapter

5

Security in the Cloud

THE OBJECTIVE OF THIS CHAPTER IS TO ACQUAINT THE READER WITH THE FOLLOWING CONCEPTS:

✓ **Domain 1: Cloud Concepts, Architecture, and Design**

- 1.2. Describe Cloud Reference Architecture
  - 1.2.5. Cloud Shared Considerations
- 1.4. Understand Design Principles of Secure Cloud Computing
  - 1.4.2. Cloud Based Disaster Recovery (DR) and Business Continuity (BC) Planning
  - 1.4.4. Functional Security Requirements
  - 1.4.5. Security Considerations for Different Cloud Categories

✓ **Domain 3: Cloud Platform and Infrastructure Security**

- 3.1. Comprehend Cloud Infrastructure Components
  - 3.1.4. Virtualization
- 3.3. Analyze Risks Associated with Cloud Infrastructure
  - 3.3.2. Cloud Vulnerabilities, Threats, and Attacks
  - 3.3.3. Virtualization Risks
  - 3.3.4. Counter-Measure Strategies
- 3.4. Design and Plan Security Controls
  - 3.4.3. Virtualization Systems Protection
- 3.5. Plan Disaster Recovery (DR) and Business Continuity (BC) Management
  - 3.5.3. Business Continuity/Disaster Recovery Strategy

✓ **Domain 5: Cloud Security Operations**

- 5.4. Implement Operational Controls and Standards

  - 5.4.5. Incident Management

  - 5.4.6. Problem Management

  - 5.4.8. Deployment Management

✓ **Domain 6: Legal, Risk, and Compliance**

- 6.4. Understand Implications of Cloud to Enterprise Risk Management

  - 6.4.2. Difference Between Data Owner/Controller vs. Data Custodian/Processor

In this chapter, we will discuss the various rights and responsibilities involved in cloud computing, how those should be apportioned between the cloud provider and customer, specific risks posed by each cloud platform and service, and BC/DR strategies for use in the cloud.

Shared Cloud Platform Risks and Responsibilities

Because the cloud customer and provider will each be processing data that, at least in some part, belongs to the customer, they will share responsibilities and risks associated with that data. Simply put, these risks and responsibilities will be codified in the service contract between the parties. That contract, however, will be the result of a complex process of deliberation and negotiation.

Although the risks and responsibilities will be shared between the cloud provider and customer, the ultimate legal liability for unauthorized and illicit data disclosures will remain with the customer as the data owner. The cloud provider may be financially responsible, in whole or in part, depending on the terms of the contract, but the legal responsibility will be the customer's. This concept will be repeated throughout the book, as it's repeated throughout the CCSP CBK.

As an example of what this means and how it could affect the customer, let's say an unauthorized disclosure of PII that belongs to the customer occurs because of some failure on the part of the cloud provider. For the sake of argument, we'll also assume that the contract stipulates that the provider is financially liable for damages resulting from this failure.

Depending on the jurisdiction where the breach occurred and the jurisdiction of the subjects of the PII (that is, the state or country of citizenship/residence of the people whose PII was lost), statutes could dictate specific monetary damages owed by the cloud customer (again, the data owner) to either the government or the subjects or both. It is possible for the customer to eventually recover those damages from the provider (because of the contract and the fault), but the government will not seek them from the provider; the government will seek damages from the customer. It is the customer that the government will serve injunctions and orders to, not the provider. In addition, depending on the jurisdiction and the breach itself, it is the customer's officers who could face imprisonment, not the provider.

Moreover, even if the customer is protected by the provider's acceptance of financial responsibility, the legal repercussions are not the only negative impact the customer faces.

The customer will likely be adversely affected by negative publicity, loss of faith among its clientele, perhaps decreased market share and a drop in share price (if the customer is publicly traded), and an increase in insurance premiums. It is therefore important for the customer to realize that the cash involved in damage awards and assignment of liability is only one aspect of the risk.

Of paramount importance is to understand that the customer's ultimate legal liability for data it owns remains true *even if the provider's failure was the result of negligence or malice.* That is a very considerable burden of risk, especially because it's a much higher standard than what we usually face in the security profession.

That said, the provider and customer still must come to terms regarding their particular responsibilities and obligations under the contract. To some degree, this will be driven by the nature of the service in question and what service and model the customer is purchasing. A graphical depiction of the general gradations of the various arrangements is shown in Figure 5.1.

FIGURE 5.1   Responsibilities according to service model

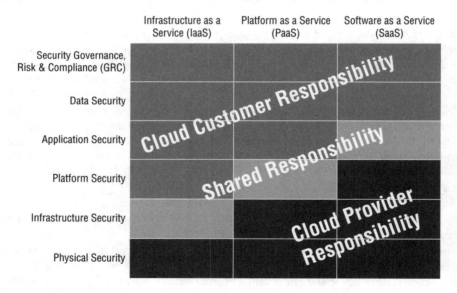

Again, this is not prescriptive, but a guide for possible contract negotiation.

There will be some dichotomy because of the two perspectives. The cloud provider and the customer are most concerned with two different things. The cloud customer is concerned about the data. The production environment being hosted on the cloud data center is the customer's lifeblood. Breaches, failures, and lack of availability are the things that most affect the customer. The provider, on the other hand, is mostly concerned with the security and operation of their data center, which is the provider's core competency and the way it survives and maintains profitability.

Therefore, the customer will be seeking maximal control over their data, with all the administrative power and insight into the data center operations it can acquire. The customer will want to impose policy, get logging data, and audit the performance and security of the data center.

The provider will be attempting to limit customer access as much as possible. The provider wants to refute control, deny insight, and refrain from disclosing any information that might be used for malicious purposes, which includes the list of security controls used for protecting the data center, procedures, and live monitoring equipment and data. In some cases, the provider might not even want to disclose the physical location of the data center, believing that secrecy can lead to security.

This creates an adversarial dynamic in the negotiation. Both parties must have a clear awareness of what outcomes they're seeking and the best means to get them. In many cases, the provider will have an advantage in this regard because the provider understands the function and design of the data center and therefore the known and expected outcomes of operation much better than most customers do. Organizations that are new to managed services in general and cloud computing specifically may not be aware of what, exactly, to ask for in the negotiation. It is therefore advisable that organizations without a core technical competency and familiarity with cloud operations seek external consultation when initially considering cloud migration and entering negotiations with providers.

Cloud Customers, Providers, and Similar Terms

In this chapter, we talk specifically about the *cloud customer* (the company, individual, or other entity that hires the cloud provider to take care of their data) and the *cloud provider* (the company that is hired to provide services, platforms, and/or applications that help with managing the cloud customer's data). In the real world, you might also see terms such as *data customer*, *data owner*, *data controller*, *data provider*, *data custodian*, and *data processor*. These terms are all attempts at describing who owns the data and who handles the data, which generally sifts out to being the cloud customer and the cloud provider, which are the terms we will use pretty consistently for our discussion.

Cloud Computing Risks by Deployment Model

To prepare for cloud migration and the requisite contract negotiation (and for familiarization with CCSP CBK content), it is useful to review the risks particular to each of the cloud deployment models. These include the private, community, public, and hybrid cloud models.

Private Cloud

A *private cloud* is a distributed computing environment with only one customer (as opposed to the more common multitenant environment, typified by a public cloud). A private cloud can be implemented by an organization (running its own data center, and supplying cloud services to its employees, vendors, and clientele), or it can be hosted by a provider.

In some situations, the provider will own the hardware that contains the private cloud, hosted in the provider's data center. The customer will be granted exclusive access to that particular set of hardware, and no other customers will have their cloud hosted on those same devices. In some cases, the customer owns the hardware, which is hosted, physically inside the provider's data center (often referred to as a *co-lo*, or colocation center).

A private cloud might be a more appropriate cloud option for customer organizations that exist in highly regulated industries or that process a significant amount/degree of sensitive information; the private cloud allows the customer to dictate and specify a much more detailed level of security controls and overall governance. This will, of course, be more expensive (in terms of the amount paid to the provider) than the public cloud model and will impede the elasticity/scaling of the cloud (instead of having theoretically infinite capacity, the private cloud capacity will reach a natural maximum of whatever components are dedicated to the customer's environment).

All private cloud operators face the following risks:

Personnel Threats   This includes both inadvertent and malicious threats. If a managed provider/data center is used, the provider's administrators remain outside the customer's control.

Natural Disasters   All the deployment and service models are still susceptible to natural disasters.

External Attacks   These attacks can take many forms, such as unauthorized access, eavesdropping, denial of service (DoS)/distributed denial of service (DDoS), and so on.

Regulatory Noncompliance   While the customer has much more control over the configuration and controls in a private cloud model (compared to a public cloud), regulators will still enforce mandates.

Malware   This can be considered an external or internal threat, depending on the source of the infection.

None of these risks are unique to the private cloud, but having a greater degree of control and specificity may give the customer a greater level of assurance in combatting them.

Community Cloud

In a *community cloud* configuration, resources are shared and dispersed among an affinity group. Infrastructure can be owned and/or operated jointly, individually, centrally, across the community, or in any combination and mixture of these options.

The benefits of this deployment model each come with attendant risks:

Resiliency through Shared Ownership Because the network ownership and operation is scattered among users, the environment is more likely to survive the loss of a significant number of nodes without affecting the others. However, this introduces additional risks because each node is its own point of entry and a vulnerability in any one node can result in an intrusion on the others. This, of course, means that unity of configuration management and baselines is almost impossible (and very difficult to enforce). With distributed ownership comes distributed decision-making in terms of policy and administration.

Shared Costs Overhead and cost of the infrastructure is shared among the members of the community, but so is access and control.

No Need for Centralized Administration for Performance and Monitoring Although this removes many burdens of centralized administration, it also removes the reliability of centralized and homogenized standards for performance and security monitoring.

 Real World Scenario

Online Gaming as a Community Cloud

Online gaming is an excellent example of the community cloud model. Each individual gamer owns their own device (a console or a computer). The individual gamer is responsible for the purchase price of the device, maintaining the device, and establishing/maintaining a connection to the Internet. Each individual gamer can also disconnect their own device voluntarily, whenever they feel like it (or even destroy their own device, if they choose, because they own the device completely).

Then there is usually a centralized identification and access management (IAM) node involved in the gaming setup. Some entity (such as Microsoft or Sony) acts as the validator of identity/permission for each individual gamer; this entity has full control/ownership of the IAM function and must pay to create/maintain that node. Individual gamers log into the centralized IAM node in order to get access to the shared game environment.

Finally, there is often another, distinct entity that is the game host; they run the server that handles the online interactions between the verified players. These backend game machines are wholly owned and maintained by the game host (often the game manufacturer or distributor).

Each entity is responsible for their own components and participation in the community; each takes part voluntarily and can leave at any time. Ownership, processing, and storage are shared among the participants, depending on their role in the interaction.

Public Cloud

This is the deployment model that has the most focus in the CCSP CBK and is most likely to provide the greatest benefit to the largest number of cloud customers. In the *public cloud*, a company offers cloud services to any entity that wants to become a cloud customer, be it an individual, company, government agency, or other organization.

Many of the same risks exist in the public cloud as in the private cloud: personnel threats (inadvertent and malicious), external threats, natural disasters, and so forth. Some of them are obviated by the public cloud's similarity to the community cloud, such as distributed infrastructure, shared costs, and reduced need for administrative capability. However, it is these same benefits that entail the additional risks of the public cloud. The organization will lose control, oversight, audit, and enforcement capabilities—basically, all the assurance of maintaining a private cloud internal to the organization.

There are some additional risks that are unique to the public cloud that also must be considered. We'll discuss those in some detail in the following subsections.

Vendor Lock-In

In ceding control of the production environment and data to an external party, the organization creates a dependency on that provider. The expense and trouble of moving the data out of the provider's data center could be crippling to the customer, especially if the customer chose to do so before the end of the contract term. In a sense, this can make the customer a hostage of the provider and allow the provider to decrease service levels and/or increase prices as the provider sees fit. It's important to stress that this is *not* a commonplace occurrence. I do not mean to suggest that cloud providers are maliciously luring customers into unfavorable arrangements. However, the possibility exists for that dependency, and dependency is a risk.

Vendor lock-in (also known as provider lock-in) can be caused by other circumstances as well. For instance, if the provider uses a proprietary data format or medium to store information, the customer may not be able to move their data to another provider. The contract itself can be considered a form of lock-in, too, if it is punitive and puts an undue onus on the customer if the customer chooses to go to another provider. Alternatively, vendor lock-in can be caused by some sort of regulatory constraint, where finding another provider that will meet the specific regulatory needs of the organization could be difficult.

To avoid lock-in, the organization has to think in terms of *portability* when considering migration. We use the term *portability* to describe the general level of ease or difficulty when transferring data out of a provider's data center (regardless of whether it's being moved to another provider or to a private cloud).

There are several things an organization can do to enhance the portability of its data:

Ensure favorable contract terms for portability.   Make sure the organization considers an exit strategy, even while creating the initial agreement with the provider at the outset of cloud service acquisition. Is there a reduced-rate trial period in the provider environment? What is the penalty for early transfer (severing the contract)? At the end of the contract term, will there be any difficulty, contractually or in terms of performance, in moving the data to another provider? (See the real-world example "Ambiguity Is Scary.")

Avoid proprietary formats.   Don't sign with a provider unless the raw data can be recovered in a format that could be used at another provider's site. This might involve using some form of conversion before moving the data, and that conversion should be simple and inexpensive if the customer chooses to move.

Ensure there are no physical limitations to moving.   Make sure that the bandwidth leaving the old provider is sufficient for the purposes of moving your organization's entire data set and that the new provider can handle that size of importation.

Check for regulatory constraints.   There should be more than one cloud provider that can handle your organization's specific compliance needs. If your needs are bizarrely unique and restrictive (for instance, if your organization is a medical college that takes credit card payments, thus requiring you to simultaneously comply with FERPA, PCI, and HIPAA), that number of providers may be extremely limited.

 Real World Scenario

Ambiguity Is Scary

In the case of one public cloud provider, the contract stipulated a set of maximum monthly upload/download parameters, with additional fees assessed if these bounds were exceeded in any given month. This is commonplace and the usual way cloud providers establish rates and provide for the appropriate level of resources to meet their customers' regular needs and still allow for cloud bursting.

Elsewhere in the contract, the terms for leaving at the end of any contract period were detailed to include a duration in which the customer could move their data away from the provider (it was 30 days).

What the contract *didn't* state was whether the same monthly limits (and fees for exceeding those limits) would be in effect during the month-long movement of data out of the provider's space in the event the customer chose to leave.

It seems obvious that the limits wouldn't be enforced during the transition period. Otherwise, how could a customer reasonably leave the provider? Assuming the customer was making maximal use of the service and uploading x bytes of data each month of a year-long contract term, there would be $12x$ bytes (12 times the established monthly limit) stored in the provider's data center at the end of the contract. If the limits were still in place, the customer would be facing considerable penalties in fees to move $12x$ bytes in that final month. Can the customer assume that this reasonable conclusion was the intention of the contract?

Of course not. We can never assume anything, especially when crafting contracts. Therefore, this is a question that would have to be resolved in writing and agreed to as an amendment or addition to the contract before both parties sign.

Vendor Lock-Out

Another problem associated with ceding control of the organization's data and production environment is referred to as *vendor lock-out* (also known as provider lock-out). Vendor lock-out can be caused when the cloud provider goes out of business, is acquired by another company, or ceases operation for any reason. In these circumstances, the concern is whether the customer can still readily access and recover their data.

We cannot really plan for all the possible reasons vendor lock-out might occur. We can, however, be aware that the possibility exists and make decisions accordingly. We may want to consider the following factors when selecting a cloud provider:

Provider Longevity   How long has the provider been in business? Does it seem to be a market leader? This aspect may be more difficult than others to assess, because IT is an extremely volatile field and new providers are constantly entering while stalwarts often leave with little warning. Cloud technology and services on a large scale, in particular, are a fairly recent development and may be more prone to significant and unexpected turbulence.

Core Competency   Can this provider offer your organization what it needs? Is it capable of meeting all your service requirements? Does it have the staff, resources, and infrastructure to handle your organization's demands, as well as those of its other customers? One measure of the possible strength and suitability of a given provider is whether a cloud service is central to its offerings or is an additional function for its company.

Jurisdictional Suitability   What country is the provider in, and which state? This question must be asked in terms of both where it is chartered and where it operates. Where is the data center? Where is its long-term storage and backup capability? Will your organization's data be crossing boundaries and borders? Can your organization use this provider and remain compliant with all applicable regulations?

Supply Chain Dependencies   Does the provider rely on any other entities for its critical functions, both upstream and downstream? Are there essential suppliers, vendors, and utilities without which the provider could not perform? This aspect will be very difficult to investigate without considerable disclosure on the part of the provider.

Legislative Environment   What pending statutes might affect your organization's ability to use that provider? This facet might carry the most potential impact for cloud customers and also be the most challenging to predict. For instance, almost nobody foresaw that Great Britain would leave the European Union in 2016, and the Brexit referendum entailed significant political and regulatory modifications for companies operating in both jurisdictions.

Not If, But When

Some people might think that a provider's record of incidents should be used as a discriminator when considering vendor lock-out and that if a given vendor has proven susceptible to breaches or attacks or failures in the past, this should be a telling portent of its ability to survive in the future. This may not be the most useful method for measuring the suitability of a vendor. Instead, knowing that a vendor has suffered through incidents may indicate that this is a vendor you should strongly consider handling your business. Simply put: Everyone can and will be breached at some point, every system fails, and every organization experiences security issues. We should not be expecting a zero-fault environment. We should be looking for a fault-tolerant environment. How did the provider respond to the incidents? What did it do? What didn't it do? How did the market (and its customers) respond to the provider's handling of the matter? We can learn more from a provider that has dealt with past security issues (and how) than from a provider that claims to have never had any.

Multitenant Environments

Going into a public cloud means entering a multitenant environment. There will be no providers that will host your organization as their sole customer. (Indeed, you should be wary of any provider that would *want* to be in that position. It doesn't scale and wouldn't be profitable.) There are therefore specific risks in the public cloud configuration that do not exist in other models, including these:

Conflict of Interest   Provider personnel who administer your data and systems should not also be involved with any of your competitors who might also be that provider's customers. The provider should be careful to not create these situations or even the perception that they might exist.

Escalation of Privilege   Authorized users may try to acquire unauthorized permissions. This might include users from organizations other than your own. A user who gains illicit administrative access may be able to gain control of devices that process other customers' data.

Information Bleed   With multiple customers processing and storing data over the same infrastructure, there is the possibility that data belonging to one customer will be read or received by another. Moreover, even if this does not happen with raw data, it might be possible for one customer to detect telltale information about another customer's activity, such as when the customer is processing data, how long the procedure takes, and so on.

Legal Activity   Data and devices within a data center may be subpoenaed or seized as evidence in a criminal investigation or as part of discovery for litigation purposes. This is of concern to any cloud customer because of the possibility that a particular asset might contain not only data that is the specific target of the investigation/litigation, it might also include data belonging to other customers. (In other words, your data might be seized because it's on the same box as the data of another customer who is a target of law enforcement or plaintiffs.)

The Brewer-Nash Model

Although the Brewer and Nash model is not part of the official material and you don't need to know it for the exam, it's useful to understand. Also known by the title of the paper in which it was proposed, "The Chinese Wall Security Policy" (https://www.cs.purdue.edu/homes/ninghui/readings/AccessControl/brewer_nash_89.pdf), it is the concept of aligning separation of duties and least privilege with dataflows to prevent conflicts of interest.

Brewer and Nash is perhaps the most relevant model for cloud computing because of the nature of cloud administrators—inside a cloud data center, administrators working for the cloud provider could have physical (and perhaps logical) access to every cloud customer served by that facility. This might include customers in direct competition in the same industry. This creates a conflict of interest for the cloud administrator as well as a potential avenue for corruption.

Proper use of the Brewer and Nash model might address these issues by reducing their likelihood and creating a policy that supports and enforces the model.

Hybrid Cloud

A *hybrid cloud* is simply a combination of two or more of the other models. Hybrid cloud configurations, of course, include all the risks of the various models they combine. An organization considering utilizing a hybrid cloud setup ought to be aware of all the risks discussed in each of the previous sections that are applicable to their particular choice of hybrid.

Cloud Computing Risks by Service Model

Another consideration in cloud migration and contract negotiation is the risks inherent in each of the cloud service models. The most common cloud service models include infrastructure as a service (IaaS), platform as a service (PaaS), and software as a service (SaaS). In addition to the concerns specific to each service model, the service models inherit the risks of whichever deployment model they are used with. This coverage is by no means exhaustive or prescriptive and should only be taken as a means to inform the reader and stimulate consideration of possible security activity.

Infrastructure as a Service (IaaS)

In the infrastructure as a service (IaaS) model, the customer will have the most control over their resources, which might alleviate some concerns about trusting the provider or lacking insight into the environment. However, there are still risks that exist in the IaaS motif, although they are not usually unique to that configuration:

Personnel Threats   Again, a malicious or negligent insider (working for the provider) may cause significant negative impact to the customer, in large part because they have physical access to the resources within the data center where the customer's data resides.

External Threats   These include malware, hacking, DoS/DDoS, man-in-the-middle attacks, and so forth.

Lack of Specific Skillsets   Because so much of the environment will be administered by the customer, and all access will be via remote connections, there will be a significant burden on the customer's administrators and staff to provide both operational and security functions in IaaS. An organization that does not have sufficient personnel with the training and experience necessary for conducting these tasks in a cloud environment is introducing a sizable risk to its operations.

Platform as a Service (PaaS)

The platform as a service (PaaS) model will have other risks in addition to those included in the IaaS model. These include the following:

Interoperability Issues   Because the OS will be administered and updated by the provider, the customer's software may or may not function properly with each new adjustment to the environment.

Persistent Backdoors   PaaS is often used for software development and development operations (DevOps) efforts because the customer can install any software (production or testbed) over the infrastructure (hardware and OS) within the cloud environment. This model lends itself well to serving as a testbed for new applications. It can mimic the production environment with a structured sampling of all the systems from the live enterprise, and it also tests the interface with various platforms through the remote access capability and opportunity to spread the test over multiple OSs. With all these benefits for DevOps, it is important to remember a significant risk that comes with that industry: backdoors left by developers after the final product ships. These are used for efficient editing and test cases so that the developer doesn't have to run the program all the way from the beginning to find the particular function that needs to be addressed. However, backdoors also serve as attack vectors if discovered and exploited by malicious parties. What was yesterday's development tool is tomorrow's zero-day exploit.

Virtualization   Because most PaaS offerings utilize virtualized OSs, the threats and risks associated with virtualization must be considered in this model. Please see the section "Virtualization" later in this chapter for more information about this.

Resource Sharing   Programs and instances run by the customer will operate on the same devices used by other customers, sometimes simultaneously. The possibility of information bleed and side-channel attacks exists and must be considered.

Software as a Service (SaaS)

All the risks inherent in the PaaS and IaaS models remain in the software as a service (SaaS) environment along with these additional risks:

Proprietary Formats   The provider may be collecting, storing, and displaying data in a format owned by and unique to that provider. This can lead to vendor lock-in and decrease portability.

Virtualization   The risks from virtualization are enhanced in the SaaS environment because even more resource sharing and simultaneous multitenancy is going to occur. For more information, refer to the next section, "Virtualization."

Web Application Security   Most SaaS offerings will rely on access through a browser, with some kind of application programming interface (API). Potential weaknesses within web apps pose a wide variety of risks and threats.

Virtualization

We have discussed the importance of virtualization throughout the book. We'll now discuss the risks related to the use of virtualization in the cloud. Many of these possibilities require attenuation through use of controls that can only be implemented by the cloud provider, so the cloud customer must rely on contractual provisions for implementation and enforcement.

Attacks on the Hypervisor   Instead of attacking a virtualized instance, which might only result in successfully breaching the content of one (virtualized) workstation, malicious actors might attempt to penetrate the hypervisor, which is the system that acts as the interface and controller between the virtualized instances and the resources of the given host devices on which they reside.

There are two types of hypervisors, known as Type 1 and Type 2. *Type 1* is also called a bare-metal or hardware hypervisor. It resides directly on the host machine, often as bootable software. *Type 2* is a software hypervisor, and it runs on top of the OS that runs on a host device.

Attackers prefer Type 2 hypervisors because of the larger surface area. They can attack the hypervisor itself, the underlying OS, and the machine directly, whereas Type 1 attacks are restricted to the hypervisor and the machine. OSs are also more complex than hypervisors, creating the increased potential for included vulnerabilities.

Guest Escape   An improperly designed or poorly configured virtualized machine or hypervisor might allow for a user to leave the confines of their own virtualized instance. This is referred to as *guest escape* or *virtual machine (VM) escape*. A user who has successfully performed guest escape might be able to access other virtualized instances on the same host and view, copy, or modify data stored there. Worse, the user might be able to access the host itself and therefore be able to affect all the instances on the machine. And the worst potential situation is known as *host escape*, where a user can not only leave their own virtualized instance, they can even leave the host machine, accessing other devices on the network. This may be unlikely, as it would only result from some rather egregious failures in hardware, software, policy, and personnel performance (or significant combinations thereof), but it is a risk and must be considered.

Information Bleed   This is another risk stemming from malfunctions or failures. The possibility exists that processing performed on one virtualized instance may be detected, in whole or in part, by other instances on the same host. In order for this risk to be detrimental, the loss does not even have to involve the raw data itself. It might instead be only indicative of the processing occurring on the affected instance. For example, it might be possible to detect that a certain operation is happening on the affected instance and that the operation lasts for a specific duration. This kind of process-specific information can tell a malicious actor about the types of security controls on the instance or what kind of operations are being conducted. This can provide the attacker with an advantage because they might be able to narrow down a list of possible attack vectors to only those that will function in that circumstance, or they might gain an insight into what types of material might be acquired from a successful attack. This tactic is often referred to as a *side channel* or *covert channel* attack.

Data Seizure   Legal activity might result in a host machine being confiscated or inspected by law enforcement or plaintiffs' attorneys, and the host machine might include virtualized instances belonging to your organization, even though your organization was not the target.

Cloud data centers can be perceived as similar to DMZs in legacy enterprises. Because everything in the cloud can be accessed remotely, it can be considered exposed to the Internet, to a greater or lesser extent. Instead of the discrete perimeter of a private network, cloud configurations may be more porous or might be considered to have no specific perimeter boundary at all.

In the following sections, we'll discuss threats to specific cloud platforms and countermeasures that may facilitate trust in cloud usage.

Threats

Although many of the threats to cloud computing are the same as those we faced in traditional IT operations, they might manifest in novel ways or pose a greater risk. In this section, we'll examine the threats to the private, community, public, and hybrid cloud models. This coverage is by no means exhaustive or prescriptive and should only be taken as a means to inform the reader and stimulate consideration of possible security activity.

Malware   Malicious software downloaded from the Internet or uploaded to the internal network can cause a wide variety of problems, including data loss, loss of control of devices, interruption of operations, and so forth. This is less likely in an SaaS environment because the customer has no ability to install software.

Internal Threats   These can be the result of malicious or accidental activity on the part of employees or others who have been granted access (such as contractors and maintenance personnel).

External Attackers   Entities outside the organization may want to attack the network for any number of reasons, including financial gain, hacktivism, political goals, perceived grievances, and so on. These attacks can take many forms and manifest a variety of effects, including DoS/DDoS, data breach, legal repercussions, syn flooding, brute force, and more.

Man-in-the-Middle Attacks   This is the colloquial term for any attack where attackers insert themselves between the sender and receiver. This can take the form of simple eavesdropping to acquire data, or it can be a more advanced attack, such as the attacker posing as one of the participants in order to gain further control/access or modifying data traffic to introduce false or damaging information into the communication. The remote access capability of a private cloud enhances the exposure to this type of threat, compared to legacy configurations where all network access was limited to internal users.

Theft/Loss of Devices   Again, the convenience and enhanced operational capability of remote access also comes with additional threats. In a BYOD environment, especially, the loss or theft of a user's device can lead to unauthorized access and exploitation of the organization's cloud network.

Regulatory Violations   Regulations affect almost all IT operations, but a private cloud adds greater risk that the organization will not be able to maintain compliance. The increased opportunity and efficiency for disseminating information also increases the likelihood of violating applicable regulations.

Natural Disasters   All operations are prone to disruption from natural disasters, and no geographical region is free of risk from this threat. They only differ in location. (Location and climate dictate the types and frequencies of disasters, such as hurricanes, floods, wildfires, tornadoes, earthquakes, volcanoes, mudslides, and so on.)

Loss of Policy Control   Because ownership is distributed in the cloud, centralized policy promulgation and enforcement is not usually an option.

Loss of Physical Control   Lack of physical control equates to a relative decrease in physical security. This threat can be accentuated in a community cloud if ownership is distributed among many participants.

Lack of Audit Access   Tied to the loss of physical control, it may be impractical or impossible to conduct audits in a distributed environment.

Rogue Administrator   This is an enhanced form of the insider threat. The public cloud incurs the possibility that an insider with more than just basic access may act in a malicious or irresponsible manner. Because public cloud providers will be managing your systems and data, a bad actor or careless employee could take the form of a network/system architect, engineer, or administrator, potentially causing far more damage than a user in the legacy environment could accomplish.

Escalation of Privilege   This is another extension of the insider threat category. This type of threat is what happens when authorized users try to increase their level of access/permissions for either malicious or operational reasons. (Not all attempts to escalate privilege are malicious in nature. Some users are willing to violate policy in order to increase their own ability to perform their tasks or to avoid annoying or cumbersome controls.) The likelihood of this type of threat increases in the cloud because users are faced with not one but at least two sets of governance—that of their own organization and that of the provider. This can cause delays in requests to modify or grant additional access/permission, which can in turn lead to user attempts to circumvent policy.

Contractual Failure   A poorly crafted contract can lead to vendor lock-in, unfavorable terms, lack of necessary services, and other risks, and it should be perceived as a threat.

Although natural disasters can still affect the public cloud architecture, the public cloud can actually provide some protection and insulation from natural disasters as well. In fact, one of the advantages of migrating to a public cloud configuration is the security offered by fast replication, regular backups, and distributed, remote processing and storage of data offered by cloud providers (assuming the provider has appropriately apportioned resources and the customer is utilizing the resources properly).

Countermeasure Methodology

The following is a discussion of some countermeasures that can be adopted in order to address the threats for each of the cloud models discussed in the preceding sections. This coverage is by no means exhaustive or prescriptive and should only be taken as a means to inform the reader and stimulate consideration of possible security activity.

Malware   Host-based and network-based anti-malware applications and agents can be employed in actual host devices and virtualized instances. Specific training can be provided for all users regarding the methods used for introducing malware into a cloud environment and how to defeat them. Continual monitoring of network traffic and baseline configurations can be used to detect anomalous activity and performance degradation that may be indicative of infections. Regular updates and patches should be implemented, perhaps including automatic checks for virtual machines as they are instantiated at every boot.

Internal Threats   Before hiring new personnel, the organization should conduct aggressive background checks, resume/reference confirmation, and skills and knowledge testing. For addressing the risks associated with existing employees, the organization should have appropriate personnel policies that might include comprehensive and recurring training, mandatory vacation and job rotation, and two-person integrity in those situations where it makes financial and operational sense. Solid workflow policies should include separation of duties and least privilege. Active surveillance and monitoring programs, both physical and electronic, can be used. Data should be masked, reducing the view of all personnel who don't need to work directly with raw data. Egress monitoring should be implemented as well (using DLP solutions).

External Attackers   Countermeasures include hardened physical devices, hypervisors, and virtual machines, with a solid security baseline and thorough configuration and change management protocols, as well as strong access controls, possibly even outsourced to a third party such as a cloud access security broker (CASB). It's also important for the organization to understand how it is perceived by adversaries; this kind of data can be used for threat assessment and identification as well as offering some predictive capability, which could provide a much more timely response than a reactive way of handling threats. Threat intelligence services offer this functionality.

 Real World Scenario

Protection vs. Security

In 2011, Sony sued a man named George Hotz after Hotz published an exploit that allowed PlayStation 3 owners to subvert internal controls on the game console and take full control of the device. Sony's actions are understandable. The company intended to protect its brand by obviating opportunities for PlayStation users to breach IRM solutions and infringe on software copyrights. Hotz's position is likewise reasonable. Hotz asserted that the owner of a device should be allowed to utilize it in any manner they see fit and that preventing such capabilities on the pretense that this ability might be abused by malicious actors ought not restrict those who have no such intent.

Sony's legal right to defend its property notwithstanding, the action was seen by some as abusive. Sony, a multinational giant with vast resources, was pursuing what was obviously a punitive course against an individual with limited resources and supposedly no ill intent. The hacking group known as Anonymous considered Hotz a kindred spirit and took umbrage at Sony's actions. A hacker claiming to act on behalf of Anonymous launched a three-day attack against Sony's PlayStation Network (PSN), resulting in a breach that exposed account information of 77 million PSN users (arguably the largest known breach at that time) and an extended shutdown of the game service. The eventual cost of the attack, according to statements attributed to Sony in news reports, exceeded $171 million, including lost revenue, legal fees, and customer restitution.

It's difficult to imagine the loss of root control over PlayStation devices costing Sony more than the damages related to the hack. This in no way suggests that the illegal attack on PSN is justifiable or reasonable. However, Sony's failure to understand public perception of its position and action exposed Sony to a much greater threat than the one the company was trying to prevent. In handling security matters, even when your organization is legally and ethically in the right, an objective, holistic view can be useful to attenuate unintentional escalation of risk.

Sony and Hotz reached an out-of-court settlement, the full terms of which are not available.

Man-in-the-Middle (MitM) Attacks   One way to mitigate these attacks is to encrypt data in transit, including authentication activity. You can also use secure session technology and enforcement.

Social Engineering   Training, training, training. Use incentive programs (perhaps including spot bonuses and accolades) to identify personnel who resist social engineering attempts and alert the security office.

Data Loss from Theft/Loss of Devices   Countermeasures include encryption of stored material to attenuate the efficacy of theft, strict physical access controls, limited or no USB functionality (up to and including physically destroying USB ports), detailed and comprehensive inventory control and monitoring, and remote wipe or remote kill switch capability for portable devices.

Regulatory Violations   Hire knowledgeable, trained personnel with applicable skillsets. Defer to general counsel in planning and managing your systems. Implement IRM solutions. Use encryption and obfuscation and masking as necessary.

Natural Disasters   The cloud provider should ensure multiple redundancies for all systems and services for the data center, including ISPs and utilities. The cloud customer can arrange for a disaster backup with the same cloud provider, with another cloud provider, or offline. For further discussion of this topic, see the section "Disaster Recovery (DR) and Business Continuity (BC)" later in this chapter.

Loss of Policy Control   Strong contractual terms should be employed that ensure the provider is adhering to a security program that is at least as effective and thorough as what the customer would institute in an enterprise the customer owned and controlled. Detailed and extensive audits should be conducted by the customer or a trusted third party.

Loss of Physical Control   You can use all of the protections listed in the internal threats, theft/loss of devices, and loss of policy control entries in this list.

Lack of Audit Access   If the provider refuses to allow the customer to directly audit the facility, the customer must rely on a trusted third party instead. If the provider limits access to full third-party reports, the customer must insist on contractual protections to transfer as much of the financial liability for security failures to the provider as possible, including additional punitive damages.

Rogue Administrator   Countermeasures include all the controls listed in the internal threats entry in this list, with additional physical, logical, and administrative controls for all privileged accounts and personnel, including thorough and secure logging of all administrative activities, locked racks, monitoring of physical access to devices in real time, implementation of video surveillance, and financial monitoring of privileged personnel (where legally allowed).

Escalation of Privilege   Extensive access control and authentication tools and techniques should be implemented. Countermeasures also include analysis and review of all log data by trained, skilled personnel on a frequent basis combined with automated tools such as SIEM/SIM/SEM solutions.

Contractual Failure   To protect against vendor lock-in/lock-out, the customer might consider full off-site backups, secured and kept by the customer or a trusted third-party vendor, for reconstitution with another cloud provider in the event of severe contractual disagreement.

Legal Seizure   Legal action (either for prosecutorial or litigatory purposes) might result in unannounced or unexpected loss or disclosure of the organization's data. The organization may consider using encryption of its data in the cloud or possibly employing data dispersion (spreading the data across multiple logical/physical locations). The revised BIA should take this possibility into account, and we need to consider the use of encryption for data in the cloud.

    Virtual machine introspection (VMI) is an agentless means of ensuring a VM's security baseline does not change over time by examining things such as physical address, network settings, and installed OS. These ensure that the baseline has not been inadvertently or maliciously tampered with.

Disaster Recovery (DR) and Business Continuity (BC)

Entire books have been written about this topic. We're not going to be able to address it completely in this one. Instead, we'll focus on those areas of BC/DR most applicable to cloud computing, specifically with the CCSP CBK and exam in mind. In the following sections, we'll go over BIA concerns specific to cloud platforms and the establishment of shared BC/DR planning and responsibilities between the cloud provider and customer.

Cloud-Specific BIA Concerns

In migrating to a cloud service architecture, your organization will want to review its existing business impact analysis (BIA) and consider a new BIA, or at least a partial assessment, for cloud-specific concerns and the new risks and opportunities offered by the cloud. Some of the potential impacts are things you should have already included in your original BIA, but these may be more significant and take new forms in the cloud. For instance, the loss of an internet service provider (ISP) might have affected your organization in its previous (non-cloud) configuration, but losing connectivity after migration might have a more detrimental effect. Unlike in a traditional IT environment, an organization conducting operations in the cloud will not be able to conduct scaled-back, local computing without connectivity to the provider.

Potential emergent BIA concerns include, but are not limited to, the following:

New Dependencies   Your data and operations will be reliant on external parties in whole new ways after migration. Not only will you have to depend on the cloud provider to meet your organization's needs, but all the downstream and upstream dependencies associated with the provider as well, including the provider's vendors, suppliers, utilities, personnel, and so on. The BIA should take into account possibilities involving the provider's inability to meet service requirements in addition to similar failings on the part of any of the provider's requisite entities.

Regulatory Failure   The efficiency and ease of data distribution in the cloud enhances potential violations of regulations as users and administrators alike promulgate and disseminate data in new ways. The cloud provider presents another potential point of failure for regulatory compliance as well. Even if your organization is fully compliant internally, the provider might be unable or unwilling to adhere to your policies. Regulatory failures could include insufficient protection for PII/ePHI data to comply with statutory requirements such as GDPR, GLBA, HIPAA, FERPA, or SOX, and they might also take the form of contractual inadequacies, such as copyright licensing violations. The BIA needs to include discussion of possible impacts from this situation.

Data Breach/Inadvertent Disclosure   Cloud computing magnifies the likelihood and impact of two existing risks: internal personnel and remote access. Moreover, because full legal liability for breaches of PII can't be transferred to the provider, the cloud customer must reassess the potential impact and effect of an unauthorized disclosure, especially in terms of costs resulting from data breach notification legislative mandates. Other potential adverse results from breaches that should be addressed in the revised BIA include, but aren't limited to, public disclosure of deleterious internal communication and reporting; loss of competitive advantage; negative effect on customer, supplier, and vendor goodwill; and contractual violations.

Vendor Lock-In/Lock-Out   The BIA should take these risks into account for any operations migrated to the cloud. Much of the data for this part of the report should be readily available and won't have to be re-created for the BIA as it should have been performed as part of the cost-benefit analysis when the organization first considered migration.

Customer/Provider Shared BC/DR Responsibilities

The negotiation between the customer and the provider will be extensive, addressing service needs, policy enforcement, audit capabilities, and so forth. One of the elements that definitely should be included in this discussion should be provisions for BC/DR, how and where it will be done, who is responsible for each part of the process, and so on. In the following sections, I'll describe aspects of cloud BC/DR that should be considered in these negotiations.

Logical Location of Backup Data/Systems

There are three general means of using cloud backups for BC/DR. For discussion purposes in this section, we'll be referring to both replicated data and systems as "backups." The basic ways of using cloud backups for BC/DR include the following:

Private Architecture, Cloud Service as Backup   If the organization maintains its own traditional IT data center for the primary production environment, BC/DR plans can include the use of a cloud provider as the backup. Negotiations with providers will have to include periodic upload bandwidth costs (which often include monthly caps as the limiting factor); frequency of backups; whether the organization will use a full, incremental, or differential backup schedule; the security of the data and systems at the backup data center; and ISP costs. In this methodology, the customer should determine when failover will occur—that is, the customer can decide what constitutes an emergency situation and when normal (internal) operations will cease and the backup will be utilized as the operational network. This may involve a formal declaration to include notifying the provider and will almost certainly require additional cost for the duration of the crisis event. Failover might take the form of using the cloud service as a remote network (in an IaaS, PaaS, or SaaS arrangement), or it might require downloading the backup data from the cloud to another physical production site for contingency operations. The negotiation between customer and provider should determine how and when that download occurs, how long it should take, and how and when data will be restored to the normal operations location at the end of the crisis event.

Cloud Operations, Cloud Provider as Backup   One of the attractive benefits of cloud operations is the resiliency and redundancy offered by cloud data centers, especially from market leaders. Cloud providers might offer a backup solution as a feature of their service—a backup located at another data center owned by the provider in case of disaster-level events. In this motif, the provider will have all the responsibility for determining the location and configuration of the backup and most of the responsibility for assessing and declaring disaster events. The customer may have some minimal participation in the failover process, but that's the exception rather than the rule. BC/DR activity, including failover, should usually be transparent to the customer in this case. Moreover, if this feature is offered as part of the normal cloud operation, it will usually be at no or little additional cost.

Cloud Operations, Third-Party Cloud Backup Provider   In this situation, regular operations are hosted by one cloud provider, but contingency operations require failover to another cloud provider. The customer may opt for this selection in order to distribute risk, enhance redundancy, or preemptively attenuate the possibility of vendor lock-out/lock-in. This may be the most complicated BC/DR arrangement to negotiate because it will have to involve preparations and coordination between all three parties and roles and responsibilities must be explicitly and thoroughly delineated. Under this arrangement, both the primary cloud provider and the cloud customer will take part in emergency assessment and declaration, and failover may require joint effort. This can impede the process, especially during crises when cooperation and clear communication is most difficult. The cloud customer will also have to negotiate all the terms in the first model in this list (private architecture, cloud service as a backup), with both the primary and backup cloud providers. Usually, this will also be a relatively expensive methodology—the backup provider will not be a cost bundled with other features offered by the primary provider, and both failover and contingency operations will entail additional expenses. (However, some of the increased costs might be offset by payments from the primary provider if conditions of SLAs are not met because of the crisis event.) Also, data format/system interoperability may be a significant concern; the customer may need to perform additional activity when porting data from one cloud provider to another in order for the data to be used properly at the destination.

Declaration

The declaration of disaster events is a crucial step in the BC/DR process. The cloud customer and provider must decide, prior to the contingency, who specifically will be authorized to make this decision and the explicit process for communicating when it has been made.

Within the customer organization, this authority should be formally assigned to a specific office or person, and there should be a deputy or backup named in case the primary is unavailable. Both the primary and backups should receive detailed emergency operations training that should include extensive and thorough understanding of the organization's specific BC/DR plan. The persons selected for this authority should be empowered by senior management to have the full capability to declare the emergency and initiate failover procedures.

The organization should have a warning system in place to assess impending disaster situations. This is not always possible with certain kinds of contingencies, but some may be anticipated with at least slight notice. The organization should be prepared to fail over in advance of the actual crisis event in order to maintain continuity of operations. The customer and the provider must agree on what will constitute formal notice so that failover occurs, but they may set up a preliminary schedule of preparatory communications before formal declaration is finalized and announced.

If the cloud provider has to conduct some failover activity, the contract should stipulate the time in which this has to be done after notice has been received (for example, within 10 minutes of formal declaration). If failover is automated and fully controlled by the customer, that should also be expressly detailed in the contract.

Resumption of normal activities following a contingency event will likewise require formal notification. Early return to operations may cause an extension of the disaster or result in the loss of data or assets. As with emergency declaration, return to normal operations should be tasked to a specific entity within the customer's organization, and the person making that decision should be fully aware of the risks and implications inherent in it. The process for doing so should also be enumerated within the contract.

 As in all things related to security practices, but especially in disaster situations, health and human safety are the paramount concern of any plan or process.

Testing

Having backups is an admirable practice, fulfills statutory requirements, and satisfies some legal due care obligations. However, merely creating a backup is not sufficient. If you never try to use your backups until an actual crisis event, you have no assurance that they will function as planned.

Failover testing (and return to normal operations) must be performed in order to demonstrate the efficacy of the plan and procedures. It also hones the skills of the personnel involved and allows for additional training opportunities. Of course, the testing itself constitutes an interruption in normal service and ought not be taken lightly. There is risk and cost involved with performing the test.

Most industry guidance stipulates that such testing occur at least annually. This amount might be increased depending on the nature of the organization and its operations.

BC/DR testing will have to be coordinated with the cloud provider. This should be planned well in advance of the scheduled testing. Care should be taken to determine and assign specific responsibilities to participants, and all liability for problems incurred during the failover or in returning to normal operations should be detailed in the contract.

Summary

In this chapter, we've discussed the shared and distinct responsibilities of the cloud customer and provider in terms of managing risk as well as BC/DR activities. We also explored the specific risks associated with each of the cloud computing platforms (private, community, public, hybrid, IaaS, PaaS, and SaaS) and detailed countermeasures for dealing with them. Finally, we discussed some of the potential threats and vulnerabilities that constitute the cloud attack surface.

Exam Essentials

Know how responsibilities are shared between the customer and provider.   Understand the notional chart depicted in Figure 5.1 at the beginning of the chapter and how the level of responsibility for each party largely depends on the amount of service being provided.

Know the risks associated with each type of cloud platform.   Memorizing the list might not be necessary, but you should understand the material sufficiently to the point where you could determine which risks are relevant to which particular platform.

Have a thorough understanding of countermeasures used in cloud computing.   Again, rote memorization is probably not the best technique for familiarizing yourself with this important material, but you, as a practitioner as well as a student, should have a degree of comprehension of each potential risk and threat sufficient to match it to specific security controls for attenuation.

Understand BC/DR in the cloud.   Be aware of the similarities to BC/DR plans and activities in the traditional environment, but pay particular attention to the increased complexity of arrangements necessary between cloud customer and provider and the significant importance of the contract in this regard.

Written Labs

You can find the answer to the written labs in Appendix A.

1. Locate two cloud providers online. Review their posted policies (preferably, boilerplate versions of their service contracts) regarding real-time or regular full backups, particularly in the context of BC/DR.

2. In less than one page, compare and contrast the two offerings, specifically discussing how each deals with bandwidth for backups, pricing structure, and their suitability for data portability to other cloud providers.

Review Questions

You can find the answers to the review questions in Appendix B.

1. What is the term we use to describe the general ease and efficiency of moving data from one cloud provider either to another cloud provider or down from the cloud?

   A. Mobility

   B. Elasticity

   C. Obfuscation

   D. Portability

2. The various models generally available for cloud BC/DR activities include all of the following except_____.

   A. Private architecture, cloud backup

   B. Cloud provider, backup from same provider

   C. Cloud provider, backup from another cloud provider

   D. Cloud provider, backup from private provider

3. Countermeasures for protecting cloud operations against external attackers include all of the following except_____.

   A. Continual monitoring for anomalous activity

   B. Detailed and extensive background checks

   C. Hardened devices and systems, including servers, hosts, hypervisors, and virtual machines

   D. Regular and detailed configuration/change management activities

4. All of the following are techniques to enhance the portability of cloud data in order to minimize the potential of vendor lock-in except: _____.

   A. Avoid proprietary data formats

   B. Use IRM and DLP solutions widely throughout the cloud operation

   C. Ensure there are no physical limitations to moving

   D. Ensure favorable contract terms to support portability

5. Which of the following is a technique used to attenuate risks to the cloud environment, resulting in loss or theft of a device used for remote access?

   A. Remote kill switch

   B. Dual control

   C. Muddling

   D. Safe harbor

6. Each of the following are dependencies that must be considered when reviewing the BIA after cloud migration except_____.

   A. The cloud provider's suppliers

   B. The cloud provider's vendors

   C. The cloud provider's utilities

   D. The cloud provider's resellers

7. When reviewing the BIA after a cloud migration, the organization should take into account new factors related to data breach impacts. One of these new factors is:
   _____.

   A. Legal liability can't be transferred to the cloud provider

   B. Many states have data breach notification laws

   C. Breaches can cause the loss of proprietary data

   D. Breaches can cause the loss of intellectual property

8. The cloud customer will have the most control of their data and systems, and the cloud provider will have the least amount of responsibility, in which cloud computing arrangement?

   A. IaaS

   B. PaaS

   C. SaaS

   D. Community cloud

9. After a cloud migration, the BIA should be updated to include a review of the new risks and impacts associated with cloud operations; this review should include an analysis of the possibility of vendor lock-in/lock-out. Analysis of this risk may not have to be performed as a new effort because a lot of the material that would be included is already available from which of the following?

   A. NIST

   B. The cloud provider

   C. The cost-benefit analysis the organization conducted when deciding on cloud migration

   D. Open-source providers

10. A poorly negotiated cloud service contract could result in all the following detrimental effects except_____.

   A. Vendor lock-in

   B. Malware

   C. Unfavorable terms

   D. Lack of necessary services

11. All of the following are cloud computing risks in a multitenant environment except
    _____.

    A. Risk of loss/disclosure due to legal seizures

    B. Information bleed

    C. DoS/DDoS

    D. Escalation of privilege

12. Countermeasures for protecting cloud operations against internal threats include all of the following except_____.

    A. Aggressive background checks

    B. Hardened perimeter devices

    C. Skills and knowledge testing

    D. Extensive and comprehensive training programs, including initial, recurring, and refresher sessions

13. Countermeasures for protecting cloud operations against internal threats include all of the following except_____.

    A. Active physical surveillance and monitoring

    B. Active electronic surveillance and monitoring

    C. Redundant ISPs

    D. Masking and obfuscation of data for all personnel without need to know for raw data

14. Countermeasures for protecting cloud operations against internal threats at the provider's data center include all of the following except_____.

    A. Broad contractual protections to ensure the provider is ensuring an extreme level of trust in its own personnel

    B. Financial penalties for the cloud provider in the event of negligence or malice on the part of its own personnel

    C. DLP solutions

    D. Scalability

15. Countermeasures for protecting cloud operations against internal threats at the provider's data center include all of the following except_____.

    A. Separation of duties

    B. Least privilege

    C. Conflict of interest

    D. Mandatory vacation

16. Benefits for addressing BC/DR offered by cloud operations include all of the following except_____.

   A. One-time pads

   B. Distributed, remote processing of, and storage of data

   C. Fast replication

   D. Regular backups offered by cloud providers

17. All of the following methods can be used to attenuate the harm caused by escalation of privilege except_____.

   A. Extensive access control and authentication tools and techniques

   B. Analysis and review of all log data by trained, skilled personnel on a frequent basis

   C. Periodic and effective use of cryptographic sanitization tools

   D. The use of automated analysis tools such as SIM, SIEM, and SEM solutions

18. What is the hypervisor malicious attackers would prefer to attack?

   A. Type 1

   B. Type 2

   C. Type 3

   D. Type 4

19. What is the term used to describe loss of access to data because the cloud provider has ceased operation?

   A. Closing

   B. Vendor lock-out

   C. Vendor lock-in

   D. Masking

20. Because PaaS implementations are so often used for software development, what is one of the vulnerabilities that should always be kept in mind?

   A. Malware

   B. Loss/theft of portable devices

   C. Backdoors

   D. DoS/DDoS

Chapter 6

Responsibilities in the Cloud

THE OBJECTIVE OF THIS CHAPTER IS TO ACQUAINT THE READER WITH THE FOLLOWING CONCEPTS:

✓ **Domain 1: Cloud Concepts, Architecture, and Design**

- 1.3. Understand Security Concepts Relevant to Cloud Computing

  - 1.3.4. Network Security

✓ **Domain 2: Cloud Data Security**

- 2.8. Design and Implement Auditability, Traceability, and Accountability of Data Events

  - 2.8.1. Definition of Event Sources and Requirement of Identity Attribution

✓ **Domain 3: Cloud Platform and Infrastructure Security**

- 3.1. Comprehend Cloud Infrastructure Components

  - 3.1.2. Network and Communications

  - 3.1.3. Compute

  - 3.1.6. Management Plane

- 3.4. Design and Plan Security Controls

  - 3.4.2. System and Communication Protection

✓ **Domain 4: Cloud Application Security**

- 4.5. Use Verified Secure Software

  - 4.5.3. Third Party Software Management

  - 4.5.4. Validated Open-Source Software

✓ **Domain 5: Cloud Security Operations**

- 5.1 Implement and Build Physical and Logical Infrastructure for Cloud Environment

  - 5.1.1. Hardware Specific Security Configuration Requirements

Contracted cloud computing is unlike other operational modes and also unlike other managed IT service arrangements. In the case of cloud computing, the data owner ostensibly owns the information being stored and processed but does not have control over how it is stored and processed or who specifically handles the information (in terms of administration). Perhaps most intriguing of all, the data owner does not actually have physical access to the places and devices where that information *is*. The customer has all the responsibility and liability for protecting the information according to legal standards and regulation but often cannot mandate the actual protections and security measures in order to accomplish this. This leads to a very complex situation with a number of unique considerations.

It's tough to think of an equivalent scenario. Perhaps one that comes close is brokered financial investment, where you give your money to someone else who manages it, invests it how they think best, and uses whatever security measures they determine are most beneficial to protect it. You don't have control over where the money goes or which particular security controls are implemented. You might shop around between investment brokers, trying to find one that offers better protections than all the rest, but it's probably unlikely you'll find much variety, much less be able to dictate the terms of the broker's operations. Depending on what kind of investment vehicle is being used, you might have no assurances that the money is protected from malfeasance and negligence on the part of the broker— many types of investments are not subject to insurance.

What about how the cloud customer is still liable for regulatory infractions and breaches that result in loss of PII, even if the root cause was the cloud vendor's wrongdoing? The financial-investment analogy is a bit stretched, but it still holds true: if someone gives you their money to invest for them, and you give it to a third party, and the third party loses it, you are still responsible for the loss of the money. In that respect, the cloud customer receives assets of value from their clientele (in the form of PII) and then gives it to a third party (the cloud vendor) while still remaining responsible for negative outcomes associated with those assets.

Because of the novelty of this arrangement and because the field of cloud computing itself is so new, many of the aspects that protect and support the financial industry do not yet exist in the cloud environment and the details are still getting sorted out. Perhaps most important, the case law that has shaped the financial sector—those thousands of cases involving finance that have been tried and ruled on over the past few hundred years— simply have not yet occurred in the IT and InfoSec realm and won't for some time.

So the relationships between the cloud customer and the cloud vendor, and the end client and the regulators, are not at all yet solidified and codified in a manner readily understood by anyone in terms of conclusive results in the event of unusual occurrences. In fact, it might be said that we don't know what to expect as usual or unusual in this field, quite yet.

In this chapter, we will explore some of the ways that these relationships are currently taking form and what to expect in terms of what each party wants and how they will prefer to operate. We're going to examine the roles involved in the arrangement, including third parties, and we'll also cover some of the contractual elements and technologies that make the relationship work, particularly application programming interfaces (APIs).

Foundations of Managed Services

Some element of adversarial relationship exists between the cloud customer and cloud vendor because they have somewhat different goals. The cloud customer wants to maximize their computing capabilities and security of information while minimizing their costs. The cloud vendor wants to maximize its profits while minimizing what it has to provide (which is expressed in terms of computing capabilities and security of information).

There is a great deal of obvious tension between these goals, which is why negotiation of the contract and the SLAs is vital. Luckily, there is also a great deal of overlap, which makes the relationship tenable and profitable for both parties. It is in the vendor's best interest not to allow security breaches. Repeated security failings would sour the market for its product/brand and expose it to continual lawsuits, which reduces profits. It is in the vendor's best interest to provide excellent service and exceed customer expectations because doing so attracts clients and increases market share.

The ambiguous areas are where the risks exist and where both parties must establish strong delineation of duties and responsibilities in order to protect themselves and their stakeholders (see Figure 6.1). As I've mentioned throughout this book, the type of service model/platform affects the nature and extent of each party's rights and tasks.

FIGURE 6.1   Responsibilities by service model

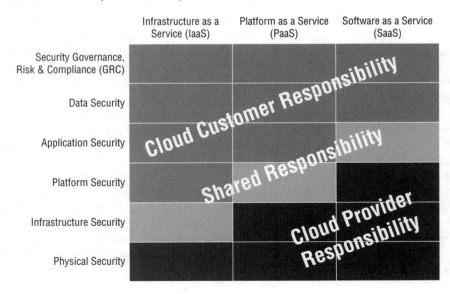

Business Requirements

The primary intent for the cloud customer should be to meet business requirements. This could involve increasing efficiency, meeting regulatory needs, and ensuring durability of capabilities during contingencies, but it should always involve reducing cost. Even if the cloud customer is a nonprofit entity and is not interested in maximizing profits, it is in the interest of all stakeholders to minimize expenses and maximize productivity.

Other business requirements will vary, depending on the industry and particular organization. Business drives all other considerations (including security) and is the primary focus of all decisions. In order to determine what is and is not a business requirement, senior management can make use of the artifacts created in various processes, including business impact analysis, risk analysis, asset inventory, and so on. To translate those requirements into cloud contract elements, SLAs, and operational functions, senior managers in a cloud customer organization can seek guidance and input from both internal and external sources.

When the business requirements have been converted into functional needs, they can be calibrated by contract terms and SLAs. These elements of legal agreement between the parties codify particular responsibilities and expectations of each, and related pricing.

Business Requirements: The Cloud Provider Perspective

What sort of business goals and operating requirements does the provider face, and how are those achieved? In a very simplistic way, that question can be answered with two short responses: be profitable and ensure all customer needs (in the form of contracts and SLAs) are being met. A more complex explanation should include a discussion of the physical establishment of the cloud provider's data center and equipment, the security aspects involved in that physical plant and architecture, and the logical design and security aspects of the data center.

Cloud Provider Responsibilities: The Physical Plant

The cloud provider needs a data center from which to provide services to its customers. The physical plant of the data center will include the campus on which the data center facility is located, the physical components inside that facility, and the services that support and connect them.

One of the first decisions a cloud provider will have to make is whether to build or buy a facility in which to situate the data center. As with all decisions, each option has benefits and risks.

In purchasing a piece of property and building an entirely new data center, the cloud provider gets to dictate every aspect of the facility, ensuring it is absolutely suited to the purpose. The provider will have much more control of how the facilities are designed, which can lead to better control over physical access to the property and buildings as well as optimized performance of the systems within the data center. This, however, is often much more expensive than purchasing or leasing an existing facility. It also requires a long-term plan for continued growth and development of the business, which often involves purchasing a larger piece of land than is initially needed for the first data center, with the understanding that additional data centers (or additional facilities) might be built on that same property in the future to increase capacity as the business grows.

The alternative, of course, is to purchase or lease an existing facility and retrofit it to the needs of the cloud provider. Although this may be less costly, especially in the short term, it may include limitations that ownership would not. For instance, if the property is being leased, the owner may not approve of all changes the provider (as a tenant) would like to make. Even if the property is owned by the provider, other external forces might limit the extent and type of changes the provider desires. This is particularly true in metropolitan settings, where zoning limitations and municipal building codes might be strict and very specific.

One popular method of avoiding the restrictions that often come with locating a physical plant in an urban setting is to locate the data center in a remote, rural setting. There are often less controls on development in these areas, and the property itself is almost always much cheaper. A factor the provider must consider, however, is the additional costs that are quite likely in situating a business in remote areas, such as creating robust, redundant utility connections for connectivity and power services.

Whichever method the provider selects, other aspects of the location itself must be taken into consideration, such as proximity to customers, ability to attract suitable personnel to staff that location, and the location's propensity for natural disasters and civil unrest.

Regardless of the build or buy decision the provider has made, the provider has to fill the facility with the physical devices that constitute a data center. While the specific vendors and manufacturers of the devices inside a cloud data center may differ from provider to provider, there are some general characteristics that will be common to most. These include the following:

Secure Hardware Components   Because of the ubiquitous use of virtualization in the cloud environment, hardware devices will have to be configured properly to ensure secure implementation of hypervisors, virtual machines, and virtual OSs. This can and should include configuring specific BIOS settings on each hardware component that follow vendor and manufacturer guidance, installing centralized virtualization management toolsets on each device, and, if cryptoprocessing will be used, ensuring the hardware has the proper settings for utilization of the Trusted Platform Module (TPM) standard. BIOS is the firmware flashed into the processor of a computer, and the TPM standard dictates how processors can be used specifically for cryptographic functions.

The notional perspective of cloud data center components usually divides the interior physical plant into three groups: compute, storage, and networking. Compute nodes are the physical host devices where customers will create virtual machines to process operational data. Storage nodes are where the data is securely stored, for either near-term or long-term purposes. Networking is all the equipment used for connecting the other nodes—the hardware devices such as routers and switches and the cables that connect them.

Manage Hardware Configuration   As with OS baselining (which we'll discuss later in this chapter), a template for the secure configuration of each specific device should be constructed, and it should be replicated whenever a new device of that particular type is added to the environment. The baseline hardware configuration should be saved in a secure manner and kept current through the formal change management process (including any required patches and updates). This is true for each of the nodes, regardless of purpose, including the compute and storage nodes, networking devices, and anything used to connect and monitor each of the nodes.

Set Hardware to Log Events and Incidents   While the granularity and specificity of which system events to capture might differ from device to device or customer to customer, the provider should ensure that sufficient data related to the activity on each machine is being saved for possible future use (including incident investigation and forensic purposes). This event data should be sufficient to determine exactly what occurred and the identity of the users involved in each event (which is also known as attribution).

Determine Compute Component Composition by Customer Need   Some cloud customers might not be suited to a multitenant environment and would prefer to have their data processed and stored in and on only devices specifically and exclusively assigned to them (the customer). While the use of stand-alone hosts is outside the norm for cloud data centers, most cloud providers will offer the option, albeit at an increased service fee (the provider will have to deploy and administer those devices and data sets separately from other customers within the same data center, which increases the cost of provision). Unlike stand-alone hosts assigned to specific customers, clustered hosts will provide scalable management benefits, allowing customers who opt for the multitenant environment to realize significant cost savings. Both stand-alone and clustered hosts must be configured and supported in such a way as to maintain high availability. This includes ensuring redundancy of the components themselves and the services that support them.

Configure Secure Remote Administrative Access   It is very likely that either the provider or the customer (or both) will have to access the hardware in order to perform some administrative function. This access will quite often be in the form of a remote connection and will therefore require particular security controls to ensure only authorized users are performing permitted actions. Security enhancements for remote access control might include implementing session encryption for the access connection, strong authentication for remote users and administrators, and enhanced logging on privileged accounts.

Cloud Provider Responsibilities: Secure Logical Framework

In addition to securing the hardware components, the cloud provider must ensure that the logical elements are likewise protected. This includes the following:

Installation of Virtual OSs   The provider must ensure that the virtual OSs installed in the data center (on virtual or hardware hosts) are configured and installed in a secure manner. In addition, as virtual OSs are deployed in the environment, virtualization management tools should be installed concurrently, to ensure the provider's ability to monitor the virtual environment for both performance and security issues and to enforce configuration policy. This is particularly important for creating and maintaining a secure hypervisor configuration—a weak hypervisor could allow malicious actors to access and attack many of the virtual assets and a great deal of the production data.

Secure Configuration of Various Virtualized Elements   In addition to the tangible hardware used in the data center, any virtual elements must also be configured in a secure fashion to attenuate potential risks such as data leakage and malicious aggregation. This is not limited to virtual hosts and OSs, but it should also include any virtualized networking or storage assets.

Cloud Provider Responsibilities: Secure Networking

Of course, in addition to securing the hardware and logical configurations, the provider will have to ensure that the networking architecture and components are secure. This will often involve many of the same tactics and methods used in the traditional (non-cloud) environment as well as some cloud-specific permutations. A brief overview of these areas follows.

Firewalls

Firewalls are tools that limit communications based on some criteria. They can be either hardware or software, or a combination of both. Firewalls can be stand-alone devices or integrated into other network nodes such as hosts and servers. The criteria for determining which traffic is allowed and which is not can take the form of rules (such as which services or protocols are allowed, which ports are to be used, from whom and when traffic should be allowed, and so forth), or behavior-sensing algorithms (the firewall is taught which behavior is "normal," for both the environment and the user, and deviations from the normal baseline are noted by the firewall), or stateful inspection (the firewall understands the expected pattern of conversation in a protocol and recognizes deviations), or even inspection of content.

IDS/IPS

Intrusion detection systems (IDSs) and intrusion prevention systems (IPSs) are very similar to firewalls in that they monitor network traffic. These can also use defined rule sets, behavior-based algorithms, content, or stateful inspection to detect anomalous activity. The explicit difference between an IDS and an IPS is that an IDS only reports suspicious activity, alerting responders (such as the security office), whereas the IPS can be set to take defensive action when suspicious activity is recognized (such as closing ports and services) in addition to sending alerts. In the modern environment, most of these solutions serve both purposes.

Honeypots

A *honeypot* is a tool used to detect, identify, isolate, and analyze attacks by distracting attackers. This is usually a dummy machine with useless data, partially secured and configured as if it was a realistic portion of the production environment. When attackers penetrate it and attempt nefarious activity (such as installing rootkits or other malware, escalating their privileges, or disabling functionality), the security team can monitor and record the attackers' behavior. This information can be used for defensive purposes in the actual production environment or as evidence in litigation and prosecution actions.

Vulnerability Assessments

A *vulnerability assessment* is a scan of the network in order to detect known vulnerabilities. These can, of course, be automated so that they're scalable for networks of any appreciable size. The unfortunate flaw in vulnerability assessments is that they will only detect known vulnerabilities. Any extant vulnerabilities that are not part of the scan will go unnoticed. Vulnerability assessments can't prevent attackers from discovering previously unknown vulnerabilities in systems and attacking them. These forms of attacks are often referred to as zero-day exploits.

Communication Protection

The connections between the various nodes and between the data center and the rest of the world must also be secured. Establishing access control and protection for remote access and data in transit can be accomplished in several ways:

Encryption   Data can be encrypted across the network, reducing the possibility that someone who does not have authorized access (an external attacker, perhaps, or a malicious insider) would be able to acquire raw data in plaintext. If network traffic was encrypted with a sufficient work factor (a measure of the time and/or resources an attacker would require to break encryption), it would not reveal sensitive data even if someone captured it. Remote connections can also be encrypted, providing the same kind of protection for user access. Of course, encryption comes with a cost: the processing overhead increases with the volume of encrypted data, some other security controls (such as IRM, egress monitoring tools, and IDS/IPS solutions) might not function in the same manner because they cannot recognize the content of the traffic, and key storage is always an issue.

Virtual Private Networks (VPNs)   Creating a secure tunnel across untrusted networks (such as the Internet) can aid in obviating man-in-the-middle attacks such as eavesdropping and interception of sensitive data, particularly when combined with encryption.

Strong Authentication   As with the other aspects of securing the cloud data center, authentication schema such as the use of robust tokens and requiring multifactor authentication can reduce the likelihood of unauthorized users gaining access and can be used to restrict authorized users to permitted activities.

Management Plane

Virtualization, cloud-specific logical configurations, and software-defined networking (SDN) are widely used. Consequently, cloud data center elements such as hardware, logical configuration, and networking elements will most likely be managed through a centralized management and control interface, often referred to as the *management plane* or the *control plane*. This interface gives a great deal of control to the administrators, analysts, and architects who will design, oversee, manage, and troubleshoot the cloud data center. The management plane can be used in each of the physical, logical, and networking areas of the data center for various tasks, such as the following types of tasks:

- **Physical:** Applying, detecting, and enforcing hardware baseline configurations

- **Logical:** Scheduling tasks, optimizing resource allocation, maintaining and updating software and virtualized hardware

- **Networking:** All network management and administration tasks (except, of course, direct physical procedures, such as connecting cabling to boxes)

Of course, the management plane also poses a significant center of risk as well as a potential single point of failure. The cloud provider must take great pains to ensure that the management plane is configured correctly and securely, that sufficient redundancy exists for every aspect of the management plane so that there is no interruption of service, and that extremely strong access control is implemented for the management plane to attenuate possible attempts to subvert or invade it.

Cloud Provider Responsibilities: Mapping and Selection of Controls

No matter what design and architecture options are employed in the cloud data center, the cloud provider (like any IT infrastructure owner or operator) must apply the proper security controls according to the relevant regulatory frameworks and the planned usage. This is especially true of, but not limited to, regulation concerning personally identifiable information (PII).

Published governance should guide the selection of appropriate controls for every aspect of data center operation (physical, logical, administrative, personnel, intangible, and tangible assets). All security policy should be based on this guidance, and all controls should be justified according to the particular regulations and standards applicable to the data center and its customers.

There are many types of regulation and appropriate standards, and they are discussed throughout this book. The cloud provider must understand which are applicable to the data center (in terms of both location and operation) and to the customers (in terms of both location and operations). For instance, each physical location will be subject to the jurisdiction of relevant laws. The "physical location" includes *both* where the data center is physically situated *and* the location of each cloud customer.

For example, a cloud data center in Park City, with customers in Omaha and Edina, would be subject to not only the data breach notification and privacy laws in Utah but also those of Nebraska and Minnesota, *as well as* any municipal codes regarding privacy and data protection for those particular cities.

In addition to physical location, the type of operations taking place in the cloud data center will dictate which regulations are applicable (and therefore, which controls are required). A cloud customer processing, say, medical information, would be subject to HIPAA, whereas those processing credit card transactions would be subject to PCI regulation (and a cloud customer doing both will require controls sufficient for fulfilling both).

There are guides and matrices of controls required by almost all relevant regulations available, usually for free. One of particular use in the cloud environment is the *Cloud Security Alliance Cloud Controls Matrix (CSA CCM)*, at https://cloudsecurityalliance .org/group/cloud-controls-matrix/, detailed elsewhere in this book. It maps requisite controls and control groups to specific contractual and legislated regulation and it is extremely useful.

Shared Responsibilities by Service Type

Again, referring to Figure 6.1, we can review what portions of the cloud environment will be tasked to which party. This is, of course, a description of the general case for many or most cloud customer–provider relationships, but it's not prescriptive by any means.

IaaS

Because the cloud provider is only hosting the hardware and utilities, its sole responsibility will be for physical security of the facility and systems. Both parties will share the responsibility for securing the infrastructure. Admittedly, this will be to a lesser extent for the cloud provider because the cloud customer will be installing the OS, which can significantly affect the security of the underlying systems, and the customer will be responsible for this aspect of infrastructure security. The customer will have sole responsibility for all other security aspects.

PaaS

In a PaaS model, the cloud customer will be installing programs on top of operating systems loaded and managed by the cloud vendor. The vendor might offer a variety of OSs, allowing the customer to ensure interoperability on a number of platforms. This can be extremely useful if the customer anticipates end users in a heterogeneous environment (for instance, in a BYOD configuration, with users accessing systems through different web browsers on a multitude of devices).

Therefore, in PaaS, the cloud provider will still maintain physical security control of the facility and hardware but will now also be responsible for securing and maintaining the OS. The cloud customer will remain obligated to provide all other security.

SaaS

As you can expect, in SaaS modes, the cloud provider will have to maintain physical security for the underlying infrastructure and OS as in the previous models but will have to secure the programs as well. In this case, the cloud customer will only be left with very specific aspects of security: access and administration.

Because the customer is the nominal data owner, the customer will always have ultimate control of who has authorization to view and manipulate the data (with the exception of those who have physical access to the hosts on which it resides, which always remains with the provider). In no circumstance will this fall to the purview of the cloud provider. Even if the task of provisioning access and accounts is contracted to the provider, the customer is still legally and ethically responsible for the security of the data itself.

Shared Administration of OS, Middleware, or Applications

In the PaaS and SaaS modes, both the cloud provider and customer will have to share some elements of control over the software elements to a greater or lesser extent. For instance, in PaaS, the customer will make updates and modifications to software they have installed (and sometimes designed) and administer on the hosted systems. The cloud provider might have some role to play in this process, as the hardware may need to be adjusted accordingly to allow for any new functionality, and that is the sole responsibility of the provider. Moreover, the provider may have to ensure security controls still function and provide the level of desired coverage upon adoption of the updates.

Operating System Baseline Configuration and Management

Perhaps one of the most useful practices for creating a secure cloud environment will be a carryover from the traditional data center—creating secure baseline configurations of the OS.

The operating system is, itself, a large attack surface, offering a great many potential avenues for malicious actors if not set correctly. As with the hosts themselves, the operating systems in a secure environment should be hardened—that is, configured in a secure manner. Hardening the operating system can include the following (and more):

- Removing unnecessary services and libraries
- Closing unused ports
- Limiting administrator access
- Ensuring default accounts are removed
- Ensuring event/incident logging is enabled

It would be cumbersome to perform the activities necessary to reach this configuration on each OS, individually and manually, so instead it is preferable to create one template, the secure OS baseline, and replicate that baseline whenever a new machine is deployed (and, in the virtual environment, whenever a new user image is created). This can be done with automated tools. We can also use those tools (or similar ones) to continually check the environment to ensure all current images and machines have an OS that meets the baseline configuration. Any OS configuration that differs from the baseline and is detected by the monitoring tool should be addressed accordingly (this might include patching or a reinstallation/rollback of the entire OS configuration).

Deviations from the baseline might have legitimate purposes. Some specialized uses and users may require adjustments to the baseline for their business tasks. In such cases, the deviation should be formally approved by the change/configuration management process and limited to situations, OS instances, and machines where that function is necessary. Configuration monitoring tools should be adjusted accordingly and the asset inventory updated so that these particular cases are not constantly setting off alerts and so that administrators don't accidentally apply the baseline configuration.

In cloud environments, where virtualization and multiple disparate customers are so prevalent, it is also important to feature the capability for capturing (and restoring) the OS of any customer and virtual guest in order to ensure the customer's particular needs are being met. There are a number of methods for copying and backing up the guest OS, such as taking snapshots of the virtual image; using software tools that install agents on the virtual machine for that purpose; and centralized, agentless configuration management solutions. When a customer needs to replicate a specific OS, the saved configuration can be copied from the backup onto the same virtual machine or others. The cloud provider and cloud customer will have to negotiate and determine how often OS configuration backups are being made and for which systems.

 VMs are saved as files when not in use; patches can't be applied to these files, so any VM taken out of storage and put into production needs to be checked against configuration versions to determine if there were patches applied to the environment while it was stored.

 All backups (not just of the OS configuration) need to be tested. The organization must restore from the backup in order to ensure that the backup method works properly, that it captures what it is designed to copy, and that integrity is maintained. If a restoration is not performed, the backup can be considered nonexistent.

Aside from maintaining the OS, baselining and configuration management are likewise important for other applications. The provider and the customer have to determine who will be responsible for establishing the secure build of the configuration template as well as performing version control activities.

Version control for applications includes following vendor recommendations, applying requisite patches and upgrades, ensuring interoperability with the rest of the environment, and documenting all changes and developments. Documentation is particularly important in support of efforts to provide consistency across the environment, to sufficiently track the current software state for business continuity and disaster recovery (BC/DR), and for any necessary forensic and discovery activities.

The Benefit of Many Eyeballs

When choosing applications and APIs for the cloud environment, cloud customers may be tempted to use software from vendors they've never done business with before and have no prior knowledge of because it offers something of enhanced value, such as a particular functionality or very low price. There is obviously a risk to using software from unverified or unvalidated sources: unknown and untested software could contain vulnerabilities and attack vectors that would otherwise be controlled for in the formal secure development or acquisition process.

One possible method for attenuating this possibility is the use of crowdsourcing—determining from other users (current and past) what their experience with particular software offered in the form of results, good or bad. This can be taken a bit further, with a decision to trust open-source programs over those with proprietary code. It is far more likely that open-source software has been vetted, verified, and validated by more people with more perspectives than even professionally developed software from known sources with rigorous testing methods. Leveraging the expertise of the community for evaluation purposes is a powerful tool.

In addition to version control for software settings, maintaining proper documentation and licensing for third-party software is also essential. Most commercial software is subject to copyright protections (although there are some packages that are freeware or shareware or have other distribution protections, such as copyleft), and only authorized, licensed versions should be used within the organization. The security office is often also tasked with the role of software custodian, maintaining a library/record of all licenses/permissions.

Shared Responsibilities: Data Access

Of course, in all models, the cloud customer (and their users) will need access and the ability to modify the data. This will require some degree of sharing administration capabilities, however minimal. For instance, the data may be processed in a database, and the database administrator may be in the employ of the cloud provider or the cloud customer, or there may be database administrators in both organizations and they might have shared or overlapping duties.

The data owner (cloud customer) will always retain fundamental liability for data protection and will therefore be the end arbiter of granting access and permissions for that data set. This may be implemented via a number of methods: direct administration of user identity and authorization processes; contracting the tasks to the cloud provider, under strict instructions and through a specified verification procedure; or perhaps contracting out the duties to a third party, such as a cloud access security broker (CASB), who will perform these administrative tasks on the customer's behalf.

Let's review some examples of processes that might facilitate each method.

Customer Directly Administers Access

If the cloud customer retains control of these duties, then the customer will provision, manage, and remove user accounts without input or cooperation from the cloud provider. This could be performed by administrators working within the customer's organization, remotely accessing the OS on the cloud host devices and manipulating the access control systems (say, updating the ACLs) manually. When a new user needs an account, the entire operation is initiated, executed, and completed within the cloud customer's organization.

In IaaS, this would always be the case because the cloud provider has no oversight or control of the OS. With PaaS and SaaS, however, this will be a bit more complicated because the cloud provider is obligated (and invested) to control the OS and software completely. Ceding administrative access to the customer will require a great deal of trust and additional controls and will almost certainly be limited to this very specific purpose.

The elements of this process must be spelled out, in great detail, in the contract and SLAs between the customer and provider.

Provider Administers Access on Behalf of the Customer

In this type of situation, any new user must submit a request to the provider, either directly or through some point of contact within the customer organization. The provider will need to verify the request is legitimate and correct by contacting the customer through a predetermined process and then create the account and assign the appropriate permissions.

Third-Party (CASB) Administers Access on Behalf of the Customer

The CASB will have some of the duties and access relegated to the other parties in the previous examples. The user will make the request to the CASB or to a local administrator, and the CASB will verify the account and then assign the appropriate access and permissions.

Lack of Physical Access

The cloud provider will typically not have any reason to allow the customer physical access to the facility and devices containing the customer's data. In fact, the provider will have every reason to prevent this. There will be a great many customers, with various levels of trust, and the more people who have knowledge of the physical location, security controls, and layout of the data center, the greater the risk to the data and operations.

From the customer's perspective, this is both beneficial and challenging. It is beneficial because it increases the customer's trust in the provider (the customer has limited access, but *all* customers have limited access, including other customers who may be hostile to or competitive with each other). It is challenging because the customer is forced to rely on the provider's assertions of security without the customer having any means to reliably validate and verify those assertions for themselves.

Audits

In a traditional environment, audits serve a valuable function, determining that controls were selected properly, the controls function properly, and the organization is in compliance with a given standard or mandate. Here is a brief overview of auditing terminology and concepts:

- **Internal Audit:** An audit (review of the environment) is performed by employees of the organization. The results of the audit (typically, an audit report) can be used by management to adjust control selection/implementation or as evidence of due diligence (often required by certain customers/regulators).

- **External Audit:** An external audit is performed by auditors from outside the organization, typically a licensed/chartered accountancy (an accounting firm). The external audit offers additional benefits beyond what the internal audit yields. External auditors are perceived (often rightly so) as being independent from the target organization, not succumbing to internal pressures and politics, and having a more trustworthy or believable perspective. As with internal audits, the results of an external audit may be used solely by management as part of the decision-making process, or they may be shared outside the organization for marketing/regulatory purposes. In the IT/InfoSec realm, external audits often take the form of vulnerability scans and penetration tests.

- **Audit Preparation:** Typically, the parameters of an audit engagement (duration, physical/logical locations, and so on) are negotiated prior to the start of the audit. Limitations are placed on which offices, artifacts, systems, and so on will be inspected as part of the audit. This is referred to as the *scope* of the audit. (*Scoping* is sometimes used as a verb, where *scoping* the audit means "determining which aspects of the organization will be included.") This is a crucial part of the overall audit process as crafting the scope can determine the impact, price, and usefulness of results of the audit.

- **Audit Processes/Methods:** Generally, audits are not exhaustive, detailed inspections of every single aspect of the target; this would be impractical and expensive and entail more impact than the results could realistically be worth. Instead, auditors will review the overall population of the environment (described in the scoping statement), select a suitable sample size, and then verify the configuration/controls/utility of the performance/controls in the sample. If the sample is suitably representative of the population, the results of the audit are taken to be meaningful for the population as a whole. There are various types of audits (and therefore, auditors), using a variety of tools/techniques depending on the desired target/population (financial, IT, and/or security audits, and so forth).

- **Audit Results:** The auditors collect findings, report on gaps between the intended outcomes and the actual environment, and present these findings to the client/target. Auditors may note shortcomings and sort those shortcomings into categories (for instance, "significant" findings that need immediate attention or "routine" findings that can be addressed in the normal course of the operational pace). Typically, auditors should *not* recommend solutions for shortcomings as this would put the auditor in the role of consultant/advisor, which is a conflict of interest (the auditor must remain impartial, including to the eventual success of the target organization). An auditor finding a grievous flaw or shortcoming might only publish an audit report with "qualifications" or "reservations," noting that the auditor feels there is a material or fundamental problem with the organization's approach to either the audit itself or the business process being audited.

In a traditional customer/provider relationship, the customer would prefer to perform an audit (or have an audit performed, at the customer's behest and supervision, by an auditor of the customer's choosing) of the provider, at the provider's location and using data/material taken directly from the provider.

Unfortunately, the cloud provider's unwillingness to allow physical access to the facility also applies to the customer's auditors, and in most cases auditors probably won't even have access to data streams and documentary artifacts necessary to perform a reasonable audit with a suitable level of veracity. This is especially troubling for those organizations that have regulatory requirements for performing audits and providing audit reports to their stakeholders (including regulators).

The lack of physical access to the cloud provider's facility also means that the preferred means of attenuating data remanence risks and ensuring secure data disposal (such as physical destruction of the host devices, drives, and media) will not be available to the customer. We've discussed the current best alternatives in other chapters, so I won't repeat them here.

For auditing purposes, then, what the customer is likely to get instead is audit reports performed by licensed and chartered auditors on the provider's behalf, made known to the customers and the public. It is, of course, in the provider's best interest to publish these audits, in the hope of increasing public perception of the reliability and trustworthiness of the provider's services and thus increasing customer satisfaction and market share. However, the provider does not want to share a detailed audit of security controls for the very same reason they don't want to allow physical access: a security control audit that revealed specific aspects and configuration of controls would provide a roadmap of attack for malicious actors.

Instead, the provider is likely to publish an audit assurance statement: something from the auditor that states, in formal terms, that an audit was performed and that the auditor finds the results suitable for the purposes of the provider's operations—a seal of approval, if you will.

Currently, this usually takes the form of an SOC 3 audit report. Let's delve into the SOC reports and their intended purpose, because this material is significant for both exam and practical purposes.

The *SOC reports* are part of the SSAE reporting format created by the American Institute of Certified Public Accountants (AICPA). These are uniformly recognized as being acceptable for regulatory purposes in many industries, although they were specifically designed as mechanisms for ensuring compliance with the Sarbanes–Oxley Act (colloquially referred to as SOX), which governs publicly traded corporations.

There are three SOC report categories: SOC 1, SOC 2, and SOC 3. Each of them is meant for a specific purpose, and there are further subclasses of reports as well.

SOC 1 reports are strictly for auditing the financial reporting instruments of a corporation, and therefore have little to do with our field. It's worth knowing that they exist (SOC 1 is mentioned in the CBK, and it's important to know the distinction between SOC 1 reports and SOC 2 and SOC 3 reports) and that there are two subclasses of SOC 1 reports: Type 1 and Type 2. Other than that, you should never have to deal with them in practice because they are not germane to computer security or cloud computing.

SOC 2 reports are the ones that are particular to our field. They are specifically intended to report audits of any controls on an organization's security, availability, processing integrity, confidentiality, and privacy. Therefore, a cloud provider intending to prove its trustworthiness can demonstrate it with a SOC 2 report.

SOC 2 reports also come in two subclasses: Type 1 and Type 2. The SOC 2 Type 1 is not extremely useful for determining the security and trust of an organization. The SOC 2 Type 1 only reviews the *design* of controls, not how they are implemented and maintained or their function. The SOC 2 Type 2 report, however, does just that. This is why the SOC 2 Type 2 is the sort of report that is extremely useful for getting a true assessment of an organization's security posture.

However, cloud vendors are reluctant to share the SOC 2 Type 2 report outside the provider's organization. The SOC 2 Type 2 report is extremely detailed and provides exactly the kind of description and configuration that the cloud provider is trying to restrict from wide dissemination. It's basically a handbook for attacking that cloud provider.

In recent years, though, many cloud providers have become willing to share the SOC 2 Type 2 reports with some customers. Usually, the provider will only share this information with customers that the provider has specifically vetted and has reason to trust, and then only if the customer is willing to sign a nondisclosure agreement or undergo additional security measures to protect the report. In some cases, the customer can only view the report material under certain conditions or in certain locations.

Cloud customers are, however, welcome to view the SOC 3 report (as is everyone else; SOC 3 reports are designed to be shared with the public). The SOC 3 is the "seal of approval" mentioned earlier in this section. It contains no actual data about the security controls of the audit target and is instead just an assertion that the audit was conducted and that the target organization passed. That's it.

This makes the SOC 3 report of dubious use for verifying the trustworthiness of an organization. Instead of taking the word of a company that the company is trustworthy, with no evidence offered in support of its word, we are asked to take the word of an auditor hired by that company that the company is trustworthy, with no evidence offered to support the auditor's assertion.

The lack of physical access to the provider's facility and the SOC reporting issues are not the only challenges to performing audits in the cloud environment. There are other challenges that should be considered:

- **Sampling:** Unlike a traditional IT environment, with a discrete number of machines/users/etc., the cloud environment is difficult to scope because of the very nature of cloud computing—scalability/flexibility/elasticity lead to an environment where the number of individual systems may be constantly fluctuating. It may be hard to properly scope an audit in a cloud environment for this reason. Selecting an appropriate, indicative sample size could pose significant difficulty.

- **Virtualization:** The use of virtualized machines might be either a hindrance or a benefit for audit purposes. From a problematic perspective, the virtualized environment may be difficult for the auditor to inspect; the level of permissions/administrative access necessary to determine the actual implementation/functionality of the configuration/controls may not be available to the cloud customer (and therefore, not available to the auditor, either). From a beneficial perspective, virtualization might address the previous problem of sample size: if all systems in the customer's (target's) IT environment are built from one specific, honed virtual image (the "Golden Build"), then an auditor could simply review that single image to determine compliance/suitability and know that all other virtualized machines made from it are satisfactory (or not).

- **Multitenancy:** In a traditional audit, the scope of the audit usually only includes property owned by the target organization; in the cloud, this is often not the case as the shared resources of the cloud data center are often in simultaneous use by other customers...and the auditor has no right/permission to view any activity of those other customers (in fact, to do so may violate laws in a significant way).

 There are other forms of certification available and widely used in the cloud computing industry, such as the CSA Security, Trust, Assurance, and Risk (STAR) program, which is available for free: (https://cloudsecurityalliance.org/star/).

Theoretically, an audit, when performed correctly by trusted and trained auditors, should lend the customer some level of assurance that the provider's controls, risk management program, and processes are sound and secure. Because the cloud customer must rely on audit reports as almost the only way to review a provider's capabilities/governance (and quite possibly the only form of due diligence the customer has in a cloud-based relationship), audits are essential for cloud-managed services' arrangements.

Shared Policy

In addition to the (most likely SOC 3) audit reports, the cloud customer will have to rely on the contract and the SLAs to ensure that the provider is securing the data to an extent and with the controls sufficient for the customer's purposes, including compliance with regulatory structures. These tools (the contract and the SLAs) will not obviate the customer's legal responsibilities in the event of a breach, but they *will* help the customer seek financial restitution for damages caused to the customer and their end clients in a breach that occurred because of negligence or malfeasance on the part of the provider.

In pursuit of this effort, and as contractual elements, the customer and provider may agree to share doctrinal mechanisms in common, such as industry standards, guidelines, vendor documentation, and other policy and procedural artifacts. This could be true whether the service is IaaS, PaaS, or SaaS. If the parties choose this type of arrangement, both must agree to work from the same version of each artifact and must involve the other in any change management process that affects the documents (even if that involvement is limited to notification). This process and any limitations must be codified in the contract from the outset of the relationship.

Shared Monitoring and Testing

Another area where providers and customers may find common ground in sharing responsibilities is security monitoring and testing. The provider may allow the customer access to data streams or administrative capabilities on devices in order for the customer to perform their own monitoring and testing activities in conjunction with or (more likely) in addition to the provider's own efforts.

Again, because of the provider's inherent requirements to ensure security throughout the cloud environment, this access is most probably going to be very limited. The customer will be granted access only to those specific aspects of the enterprise that will not affect or give any insight into any of the provider's other customers residing in the cloud. The provider's concern is twofold: not allowing any specific customer or user enough capability to cause significant harm to the enterprise through accident or malicious intent and not disclosing any customer's data or operation to any other customer.

Even with this limited amount of transparency, though, it is possible for the customer to have a greater certainty and trust in the security controls and performance of the cloud provider. This assurance is gained by allowing the customer to monitor and test the data and behavior of the network and to ensure that the general set of security controls and protective measures available to all customers are sufficient and not problematic for the customer's specific data set.

For instance, the provider may allow the customer to access audit and performance logs or to even configure settings on resources limited to that customer's use. Or the provider may deliver SIEM log data to the customer so that the customer might perform their own analysis and internal reporting with it.

Also, the provider might act in concert with the customer to configure and deploy a DLP solution that could issue alerts or reports on any data egress activity—limited, of course, to the customer's own specific data. This may be more cumbersome and challenging because of the nature of shared resources in the cloud environment (shared between customers) and because of the wide use of virtualization (requiring DLP solutions expressly designed for the purpose).

For testing purposes, the provider may allow the customer access to a scaled-down, limited portion of the cloud environment that mimics the overall infrastructure in order for the customer to perform small-scale testing of their data and usage in a sandboxed, isolated manner. This could improve the customer's confidence in the production environment, enhancing their trust in the provider's ability to protect the customer's data and to administer the network in such a way that there is no untoward impact to the customer's critical functions.

Again, these capabilities would necessarily be limited and must be formally agreed to by both parties, in the contract and SLAs, prior to the commencement of the business arrangement.

Summary

In this chapter, we have explored how both parties will be able to act independently and in concert to assure for themselves and each other that the security of the network and the data on it will not be unduly affected. We discussed which responsibilities might be distinct to each party in different cloud models and which aspects might be shared.

Exam Essentials

Know the cloud provider's responsibilities for providing secure physical, logical, and networking elements in the data center.   Understand how the provider will use secure processes, methods, and controls to provide the customer with a trusted environment in which to conduct business. Know the various network security components and tools. Be familiar with the process of mapping specific security controls and control groups to applicable regulatory guidance.

Understand which party will most likely have which specific security responsibilities in each of the cloud service models.   Know what the provider and customer each are tasked with in IaaS, PaaS, and SaaS configurations.

Understand which responsibilities the cloud customer and cloud provider are likely to share.   Know that OS and application baselining and management responsibilities are likely to be shared, as are identity and access management, to some degree.

Know the different types of audit reports most likely to be used for cloud data centers.
Understand the difference between SOC 1, 2, and 3 reports and Types 1 and 2 of SOC 2.
Know which is preferred for detailed analysis and which the cloud customer is most likely
to have easy access to.

Written Labs

You can find the answers to the written labs in Appendix A.

1. Visit the web page for the CSA's STAR program (https://cloudsecurityalliance
    .org/star/).

2. Download the Consensus Assessments Initiative Questionnaire: https://
    cloudsecurityalliance.org/download/
    consensus-assessments-initiative-questionnaire-v3-0-1/.

3. Review the questionnaire. Understand the operational security aspects a cloud data
    service provider will be expected to verify and attest to. Think of these aspects in terms
    of what you've learned so far from this book.

4. Visit the actual Registry itself: https://cloudsecurityalliance.org/star/registry.

5. Select any registered provider, and download its (completed) questionnaire.

6. In one page or less, describe three security aspects of the registered provider's responses
    that you find interesting or troubling or that should be of concern to a cloud customer
    considering using that provider.

Review Questions

You can find the answers to the review questions in Appendix B.

1. What is the cloud service model in which the customer is responsible for administration of the OS?

    A. IaaS

    B. PaaS

    C. SaaS

    D. QaaS

2. To address shared monitoring and testing responsibilities in a cloud configuration, the provider might offer all these to the cloud customer except _____.

    A. Access to audit logs and performance data

    B. SIM, SIEM, and SEM logs

    C. DLP solution results

    D. Security control administration

3. In addition to whatever audit results the provider shares with the customer, what other mechanism does the customer have to ensure trust in the provider's performance and duties?

    A. Statutes

    B. The contract

    C. Security control matrix

    D. HIPAA

4. Which kind of SSAE audit report is a cloud customer most likely to receive from a cloud provider?

    A. SOC 1 Type 1

    B. SOC 2 Type 2

    C. SOC 1 Type 2

    D. SOC 3

5. Which kind of SSAE audit report is most beneficial for a cloud customer, even though it's unlikely the cloud provider will share it without additional protections?

    A. SOC 1 Type 1

    B. SOC 2 Type 2

    C. SOC 1 Type 2

    D. SOC 3

6. The auditor should not _____.

    A. Review documents

    B. Physically visit the business location

    C. Perform system scans

    D. Deliver consulting services

7. Hardening the operating system refers to all of the following except _____.

    A. Limiting administrator access

    B. Removing anti-malware agents

    C. Closing unused ports

    D. Removing unnecessary services and libraries

8. The cloud customer's trust in the cloud provider can be enhanced by all of the following except _____.

    A. Audits

    B. Shared administration

    C. Real-time environmental controls

    D. SLAs

9. User access to the cloud environment can be administered in all of the following ways except: _____.

    A. Customer directly administers access

    B. Customer provides administration on behalf of the provider

    C. Provider provides administration on behalf the customer

    D. Third party provides administration on behalf of the customer

10. Which kind of SSAE audit reviews the organization's controls for assuring the confidentiality, integrity, and availability of data?

    A. SOC 1

    B. SOC 2

    C. SOC 3

    D. SOC 4

11. Which kind of SSAE report provides only an attestation by a certified auditor?

    A. SOC 1

    B. SOC 2

    C. SOC 3

    D. SOC 4

12. Which of the following is a cloud provider likely to provide to its customers in order to enhance the customer's trust in the provider?

A. Site visit access

B. Financial reports to shareholders

C. Audit and performance log data

D. Backend administrative access

13. In all cloud models, the customer will be given access and ability to modify which of the following?

A. Data

B. Security controls

C. User permissions

D. OS

14. In all cloud models, security controls are driven by which of the following?

A. Virtualization engine

B. Hypervisor

C. SLAs

D. Business requirements

15. In all cloud models, the _____ will retain ultimate liability and responsibility for any data loss or disclosure.

A. Vendor

B. Customer

C. State

D. Administrator

16. Why will cloud providers be unlikely to allow physical access to their data centers?

A. They want to enhance security by keeping information about physical layout and controls confidential.

B. They want to enhance exclusivity for their customers, so only an elite tier of higher-paying clientele will be allowed physical access.

C. They want to minimize traffic in those areas to maximize efficiency of operational personnel.

D. Most data centers are inhospitable to human life, so minimizing physical access also minimizes safety concerns.

17. Which type of software is most likely to be reviewed by the most personnel, with the most varied perspectives?

A. Database management software

B. Open-source software

C. Secure software

D. Proprietary software

18. A firewall can use all of the following techniques for controlling traffic except _____.

A. Rule sets

B. Behavior analysis

C. Content filtering

D. Randomization

19. A honeypot should contain _____ data.

A. Raw

B. Production

C. Useless

D. Sensitive

20. Vulnerability assessments cannot detect which of the following?

A. Malware

B. Defined vulnerabilities

C. Zero-day exploits

D. Programming flaws

Chapter 7

Cloud Application Security

THE OBJECTIVE OF THIS CHAPTER IS TO ACQUAINT THE READER WITH THE FOLLOWING CONCEPTS:

✓ **Domain 1: Cloud Concepts, Architecture, and Design**

- 1.3. Understand Security Concepts Relevant to Cloud Computing
  - 1.3.2. Access Control
  - 1.3.6. Common Threats

✓ **Domain 3: Cloud Platform and Infrastructure Security**

- 3.4. Design and Plan Security Controls
  - 3.4.4. Identification, Authentication, and Authorization in Cloud Infrastructure

✓ **Domain 4: Cloud Application Security**

- 4.1. Advocate Training and Awareness for Application Security
  - 4.1.1. Cloud Development Basics
  - 4.1.2. Common Pitfalls
  - 4.1.3. Common Cloud Vulnerabilities
- 4.2. Describe the Secure Software Development Lifecycle (SDLC) Process
  - 4.2.1. Business Requirements
  - 4.2.2. Phases and Methodologies
- 4.3. Apply the Software Development Lifecycle (SDLC)
  - 4.3.1. Avoid Common Vulnerabilities During Development
  - 4.3.2. Cloud-specific Risks
  - 4.3.3. Quality Assurance

In this chapter, we continue to explore cloud computing by learning about application design and architecture for the cloud as well as application testing and validation to ensure our cloud applications are secure. In the cloud context, applications are the main focus of the software as a service (SaaS) model. These web applications are the software that is consumed as part of the cloud offering. We will discuss and review their design, architecture, validation, processes, and lifecycle as well as the tools used to build and deploy successful cloud applications.

We also examine the importance of training and awareness and issues involved with moving to or building applications for the cloud environment. Finally, there is an in-depth look at the software development lifecycle, identity and access management, cloud application architecture, and software assurance and validation.

Training and Awareness

Training and awareness relates directly to application developers and how programmers need to have sufficient understanding of risks in the cloud environment to properly design secure software.

Because applications manipulate data, we must determine the sensitivity of our data or we may end up using it in such a way that we unnecessarily expose data. For instance, does the data or the results of its manipulation and processing contain personally identifiable information (PII) such as name, address, Social Security number, or health information? If so, the application, along with the data to be stored and manipulated, may not be a good fit for a cloud application solution. Moving an application to the cloud may or may not reduce risks, which is why it is so important to evaluate your situation and application before migration.

It is also important to consider the responsibilities associated with using cloud data. When we begin discussing cloud applications, data concerns must be adequately addressed as it is vital that the data owner understand very clearly the responsibilities of each of the players in this endeavor. See Figure 7.1.

FIGURE 7.1   Customer/provider responsibilities, by service Model

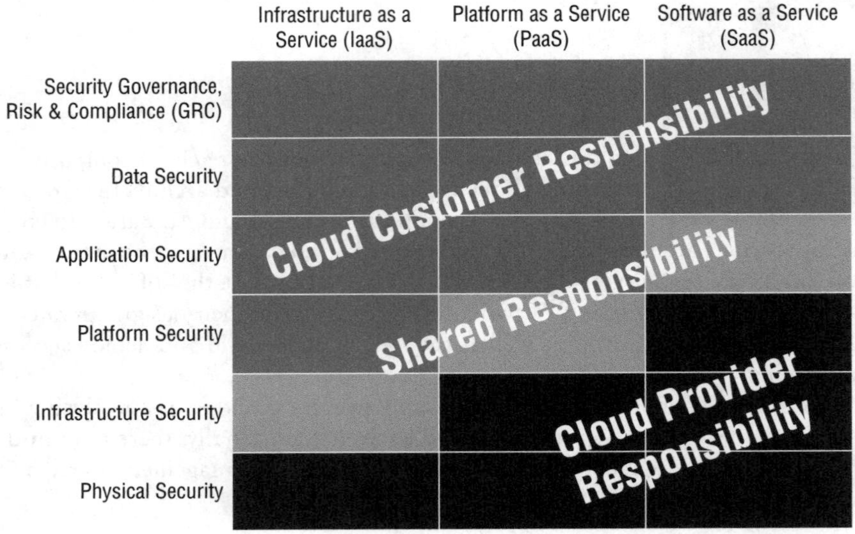

As you can see from Figure 7.1, there are differing responsibilities for each service and delivery model. However, under current laws, the data owner is always legally responsible for securing data. This is true even when the provider is tasked with financial liability according to the contract.

On the other hand, if the nature and sensitivity of the data is such that it changes constantly or is of little real value, then moving the associated applications and related data to the cloud may make good sense, both from a computing and storage perspective and more importantly from the business perspective. An example of this might be a wholesaler that uses images of products with SKUs so that customers can order items online. As long as the actual purchase occurs in a different application, the catalog of items would be of little value to anyone other than the customer placing the order. In addition, as prices change rapidly, any associated prices would also be worth very little. Therefore, the catalog application and its associated images and pricing could more than likely be easily moved to the cloud and secured with minimal effort and risk.

There are also instances where it makes more sense to move an application into the cloud because the security is *better*. For instance, many banking institutions host their primary, or what is called their "core banking" application, in the cloud specifically because they do not have the resources, experience, and tools to securely manage the applications themselves. The core application is generally what they use for day-to-day teller transactions, deposit, withdrawals, and so forth. Cloud providers of these core services generally have 24×7 staff who monitor everything and are highly trained and skilled in these areas, providing resources many companies simply cannot afford. For these specific providers, there are also regulatory incentives to ensure that data is secure and that applications work as designed. Even in instances where they may have code issues, it is usually a matter of the application *not* doing something as opposed to it performing a transaction that would cause problems. These applications are thoroughly tested before being allowed to touch a customer's account information.

An often-used term for moving an entire application to the cloud without any significant changes is *forklifting*. This refers to the idea of moving an existing legacy enterprise application to the cloud with little or no code changes. These are often self-contained stand-alone applications that have operated successfully in the enterprise environment. However, dependency on infrastructure aspects of the legacy enterprise that might not be replicated in the cloud can cause serious problems in transition efforts. Other issues such as the use of proprietary libraries that the cloud environment does not also have can also inhibit transition efforts. In addition to the fact that not all apps are natively ready for the cloud, many cannot move to the cloud at all without some type of extensive code changes. Last, many applications, particularly office applications such as accounting and word processing programs, now have alternative cloud-based versions, minimizing or eliminating the need to move those applications at all.

Developers often face challenges when working in a new and unfamiliar environment. For instance, they may be used to working in a certain language or framework that may not be available to them on a particular platform. Developers working in the traditional IT environment may not be used to the particular risks, threats, and vulnerabilities associated with cloud computing. Moreover, there may be a lack of pertinent documentation for moving specific applications to the cloud; developers might not know how to approach migration. This is even more true for proprietary applications exclusive to the developers' organization. Developers might have a steep learning curve for their own professional skills and knowledge if they've never worked in the cloud before, and they might not have the time, budget, or discipline to conduct suitable training.

The Treacherous 12

The Cloud Security Alliance (CSA) publishes a report about every three years on the top threats associated with cloud computing. The 2016 report (the most current as of publication of this book) is titled *The Treacherous 12, Cloud Computing Top Threats in 2016*: https://cloudsecurityalliance.org/artifacts/the-treacherous-twelve-cloud-computing-top-threats-in-2016/. This is a compilation by the CSA Top Threats Working Group, which consists of some of the most noted experts in the industry. These experts from around the world and many different backgrounds come together to conduct research into data breaches and malicious intrusions, publish surveys, and develop this list. Often, threats included in previous versions of the Top Threats list still appear in the current list; we know what the problems are, yet we continue to make the same mistakes repeatedly.

These are some of the issues and challenges that developers and administrators face when migrating to the cloud:

Multitenancy   This is the concept of sharing resources with other cloud customers simultaneously.

Third-Party Admins   Administrators in the cloud data center have physical access to the devices that contain customer data, but they are not under the control of the customers.

Deployment Models (Public, Private, Community, Hybrid)   In many cloud deployments, the customer will no longer have control of the physical hardware that contains their data; in the traditional environment, software developers did not have to consider or contend with the possibility that the programs would be running on hardware that was not owned and/or controlled by the organization using the software.

Service Models (IaaS, PaaS, and SaaS)   Developers may or may not have control over the particular infrastructure, platform, or even application stack that they must work with.

Another area of complexity and concern for the CCSP is that of understanding the appropriate use and design of encryption technologies in the cloud and with cloud applications. Encryption is one of the more effective control mechanisms for securing digital data and, in many cases, is the only viable option for the cloud customer for securing data because the customer won't have administrative or physical control of the cloud resources and infrastructure.

Not all applications will run effectively or securely in the cloud. They must be examined on a case-by-case basis with these factors and characteristics in mind.

Common Cloud Application Deployment Pitfalls

Common pitfalls that developers face when deploying cloud applications include whether the same functionality will be available on-premises versus off-premises, poor documentation and training, tenancy separation, and the use of secure and validated APIs are all significant challenges developers face in deploying applications in the cloud environment. We'll examine these issues in the following sections.

On-Premises Apps Do Not Always Transfer (and Vice Versa)

On-premises applications (or "on-prem" applications as they are often called) are usually designed to be run in a traditional enterprise environment where data is accessed, processed, and stored locally. Moving these to the cloud is not always practical or even possible.

Traditional enterprise application developers often do not have to contend with speed or bandwidth issues due to running on a local area network (LAN). A lack of routing involvement and high-speed switches make these very quick and responsive even if code is sometimes not well written. One example would be when the application makes numerous calls in order to assemble a single piece of data, as opposed to making a single call and collecting it all at once. These design issues can slow a cloud application down to the point that it simply does not function properly. These calls create numerous sessions and take up processor and memory resources, and eventually entire systems can slow to a crawl.

Traditional on-premises applications are not typically asked to share resources such as CPU, RAM, and bandwidth, allowing poorly designed code to run adequately on a faster local network but then failing to meet expectations when moved to the cloud.

Poor Documentation

The lack of proper documentation is not a new risk introduced by cloud computing, but it is instead a harsh reality in our field. Developers are constantly being goaded to rush applications into production, while documentation is a slow, methodical process that does not add to functionality or performance. Moreover, the skills necessary for software design don't often overlap into the skillset for technical documentation, so the two efforts are largely performed by different people, which adds another layer of complication and delay to the process.

Moreover, in organizations that use custom, proprietary software in a traditional environment, it is very possible that no documentation exists for moving the application to the cloud because it has never been tried before. During migration, developers do not have any guidance to assist them in this situation.

Not All Apps Are Cloud Ready

Some applications, specifically database applications, might run even better in the cloud. Typically cloud storage is faster than older enterprise spinning disks, and the data usually has a much smaller distance to travel in order to reach compute and storage components because they are all stored in the same logical units.

However, they are not all ready for the cloud. Often, code must be reevaluated and altered in order to run effectively in the cloud. Encryption may be needed that had not been used in the past, and a host of other issues exist. Even though some apps will eventually run successfully in the cloud, they are not always immediately ready and may require code or configuration changes in order to work effectively.

Tenancy Separation

In the traditional enterprise, where all infrastructure and resources are owned and controlled by the organization, there is no risk of other tenants accessing the organization's data through inadvertent "data bleed" between applications, OSs, guest images, and users. The exact opposite is true of the cloud environment: all those possibilities exist, so the risk of each must be addressed by significant use of countermeasures that ensure access control, process isolation, and denial of guest/host escape attempts...and all these countermeasures will be dependent on remote administration (and will most likely require significant negotiation and cooperation with the provider).

Use of Secure, Validated APIs

One feature that makes cloud-based operations so desirable is the flexibility to use current data sets in new and novel ways; this capability is offered and enhanced through the deployment of a wide variety of APIs, many of which can be chosen by the cloud customer and more that can be selected by the user (on the user's own platform or device, in a BYOD environment). Although the variety of options is enticing, it brings an attendant risk: the APIs used to provide this capability might be of questionable origin.

It behooves the cloud customer to formalize a policy and process for vetting, selecting, and deploying only those APIs that can be validated in some fashion—a method for determining the trustworthiness of the source and the software itself. This process should be included in the organization's acquisition and development program as well as the change management effort.

Cloud-Secure Software Development Lifecycle (SDLC)

The cloud-secure software development lifecycle (SDLC) has the same foundational structure as the traditional SDLC, although there are some factors when dealing with the cloud that need to be taken into account. Just like data, software has a useful lifecycle based on phases or stages of development and use (see Figure 7.2). Although the name and number of stages can be debated, they generally include the following core stages (although some models forego secure operations and disposal or use slightly different names for the stages):

1. Defining
2. Designing
3. Development
4. Testing
5. Secure Operations
6. Disposal

FIGURE 7.2   The cloud-secure software development lifecycle (SDLC)

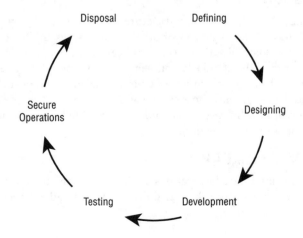

In the definition phase, we are focused on identifying the business requirements of the application, such as accounting, database, or customer relationship management. Regardless of the application's purpose, it is vital that the definition phase describe aspects of the business needs. We try to refrain from choosing any specific tools or technologies at this point; the temptation to do so creates a situation where we have a foregone conclusion ("We're going to use Tech X") instead of truly considering all possibilities that might best satisfy the business requirements.

In the design phase, we begin to develop user stories (what the user will want to accomplish and how to go about it), what the interface will look like, and whether it will require the use or development of any APIs.

The development phase is where the code is written. The code takes into account the previously established definition and design parameters. Some testing of code snippets may occur in this phase to determine whether the code is working as designed. However, major testing will occur later in the process.

In the testing phase of application development, activities such as initial penetration testing and vulnerability scanning against the application are performed. We will use techniques and tools for both dynamic and static testing or dynamic application security testing (DAST) and static application security testing (SAST). We will look at these testing methods later in the chapter. Generally, at least two types of testing take place: functional and security testing. Functional testing should ensure that the software performs whatever tasks it was intended for, completely and accurately, in a manner resistant to loss/interruption. Security testing ensures that whatever controls were included in the software are working effectively and accomplishing their purpose.

Once all the other stages are finished, the application would then enter into what some call the *secure operations phase*. This is after thorough testing has been successfully completed and the application and its environment are deemed secure.

The disposal phase is not included in the CCSP CBK but is worthy of mention here. Once the software has reached the end of its useful life or has been replaced by a newer or different application, it must then be securely disposed of. Most software companies have a published software lifecycle as part of their customer-facing information. It includes life spans of the applications with specifics about things like how long and what kind of security patches will be available to the customer. Software that is no longer supported by the vendor poses a risk to the enterprise in many ways, particularly because the vendor will no longer offer security patches for newly discovered vulnerabilities.

Most web and cloud applications are a bit different than traditional applications in that they can often be updated in place continually and may stay in service for a very long time.

Throughout development, the process itself should be managed and inspected in such a way as to reduce the possibility of introducing errors or harming the end product. This management/inspection is referred to as *quality assurance* (QA).

Configuration Management for the SDLC

It is crucial to apply configuration/change management (CM) practices and processes to software in conjunction with the SDLC. Proper version control, documentation, and managerial/project oversight of the software package is necessary to ensure that requirements are being met, problems are addressed, and fixes to problems are retained in subsequent versions so the problems don't recur. (Some of these aspects, particularly version control and documentation, can be tricky when using Agile software development; see the Agile discussion later in this chapter.)

As a new asset, the software should be entered into the organization's inventory and formal CM process as early as possible (indeed, the CM board should have had to approve the initiation of the project). Many of the SDLC phases and practices should synchronize fully with the organization's CM process (such as testing before entering production and long-term maintenance and operational support).

ISO/IEC 27034-1 Standards for Secure Application Development

The International Organization for Standardization (ISO) has created an approach organizations can use for tracking security controls used in their software. ISO/IEC 27034-1 provides an overview of application security that introduces definitive concepts, principles, and processes involved in application security. In doing so, it describes two documents an organization can use internally as inventories of controls.

The Organizational Normative Framework (ONF) is the framework for all components of application security controls and best practices catalogued and leveraged by the organization. The application normative frameworks (ANFs) are the subsets of the ONF for each specific application. The ANF shares the applicable parts of the ONF needed to achieve an application's required level of security and the level of trust desired.

The ANF-to-ONF relationship is a one-to-one relationship; every application has an ANF that maps back to the ONF. However, the ONF-to-ANF relationship is one-to-many. The ONF has many ANFs, but the ANF has only one ONF. Make sure you understand this concept.

ONF/ANF Example

Company X has three software applications, Programs A, B, and C. Each of the Programs has these controls:

Program A

- Password

- Encryption

- Process isolation

- Input validation

Program B

- Password

- Integrity check

- Screencap disabling

Program C

- Password

- Integrity check

Each list, for each Program, is that software's ANF. Company X has three ANFs, one for each software application.

The company also has an ONF; the list of all the controls used in all the Programs within the company. It looks like this:

- Password

- Encryption

- Integrity check

- Integrity check process isolation

- Screencap disabling

- Input validation

Identity and Access Management (IAM)

IAM is about the people, processes, and procedures used to create, manage, and destroy identities of all kinds. IAM systems typically consist of several components. First, they allow creation of identification mechanisms. IAM then allows the organization to verify or authenticate users' identities prior to granting access to systems/assets. Once authenticated, the users are then authorized and given subsequent access to resources. The user is generally managed through a central user repository.

IAM functionality is often divided into identity management and access management:

Identity Management   Identity management is the process whereby individuals are given access to system resources by associating user rights with a given identity. *Provisioning* is the first phase of identity management, where each subject is issued a unique identity assertion (something that serves as an identification, such as a user ID). During this process, the user is usually also issued a password for use in authenticating the identity assertion. The entity issuing the password and identity assertion will retain a record of each for use in recognizing the user later (when the user logs in to resources with that user ID/password combination). The generation, storage, and security controls of these passwords are collectively known as *password management*.

Access Management   Access management is the part of the process that deals with controlling access to resources once they have been granted. Access management identifies who a user is and what they are allowed to access each time they attempt to access a resource. This is accomplished through a combination of means:

Authentication   Establishes identity by asking who you are and determining whether you are a legitimate user (often by combining the use of an identity assertion and an authentication factor; for example, a user ID and password).

Authorization   Evaluates what you have access to after authentication occurs (in many cases, this means comparing the identity assertion against an access control list [ACL]).

Policy Management   Serves as the enforcement arm of authentication and authorization and is established based on business needs and senior management decisions.

Federation   An association of organizations that facilitate the exchange of information as appropriate about users and access to resources, allowing them to share resources across multiple organizations.

Identity Repositories   The directory services for the administration of user accounts and their associated attributes.

These components are stored in what is called an identity repository directory. The schema used is much more detailed and has many more uses, and it must be heavily protected. A breach of this component would be devastating to the organization.

Besides identity repositories and their directories, other core facets of IAM include federated identity management, federation standards, federated identity providers, various types of single sign-on (SSO), multifactor authentication, and supplemental security components. These concepts will be explored in the following sections.

Identity Repositories and Directory Services

Identity repositories are the store of information or attributes of identities. Directory services are how those identities and attributes are managed. They allow the administrator to customize user roles, identities, and so on. All of this becomes even more important when we deal with federation, as there must be a consistent means of accessing these identities and their associated attributes in order to work across disparate systems.

Here are some of the most widely used directory services:

- X.500 and LDAP
- Microsoft Active Directory
- Novell eDirectory
- Metadata replication and synchronization

Single Sign-On (SSO)

When an organization has a variety of resources that each require authentication, usage and utilization can become cumbersome for users, especially when they have to keep track of passwords and user IDs that have different requirements (length, complexity, and so forth). Single sign-on (SSO) is a way to address this and simplify the operational experience for the user.

While there are several ways to implement SSO, the term generally refers to a situation where the user signs in once, usually to an authentication server, and then, when the user wants to access the organization's resources (say, on different servers throughout the environment), each resource will query the authentication server to determine if the user is logged in and properly authenticated; the authentication server then approves the request and the resource server grants the user access. All of this should be transparent to the user, streamlining their use of the resources on the network. Theoretically, the user could log in just once per day, when they sit down at their desk to begin work, and never have to reenter any additional sign-on credentials.

This convenience does not, of course, come without costs and risks: SSO solutions are difficult to implement and maintain; an attacker gaining a user's single credential will have access to multiple systems; and the impact of losing an SSO server will be much greater than losing an individual system.

Federated Identity Management

Federated identity management (or *federation*, in general) is much the same as normal identity management except it is used to manage identities across disparate organizations. You can think of it as single sign-on (SSO) for multiple organizations.

Let's look at an example. A group of research universities want to share their research data. They can create a federation so that a scientist signing in at their own university, on their own system, can then access all the research resources of the other universities in the federation without having to present other, new identity and authentication credentials.

There are two general types of federation: the web-of-trust model and use of a third-party identifier.

In the web of trust, each member of the federation (that is, each organization that wants to share resources and users) has to review and approve each other member for inclusion in the federation. While it's a good method to be sure that everyone else in the federation reaches your particular level of trust, this can become costly and unwieldy once the federation reaches a significant number of member organizations—it just doesn't scale well.

By using a third-party identifier, on the other hand, the member organizations outsource their responsibilities to review and approve each other to some external party (that each of them trust, of course) who will take on this responsibility on behalf of all the members. This is a popular model in the cloud environment, where the identifier role can often be combined with other functions (for instance, crypto key management) and outsourced to a cloud access security broker (CASB).

When discussing federation, we apply the terms *identity provider* and *relying parties*. The identity provider is the entity that provisions and authenticates identity assertions (validating users, provisioning user IDs and passwords, managing both, deprovisioning them, and so forth), and the relying party is any member of the federation that shares resources based on authenticated identities.

In the web-of-trust model, the identity provider is each member of the federation (provisioning identity assertions for each of their users, respectively) *and* they are also the relying parties (sharing resources with each other, based on those authenticated identities).

In the trusted third-party model of federation, the identity provider is the trusted third party, and the relying parties are each member organization within the federation.

Federation Standards

There are a number of federation standards, but the most widely used one is Security Assertion Markup Language (SAML). The latest version of SAML is SAML 2.0. It is XML-based and consists of a framework for communicating authentication, authorization or entitlement information, and attribute information across organizations. In other words, it is a means for users from outside organizations to be verified and validated as authorized users inside or with another organization without the user having to create identities in both locations.

Some of the other standards that exist in this area are as follows:

WS-Federation This uses the term *realms* in explaining its capabilities to allow organizations to trust each other's identity information across organizations.

OAuth Often used in authorization with mobile apps, the OAuth framework provides third-party applications limited access to HTTP services.

OpenID Connect This is an interoperable authentication protocol based on the OAuth 2 specification. It allows developers to authenticate their users across websites and applications without having to manage usernames and passwords.

Multifactor Authentication

Multifactor authentication has become more popular and widespread in recent years due to increased demand for better authorization security and decreased costs of the technology. Many banks have used such technology since the early 2000s to facilitate secure wire transfers.

Multifactor authentication is composed of, at a minimum, two of the following aspects: something you know, something you are, or something you have. Something you know can be a password, passphrase, and so on. Something you have can be something like a number-generating key fob, a smartphone capable of receiving text messages, or even a verified phone number unique to an individual that can receive a number or key. Something you are is a biometric trait of yourself, as a living creature. This could be as unique and specific as your DNA fingerprint or as cursorily general as a photograph.

The authentication solutions featuring the "know" and "have" aspects are especially useful with remote access security where presenting a biometric factor would be awkward because they help to prevent an unauthorized user from accessing an account or data without both pieces of the authentication mechanism. It is one thing to steal or guess a password for an account, but it is much harder for someone to obtain both a password and a key generated by a device to which only the user has access.

Supplemental Security Components

There are a few additional security components the CCSP candidate should be familiar with. The first is firewalls. The firewall is designed as the access point for traffic entering or leaving the perimeter of a network. Firewalls come in a variety of designs and capabilities. Early versions were limited to simply using port or IP address blocking, with no ability to see inside the packets traversing the interface. Then *stateful inspection* came into the picture, which allowed firewalls to prevent inbound traffic from entering unless the connection had been initiated from inside the network.

Today's application-aware firewalls are far superior to their predecessors. However, attackers and attacks are constantly evolving, which led to the web application firewall (WAF).

These firewalls are deployed in addition to any network firewall and are designed to protect specific web-based applications. PCI DSS requires them as a way of protecting against credit card data egress from a web application that may be handling online transactions. These firewalls are specific enough that they know the way the application should be behaving and can detect even the slightest unusual activity and bring it to a stop. In addition, WAFs can also provide protection against such network-based attacks as DoS or DDoS attacks. WAFs function at Layer 7 of the OSI model.

Another form of protection is database activity monitoring (DAM). Again, as with the web application firewall, the idea is to have a piece of software or a dedicated appliance watching databases for any type of unusual requests or activity and then to be able to send alerts and even take actions to stop malicious activity. These DAMs can be either agent-based or network-based, meaning an agent resides on the machine or instance of the database or a network component monitors traffic to and from the database.

API gateways are also an important part of a layered defense. They can be used to impose such controls on API activity as these:

- Acting as an API proxy so as to not directly expose the API
- Implementing access control to the API
- Limiting connections so that bandwidth is available for all applications, which can also help in the event of an internal DoS attack
- API logging
- Gathering metrics from API access logs
- Additional API security filtering

XML gateways work in much the same way, except they work around *how* sensitive data and services are exposed to APIs. They can be either software- or hardware-based and can implement some types of data loss prevention (DLP).

Cloud Application Architecture

It is important that we examine the mechanisms that make application security and software development for the cloud work as well as the weaknesses and vulnerabilities associated with each. The CCSP candidate needs to understand how to evaluate and discover these, from the perspective of a cloud customer.

Application programming interfaces (APIs) are the coding components that allow applications to speak to one another, generally through a web interface of some kind and preferably in a safe and secure manner. The cloud security professional should know how to determine risks and threats associated with the use of APIs.

Application Programming Interfaces

There are two common types of application programming interfaces (APIs) in use with cloud-based applications that the CCSP candidate must understand. The first is RESTful APIs. REST stands for Representational State Transfer. It is a software approach designed to scale the capabilities of web-based applications. It is based on guidelines and best practices for creating these scalable web applications. Other characteristics of the REST approach include the following:

- Low processing/traffic overhead ("lightweight")
- Uses simple URLs/URIs
- Not reliant on any single programming language
- Scalable
- Offers outputs in many formats (CSV, JSON, and so on)
- Efficient, which means it uses smaller messages than alternative approaches, such as SOAP

The following situations are among those in which REST works well:

- When bandwidth is limited
- When stateless operations are used
- When caching is needed

SOAP is the other API approach you should be familiar with. Simple Object Access Protocol (SOAP) is a protocol specification providing for the exchange of structured information or data in web services. It also works over other protocols such as SMTP, FTP, and HTTP.

Some of the characteristics of SOAP include the following:

- Standards-based
- Reliant on XML
- Highly intolerant of errors
- Slower
- Built-in error handling

Here are some examples of where SOAP works or fits in better:

- Asynchronous processing
- Format contracts
- Stateful operations

Neither API format is necessarily better than the other. It is important to understand that regardless of what type of API you use to offer web services, you are granting another application access to the primary application and any data it may have access to. This can present many security challenges for end users unable to evaluate the security of any specific API, or even which API (or APIs) they are using. This can lead to data leakage or other problems if the APIs in question have not been sufficiently vetted and validated to ensure they provide adequate security.

Tenancy Separation

Multitenancy refers to the concept that multiple cloud customers may share the same host devices and underlying resources. It is vitally important that configurations be made in such a way as to ensure logical isolation of the various tenants; otherwise, data leakage and corruption could occur.

Cryptography

Although we will not be discussing the specifics of encryption here, the CCSP candidate must be familiar with the different types of encryption, the places where it is used, and the use case for each. Data is typically encrypted either when it is at rest or when it is in transit, and both types of encryption can be effectively used as part of overall cloud security.

Encryption of Data at Rest   Data at rest, whether it be short-term or long-term storage, should be protected from multitenancy issues and similar problems. Encrypting data at rest is a great way to prevent unauthorized access to data. Data stored in a multitenant environment poses a risk that did not exist in the traditional environment; a government/law enforcement/regulatory entity might seize a particular hardware component while investigating one tenant and end up with data belonging to various tenants. If each tenant applies its own cryptography, those tenants not under investigation should remain protected from unauthorized disclosure in this type of situation.

Encryption of Data in Transit   Encryption of data in transit is necessary to mitigate against intermediaries (often referred to as the man-in-the-middle attack).

There are a number of encryption technologies that you should also know about:

Transport Layer Security (TLS)   TLS is a protocol designed to ensure privacy when communicating between applications. This can occur between two servers or between a client and a web server.

Secure Sockets Layer (SSL)   Invented and first adopted by Netscape back in the mid-1990s, SSL was originally meant to encrypt data transmissions between two endpoints, such as two servers or a server and a user. SSL was deprecated in 2015 and replaced with TLS, but SSL is still used in many enterprises since it was ubiquitous and upgrading or transitioning can be costly and time-consuming.

Whole-Instance Encryption   Also known as whole-disk encryption, this is the idea of encrypting all of a system's data at rest in one instance. Rather than designated folders being used for encrypted material, the entire storage medium is encrypted. With the advent of stronger and faster processors, even a small smart device can be totally encrypted without significantly harming performance. Whole-disk encryption protects data on the device in the event the device itself is lost or stolen.

Volume Encryption   Much like encrypting an entire device, volume encryption refers to only encrypting a partition on a hard drive as opposed to the entire disk. This is useful when the entire disk does not need to be encrypted as only the protected sections have data of any value.

Customers or users can also add another layer of protection by encrypting specific files or folders. This way, the customer holds the keys to unencrypt the data should the disk or volume be breached in some manner.

Keep in mind that the primary requirement for securing any encryption scheme is the safe storage and management of the keys used to encrypt and decrypt.

Sandboxing

In context of computing, the term *sandbox* can mean a couple of things.

A physical sandbox is a test environment of isolated devices and cabling, completely distinct from the production environment. (In fact, there is often space, actual empty space, between the physical sandbox/testbed, so we refer to the two environments—production and test—as "airgapped"). The benefit of a physical sandbox is that errors/vulnerabilities introduced there will not contaminate/affect the production environment.

A logical sandbox is an isolated memory space where untrusted/untested code can be run in isolation from the underlying hardware so that detrimental aspects of the program do not affect the machine/other programs.

Either type of sandbox might be used during the SDLC for testing code in development or for security purposes such as performing forensics analysis on malware or experimenting with patches/updates before they are deployed in the production environment.

Application Virtualization

Application virtualization is a somewhat misunderstood term. The idea of application virtualization has to do with running applications in a trusted virtual environment. It is somewhat like sandboxing, but instead of sandboxing a process, application virtualization allows you to run full applications in a protected space. In addition, because you are doing this virtually, you can run applications that would otherwise not run on the host system. An excellent example is the Linux application WINE. WINE is itself an application virtualization platform that then provides a Linux machine with the ability to run Windows-based applications. This also provides for a space where new apps can be tested, for instance with Windows, without allowing the application to touch what would normally be the external Windows machine. Microsoft App-V and XenApp also allow users to perform application virtualization.

Cloud Application Assurance and Validation

To effectively test web applications, we need to be familiar with a number of application security testing methods and tools. In the following sections, we explore a variety of common approaches.

Threat Modeling

There are several threat modeling tools such as Trike, AS/NZS 4360, and CVSS. However, for the purposes of the CCSP exam, we will cover only the STRIDE model.

Created by Microsoft some time ago, the STRIDE threat model has been widely adopted throughout the industry. The model provides a standardized way of describing threats by their attributes. Developers can use this model to attempt to discover flaws and vulnerabilities in the software they're creating.

The STRIDE acronym stands for the following:

S (Spoofing)   Can the identity of the entity using the application be obscured in some way? Does the user have the capability to appear as a different user?

T (Tampering)   Does the application allow a user to make unauthorized modifications to actual data, affecting the integrity of information or communications?

R (Repudiation)   Is the user capable of denying they took part in a transaction, or does the application track and log the user's actions?

I (Information Disclosure)   Does the application reveal information (either the data being processed, or information about the application's function) while it runs?

D (Denial of Service) Is there a way to shut down the application through unauthorized means? This might include crashing, overloading, or restarting the application.

E (Elevation of Privilege) Can a user change their level of permissions in order to perform unauthorized action (such as gaining administrative control of the application)?

The "user" in each of these categories may be a legitimate employee who is granted access to the application or someone who has gained unauthorized access. The various threats may be the result of accidental input by a user or intentional effort to misuse the application.

STRIDE is particularly useful as part of the SDLC in attempting to identify vulnerabilities throughout the build process. The STRIDE model enables us to do this. When we are evaluating cloud application security, these six concepts help in identifying and classifying threats or vulnerabilities and help form a common language used to describe them. That way, we can systematically address them through better coding techniques or other control mechanisms.

STRIDE Resources

Microsoft has made the STRIDE model and suggestions for its implementation freely available on its website: https://msdn.microsoft.com/en-us/library/ee823878(v=cs.20).aspx

An example of how STRIDE might be used to evaluate the potential attacks on a web commerce server is provided as well: https://msdn.microsoft.com/en-us/library/ee798544(v=cs.20).aspx

Microsoft also offers an automated tool designed to aid in applying the STRIDE model to any software. It is available, free of charge, from Microsoft's website: https://docs.microsoft.com/en-us/azure/security/azure-security-threat-modeling-tool

---

Threat modeling helps prepare for some of the more common application vulnerabilities that developers will encounter when working with cloud applications, which include the following:

Injection When a malicious user attempts to inject a string of some type into a field in order to manipulate the application's actions or reveal unauthorized data. Examples include such things as SQL, LDAP, and OS injections. If the injection is successful, either unauthorized data is seen or other manipulative actions are taken.

Broken Authentication When a malicious user is able to break a session and steal items like tokens, passwords, or keys. This then allows the malicious user to hijack the system.

Cross-Site Scripting (XSS) XSS is one of the most widely seen application flaws, next to injections. XSS occurs when an application allows untrusted data to be sent to a web browser without proper validation or escaping. This then allows the malicious user to execute code or hijack sessions in the user's browser.

Insecure Direct Object Access   Involves a reference to an internal object, like a file, without access control checks or other controls in place to ensure attackers cannot manipulate data.

Security Misconfigurations   Security misconfigurations are often unintentional, caused by authorized entities, and a result of basic human error.

Sensitive Data Exposure   The disclosure of information such as PII, medical data, credit card material, and so on. Without proper controls in place (such as encryption, data masking, tokenization, and so on), sensitive data can be leaked by an application or system.

Missing Function-Level Access Control   An application should always verify function-level access privileges before granting access of that functionality to the user interface (UI). If this is not implemented properly, malicious users may be able to forge requests that will allow them functionality without authorization.

Cross-Site Request Forgery (CSRF)   A CSRF manipulates a logged-on user's browser to send a forged HTTP request along with cookies and other authentication information in an effort to force the victim's browser to generate a request that a vulnerable application thinks is a legitimate request from the user.

Using Components with Known Vulnerabilities   This can occur when developers use application/programming libraries of known components but do not heed security comments or fail to understand the context in which the component will eventually be used in production.

Invalidated Redirects and Forwards   Oftentimes developers will use redirects without validation, which may expose applications to untrusted data or other applications. Without this validation, malicious users can alter the redirects to point the user to malicious sites such as phishing sites.

This list largely comes from the Open Web Application Security Project's (OWASP) Top Ten Critical Application Web Application Security Risks effort. OWASP updates the list almost every other year; as of the time of publication of this book, the most current list was from 2017 and can be found here: `www.owasp.org/index.php/ Category:OWASP_Top_Ten_Project`.

I highly recommend the CCSP candidate review the source material available from OWASP.

Quality of Service

There is always a trade-off between security and productivity; every control that offers a security benefit to an organization will also impede productivity, often by degrading quality of service (QoS).

Encryption is an excellent example. Enabling encryption in most databases causes a slowdown in performance due to the processing power required for the encryption and decryption process to occur; it may also limit the ability to query the database because encrypted data can't be catalogued or interrogated in the same way plaintext can. Another example is running host-based intrusion detection systems (HIDSs) on a server. Usually this requires the viewing of all connections and data coming into and leaving the device, which can have a significant impact on performance.

Software Security Testing

Testing the security aspects of software requires a specialized skillset. In this section, we review some of the methodologies, testing concepts, and tools used to verify and validate that we have the appropriate controls.

We begin with penetration testing and vulnerability scanning. Although both are quite useful and have their place in the realm of application testing, they serve very different purposes and are used in different ways.

Vulnerability scanning involves searching the environment for known flaws, often with an automated tool. Vulnerability scanning does not necessarily identify configuration errors (although some may be encountered and discovered) but is more of a set of vulnerability definitions compared against the application or network being scanned. These types of scanners are also often employed by hackers as part of ongoing reconnaissance for vulnerabilities to be used later in attacks. However, when we perform vulnerability scanning to test our own system, no exploitation occurs and, as long as the scans are performed properly, no damage should occur. Sometimes errors occur, but usually at worst the system will need a reboot.

The downside, of course, to vulnerability scanning is that it can only detect the vulnerabilities for which it has definitions—that is, known vulnerabilities. Any vulnerabilities not currently known and included in the scanning tool can later become zero-day exploits if and when attackers figure out how to use them.

Penetration testing is designed to find vulnerabilities and to then exploit them to the point of actually gaining unauthorized access to systems or data. These tests usually begin with a reconnaissance and/or vulnerability scan to identify system weaknesses and then move on to the penetration phase. Penetration testing might be distinguished from vulnerability scanning in that it includes an active component (the penetration of the environment), whereas vulnerability scanning is almost exclusively passive.

It is extremely important to mention again that under no circumstances should you ever attempt any type of vulnerability scanning or penetration testing against an application or system without full authorization to do so. You could be violating several laws and get into some very deep trouble. In addition, you might even jeopardize your ISP account if they do not allow such activity in your end-user license agreement (EULA). Get permission first.

In addition to testing the environment as a suitably secure place for the application to function, we need to test the application itself to determine whether it has inherent security weaknesses and flaws. There are two general approaches:

White-Box Testing (Static Application Security Testing [SAST]) SAST entails reviewing the source code. This requires a testing team with two kinds of skills and knowledge: how to read the code the program was written with and a deep understanding of security. Personnel with both capabilities are rare (and expensive). We also have to be careful not to use the same developers who wrote the code in performing the test; the testing team needs to be composed of people with entirely "fresh" eyes and no inherent conflict of interest.

Black-Box Testing (Dynamic Application Security Testing [DAST]) DAST entails testing the program as it functions, in runtime. In black-box testing, the source code is not reviewed; instead, the testing team uses inputs and results from the application itself, as it's running.

Because white-box and black-box testing can reveal different security issues, it's usually best to employ both in the testing regimen. See Figure 7.3 for some of the testing issues of SAST and DAST.

FIGURE 7.3 Testing Issues

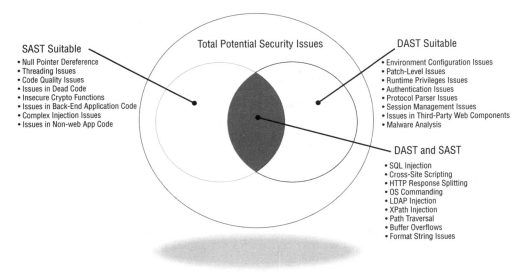

 Although SAST and DAST are completely different types of testing methodology, they are often used in conjunction to observe or test the applications from more than one perspective.

Approved APIs

APIs are a large part of cloud application development because they allow other applications to consume web services from the application, thereby expanding its capabilities. In addition, they provide for automation and integration with third-party tools, again aimed at extending the functionality of the application. However, this does not come without risk. There are both consumers and providers of web services provided by APIs, and they each present special considerations.

When consuming APIs, the customer is relying on the API vendor to have included appropriate security controls and conducted testing and validation to ensure the integrity and security of the application. However, there is often little opportunity to ascertain this in advance. For instance, there are no certifications of APIs. You are reliant on the vendor's promise that data exchanges have been tested and validated.

One of the most significant problems with using APIs is that not everyone who creates them uses the same level of scrutiny. APIs are sometimes coded with little or no validation or security testing. Consumption of these APIs without any type of validation can lead to data leakage, poor authentication, and authorization and application failure. In addition, manipulating an unsecured API could at the worst lead to a data breach. What's more, when an application is updated or changed, the API may expose items that were not exposed before.

One way to overcome these issues is to ensure that organizational processes are in place that allow for constant testing and review of APIs.

Software Supply Chain (API) Management

Another issue that is becoming more pronounced is that of software supply chain management. Developers are finding ways to leverage APIs with third-party applications. This is what APIs are designed to do. The problem lies in third-party developers who build applications leveraging upstream APIs and then adding their own to be consumed by yet another application, and so on. This chain of APIs can quickly spin out of control to the point that the end consumer has almost no way of knowing what other applications may or may not be sending data upstream and vice versa. Often, the consumer will overlook these deficiencies if the functionality offered by the application is appealing enough.

Suggested ways of dealing with these issues include auditing/contractual language for acquired applications as well as security reviews for developed apps to ensure they only make use of authorized APIs.

Securing Open-Source Software

There is a philosophical disagreement in the InfoSec community about whether proprietary software (where the source code is hidden from everyone except the vendor) is preferable and more secure than the open-source variety (where the source code is published and anyone can review it, make modifications, and publish derivative versions).

Both offer some value. However, it is generally agreed that open-source programs are more flexible, provide largely the same protections, and have a greater range of functionality than their proprietary counterparts (think Mozilla Firefox versus Microsoft Internet Explorer).

Perhaps one of the main points in favor of proprietary options is the possibility that liability will map back to the vendor—that breaches or other impacts due to failures in the program can be blamed on the vendor, who may be held accountable (although it's difficult to point to examples where this has occurred). Another benefit might be the active and constant efforts of vendors to update and secure their proprietary applications.

Conversely, the benefit of choosing open-source programs often includes a reduced price (or, indeed, having it free of charge) and the opportunity to review, for yourself, the code to test it for security vulnerabilities. Open-source code also allows the user to make whatever modifications they choose in order to add or enhance functionality.

Agility

Many software vendors are implementing something called *Agile development*. This framework is designed to greatly speed up the development of software so that it can be delivered in a more timely manner to the customer. In these instances, open-source libraries are sometimes considered the most expedient and cost-effective way to accomplish this in the short run. The customer gets the software quicker and cheaper and with all the functionality they have requested. The problem is that Agile focuses on timely delivery and not longevity or security of the application. These elements are not necessarily overlooked, but they are not a core part of the Agile development process. This can easily lead to the situation where vulnerabilities are later discovered with no means to correct the issues short of redesigning or rebuilding the application.

Application Orchestration

When two or more applications must interact in order to successfully complete a business process/transaction, there are two general approaches we can take:

- Link elements of the applications directly, so that the output of one (or step of one) is the input of another.
- Abstract the functions of the applications such that their inputs/outputs can be handled distinctly from the way the programs work, often with another set of code/software.

The first option can lead to additional problems, such as creating unnecessary dependencies and increasing the difficulty of version control and testing. Therefore, the second option, referred to as application orchestration, is often preferable.

Orchestration often requires that data from the various participating applications be converted to a new format (or formats) so that the information can work in the orchestration. It may also involve creating a new overlay/interface with the data/applications so that the interaction can be managed. Finally, new or intermediary protocols might be necessary so that the processes can be negotiated between the applications.

The Secure Network Environment

Cloud applications will also need to run in a secure environment. The CCSP should understand basic networking practices to appreciate/perceive the methods used inside cloud data centers. These include the following items:

- **VLAN:** A virtual local area network; a logical means of isolating particular portions or segments of a network, even though the machines may all be physically connected. Member devices in a VLAN can only communicate directly with other members of the same VLAN, unless the traffic first passes through a portal/gateway leading outside the VLAN.

- **DHCP:** When assigning IP addresses to devices, we can use a permanent, specific address for a given device; this is called static addressing. An alternative to static addressing is assigning an IP to a specific device for only a certain duration, temporarily; this is dynamic addressing. The method we use for the latter is the Dynamic Host Configuration Protocol (DHCP). A DHCP in an environment selects an IP address from the allowed range (the range of IP addresses owned by the organization), assigns it to a specific device, and keeps a record of which devices have which addresses; when the use of the address is terminated, the address goes back into the pool of allowed addresses, and the DHCP server can reassign it to another machine (or the same machine).

- **DNS:** The Domain Name Service is how computers translate IP addresses to domain names. DNS functions through the use of hierarchical, distributed tables; when a change is made to how a domain name relates to a specific IP address, the change is registered at the top domain of the DNS hierarchy and then filters down to all other DNS servers. When a user wants to communicate with another machine, the user's machine (or, often, the application on the user's machine) queries a device with a DNS table (often at the user's ISP) to get the correct address. Security extensions (DNSSEC) add to security by providing origin authority, data integrity, and authenticated denial of service, reducing susceptibility to spoofing.

- **VPN:** A remote user can be granted permissions to the IT environment even though the connection is over an untrusted network (such as the Internet). This is accomplished through the use of a virtual private network (VPN). The VPN is an encrypted tunnel between the remote user and the IT environment. A tunnel is an encapsulated communication; one protocol embedded inside another protocol. This connection is then encrypted to add protections against intermediaries/attackers observing the communication.

Summary

This chapter discussed awareness of application training and deployment issues, the application software development lifecycle, how to verify software through testing, how to select trusted software, how to design and use identity and access management systems, appropriate cloud application architecture, and cloud software assurance and validation.

Exam Essentials

Understand the differences between ANF and ONF. An ONF is the catalog of all application security controls used in all the applications throughout an organization. It is composed of ANFs, subordinate lists of controls used in each individual application in the organization.

Be able to articulate the components of the STRIDE threat model. The STRIDE threat model contains six threat categories:

- Spoofing
- Tampering
- Repudiation
- Information disclosure
- Denial of service
- Elevation of privilege

Be able to describe the stages of the SDLC. Be sure to understand the stages in a common SDLC model. The SDLC consists of the following stages:

- Defining
- Designing
- Developing
- Testing
- Secure Operations
- Disposal

Understand identity and access management and how it fits into the cloud environment. IAM plays a critical role in managing users with the advent of role-based access. Understand the importance of this and federated identities.

Comprehend the specifics of cloud application architecture. Not all applications are designed to run in the cloud. Be sure to understand the differences in architecture when designing or attempting to move applications.

Written Labs

You can find the answers to the written labs in Appendix A.

1. Identify one cloud application that you use and identify any and all APIs in use. Be sure to include third-party APIs that may be used that cannot be identified or validated.

2. Describe the similarities and differences between the cloud software development lifecycle and other models.

3. Identify and describe at least two components of the cloud application architecture.

4. Describe the functions of an identity management solution in the cloud environment.

Review Questions

You can find the answers to the review questions in Appendix B.

1. Which of the following best represents the REST approach to APIs?
   A. Built on protocol standards
   B. Lightweight and scalable
   C. Relies heavily on XML
   D. Only supports XML output

2. Which of the following is not commonly included in the phases of SDLC?
   A. Define
   B. Reject
   C. Design
   D. Test

3. Which of the following is *not* a component of the of the STRIDE model?
   A. Spoofing
   B. Repudiation
   C. Information disclosure
   D. External pen testing

4. Which of the following best describes SAST?
   A. White-box testing
   B. Black-box testing
   C. Gray-box testing
   D. Red-team testing

5. Which of the following confirms that the identity assertion belongs to the entity presenting it?
   A. Identification
   B. Authentication
   C. Authorization
   D. Inflammation

6. Which of the following best describes a sandbox?
   A. An isolated space where transactions are protected from malicious software
   B. A space where you can safely execute malicious code to see what it does
   C. An isolated space where untested code and experimentation can safely occur separate from the production environment
   D. An isolated space where untested code and experimentation can safely occur within the production environment

7. Identity and access management (IAM) is a security discipline intended to ensure _____.

  A. All users are properly authorized

  B. The right individual gets access to the right resources at the right time for the right reasons

  C. All users are properly authenticated

  D. Unauthorized users will get access to the right resources at the right time for the right reasons

8. In a federated identity arrangement using a trusted third-party model, who is the identity provider and who is the relying party?

  A. A contracted third party/the various member organizations of the federation

  B. The users of the various organizations within the federation/a CASB

  C. Each member organization/a trusted third party

  D. Each member organization/each member organization

9. Which of the following best describes the Organizational Normative Framework (ONF)?

  A. A container for components of an application's security controls and best practices catalogued and leveraged by the organization

  B. A framework of containers for all components of application security controls and best practices catalogued and leveraged by the organization

  C. A subset of application security controls and best practices catalogued and leveraged by the organization

  D. A framework of containers for some of the components of application security controls and best practices catalogued and leveraged by the organization

10. APIs typically are built with REST or _____.

  A. XML

  B. SSL

  C. SOAP

  D. TEMPEST

11. The ANF is best described as which of the following?

  A. A stand-alone framework for storing security practices for the ONF

  B. A subset of the ONF

  C. A superset of the ONF

  D. The complete ONF

12. Which of the following best describes SAML?

  A. A standard for developing secure application management logistics

  B. A standard for exchanging authentication and authorization data between security domains

  C. A standard for exchanging usernames and passwords across devices

  D. A standard used for directory synchronization

13. Which of the following best describes the purpose and scope of ISO/IEC 27034-1?

    A. Describes international privacy standards for cloud computing

    B. Provides an overview of application security that introduces definitive concepts, principles, and processes involved in application security

    C. Serves as a newer replacement for NIST 800-53 r4

    D. Provides an overview of network and infrastructure security designed to secure cloud applications

14. Which of the following terms means "to perceive software from the perspective of the attacker in order to locate/detect potential vulnerabilities"?

    A. Rendering

    B. Galloping

    C. Agile

    D. Threat modeling

15. Database activity monitoring (DAM) can be _____.

    A. Host-based or network-based

    B. Reactive or imperative

    C. Used in the place of encryption

    D. Used in place of data masking

16. WAFs operate at OSI Layer _____.

    A. 1

    B. 3

    C. 5

    D. 7

17. Multifactor authentication consists of at least two items. Which of the following best represents this concept?

    A. A complex password and a secret code

    B. Complex passwords and an HSM

    C. A hardware token and a magnetic strip card

    D. Something you know and something you have

18. SOAP is a protocol specification providing for the exchange of structured information or data in web services. Which of the following is *not* true of SOAP?

    A. Standards-based

    B. Reliant on XML

    C. Extremely fast

    D. Works over numerous protocols

19. DAST requires _____.
    A. Money
    B. Compartmentalization
    C. A runtime environment
    D. Recurring inflation

20. Physical sandboxing provides which of the following?
    A. The production environment
    B. An airgapped test environment that isolates untrusted code for testing in a nonproduction environment
    C. Emulation
    D. Virtualization

Chapter 8

Operations Elements

THE OBJECTIVE OF THIS CHAPTER IS TO ACQUAINT THE READER WITH THE FOLLOWING CONCEPTS:

✓ **Domain 1: Cloud Concepts, Architecture, and Design**

- 1.2. Describe Cloud Reference Architecture
  - 1.2.6. Impact of Related Technologies
- 1.3. Understand Security Concepts Relevant to Cloud Computing
  - 1.3.5. Virtualization Security
- 1.5. Evaluate Cloud Service Providers
  - 1.5.1. Verification Against Criteria

✓ **Domain 2: Cloud Data Security**

- 2.1. Describe Cloud Data Concepts
  - 2.1.2. Data Dispersion
- 2.2. Design and Implement Cloud Data Storage Architectures
  - 2.2.1. Storage Types
  - 2.2.2. Threats to Storage Types

✓ **Domain 3: Cloud Platform and Infrastructure Security**

- 3.1. Comprehend Cloud Infrastructure Components
  - 3.1.1. Physical Environment
  - 3.1.5. Storage
- 3.2. Design a Secure Data Center
  - 3.2.1. Logical Design
  - 3.2.2. Physical Design
  - 3.2.3. Environmental Design

Although most IT and InfoSec practitioners will probably spend the majority of their time providing professional services to cloud customers, the CCSP CBK and exam also require the ability to understand the perspective of the cloud provider to some extent. In this chapter, we'll continue our review of the internal working of a cloud provider (and the provider's data center) in a bit more detail.

Physical/Logical Operations

The cloud data center has to be robust and resilient to all types of threats, from natural disasters to hacking attacks to simple component failure. This strength and capability has to be comprehensive and exhaustive enough to provide close to continuous system operation and data access (referred to as *uptime*) for multiple customers with a wide spectrum of service needs.

Currently, the industry standard for uptime in cloud service provision is *five nines*, which means 99.999% uptime (in some cases, uptime offered by providers exceeds this boundary, to 99.9999%). That's a vast difference in the level of service expected just as recently as a decade ago. At that time, managed services were often not based in the cloud and instead took the form of contractors leasing and maintaining IT devices and networking capability to customers, often inside the customers' own facilities. Back then, expected outages for regular maintenance, upgrades, and routine component loss likely incurred scheduled downtime of up to three days each month. Five nines, over a calendar year, on the other hand, equates to less than six downtime minutes *per year*.

In the following sections, we'll review standards and methods created for the purpose of achieving an uptime of five nines (or more).

Uptime and Availability

The CCSP CBK expressly differentiates between uptime and availability. In the most literal of senses, this is true. A data center could be providing continuous uptime, but the cloud customer may encounter availability problems. For instance, the customer's ability to connect to the data center may be limited by a failure within the customer's ISP. This would be a lack of availability from the customer's perspective but not a lack of uptime on the part of the provider. The data center is up, but the customer can't reach it.

This may seem like splitting hairs because, realistically, most professionals (or, for that matter, courts or regulators) already would not expect an entity to be responsible for agencies and externalities outside its control. Nobody would consider the cloud provider to be liable for the failure of the customer's ISP in the first place. Certainly, the cloud provider could not be held liable for not meeting the terms of the SLA in such a circumstance.

That aside, for practical purposes, the terms *uptime* and *availability* are usually meant to communicate the same notion: the cloud provider's ability to offer service within the parameters specified in the SLA, without undue interruption, with the implicit understanding that the provider is not responsible for the customer's inability to access the data center for reasons outside the provider's purview.

However, for academic and testing purposes, in the strictest sense, they are not synonymous.

Facilities and Redundancy

A vast majority of the effort to ensure continuous uptime will be spent providing redundancy of physical components and infrastructure. With sufficient replication of hardware and media, elements can be lost without impact to operations.

When designing a data center, consider redundancy not only for the IT systems and infrastructure, but for all aspects of functionality that support the operation of the data center. These include utilities (electrical power receipt/distribution, water, communications connectivity), staff, emergency capabilities (mostly power generation and fuel for the generator as well as egress paths for personnel), HVAC, and security controls.

 Heating, ventilation, and air-conditioning (HVAC) systems separate the cool air from the heat caused by servers. They provide air management that includes racks with built-in ventilation or alternate cold/hot aisles.

Power Redundancy

IT systems cannot operate without electricity. The data center will require a power source sufficient to operate all the core processing and storage systems for all customers as well as those support systems necessary to run the data center (such as HVAC and lighting). The cloud provider will want to consider two major aspects of redundancy for primary power needs: energy utility providers and the actual physical connections from the providers to the data center's campus. Furthermore, this replication of power should carry on throughout the data center itself, down to the component level; each device should have both primary and backup power feeds to ensure availability.

Power Provider Redundancy

Finding multiple power utilities for a single physical plant might prove challenging. Most municipalities are not served by more than one power provider, by legal construct. Power companies are usually granted some form of local monopoly, based on the premise that competing providers would harm the community's ability to receive power on a cost-effective basis. This is because of the costs of creating and maintaining multiple sets of infrastructure to generate and deliver power. Theoretically, every power provider would have to have its own generation plant, electrical grid, and all that entails, to include lines running to each building for all its customers. This could lead to an overabundance of cables and wires in the service area and decrease the opportunity to create economies of scale by limiting infrastructure to one set. Regardless of whether this theory is true (and it is questionable; telephone service provision was once limited based on the same reasoning, and that market not only survived the breakup of the telephone service monopoly but flourished and expanded, while consumer costs dropped considerably, without an overabundance of telephone infrastructure affecting neighborhoods), most metropolitan areas will not have more than one power provider.

Moreover, the geographic locations often deemed most desirable for data centers are even less likely to have multiple power providers for other reasons. Because data centers are costly to erect, require a large footprint, and need very little in terms of external services (other than power and communications connectivity), remote rural areas are often seen to be optimal for building them: land is cheap, zoning limitations are greatly reduced or nonexistent, and there is less chance of impact from certain types of external threats (civil unrest, fire from neighboring buildings, basic crimes/vandalism, and so on). However, rural areas are also often served by only one power provider, not because of statutory fiat, but because it is not profitable for more than one vendor to offer services in areas with low population density. This could, in turn, make it difficult for cloud providers to find multiple power utilities to serve their data center.

Power Line Redundancy

There is a form of attack that almost everyone who has worked in the IT field for any length of time has suffered: having your entire IT enterprise being DoSed by a backhoe. For some reason, backhoes (and bulldozers, and steam shovels) seem to magically be able to locate and slice power and communication lines that lead to buildings, even if the lines are buried sufficiently underground or raised far enough into the air, and even if these locations are clearly marked by utility inspectors before construction activity begins. It's like a natural law: if you, as a security professional, see construction equipment in the parking lot of your campus, prepare to lose power and communications.

WARNING Also, squirrels. Squirrels. I have known of more than one organization that has been DoSed by squirrels dining on the power and communication lines. In one case, it happened to the same organization more than once. This is not a joke, but it is kind of funny. It's also an example of a natural environmental threat that must be taken into consideration when designing a data center.

So it behooves the cloud provider to ensure that all power and communication lines that connect to each of the buildings on the campus are not only replicated, but that the connections are replicated *on opposite sides of each building.* We want to avoid the backhoe taking out both lines simultaneously, and the likelihood of construction scheduled on both sides of a facility at the same time is somewhat less than on just one side at a time.

Power Conditioning and Distribution Redundancy

Another aspect of power provisioning for the data center is the ancillary necessary infrastructure, including power conditioning apparatus and distribution mechanisms.

Raw power from most power mains is not suitable for commercial IT systems. The electricity must be adjusted so as to optimize its suitability for system performance. We call this *conditioning.* Conditioning usually involves adjusting the voltage on the line. It also includes surge protectors, which attenuate the effects of power spikes that might occur as the result of natural forces (such as storms) or uncontrolled activity elsewhere in the grid.

When designing a data center, it is a good practice to also plan for redundancy in these power conditioners as well as the other aspects of the electrical system. Likewise, other aspects of the power system within the data center that should be similarly replicated include any distribution node, such as transformers or substations, as well as the conduit that actually carries power to each facility.

When discussing electrical power and resilient design, it's important to also address backup power systems, such as batteries and generators. We will cover that aspect in Chapter 9, "Operations Management," in the section "Business Continuity and Disaster Recovery (BC/DR)."

Communications Redundancy

Many of the same challenges associated with finding multiple power providers will affect plans for redundant communication providers. In geographically isolated areas, finding even one broadband ISP might be difficult, let alone two or more. However, cloud data centers bring enough demand and need for service that ISPs may build out their current infrastructure specifically to serve those data centers.

Personnel Redundancy

When considering redundancy and resiliency design for data centers, remember the personnel who administer and support the IT components and those that operate/maintain environmental support systems. Some of the techniques we can adopt to provide this increased level of robustness among personnel resources are as follows:

Cross-Training   Whenever possible, have personnel trained not only in their primary duties but in another employee's duties as well (and vice versa). That way, they can serve as relief or backups for each other for crisis purposes or for ease of scheduling (this is particularly useful in data centers, where constant uptime often means shiftwork, which entails scheduling challenges). This technique, however, is very expensive. Having all personnel trained in multiple disciplines requires not only a significant training budget but also high salaries reflecting investment in top-flight personnel. Only high-quality employees will have the discipline and ability to fulfill a range of functional tasks in areas other than their main duties. If this methodology is utilized to create personnel redundancy, it's important to ensure that all staffers are engaged in tasks that exercise each of their skillsets on a recurring basis so that they maintain currency in each area and the training does not atrophy.

Water   Utility redundancy is an important consideration for cloud data centers. Similar to power service, water providers are another utility that may be overlooked in contingency planning. Water supports both personnel and systems for drinking, cooling, and fire suppression. As with electricity, finding multiple water providers in a given area might be difficult. Unlike electricity, however, water is not as difficult or dangerous to generate, transport, and store. In addition to subscribing to the local water district, data center owners can acquire potable water from wells on their own property, or they can contract with hauling companies who can bring water tanks in by rail or truck. Water can be stored onsite for a fairly long time, in cisterns or cooling towers (and a well serves the dual purpose of provision and storage). When designing redundancy for water supply, it is also important to remember to include multiple pumping facilities to ensure sufficient pressure and the power to run those pumps.

Egress   The paramount concern for all security efforts is health and human safety. The data center buildings—all of them—should have multiple points of escape in case of emergency. This does not have to make your physical defenses porous; emergency exits can be one-way portals (such as doors with interior-facing push-bars, and no means to open them from the outside), and ingress can still be severely limited and tightly controlled. Remember to design deluge fire suppression systems over paths of egress.

Lighting   In terms of continuous uptime, lights may not seem like an essential element of operations. However, consider a data center without interior lighting or a lighting system without power. Because most data centers don't have windows (windows are both a safety and a security risk and are largely unnecessary in data centers), a lighting system failure would result in a facility that was both uncomfortable and hazardous for people to occupy, much less get work done. Emergency lights, particularly along egress routes, are important (and often required by building codes), as is ensuring that the lighting is connected to any backup power supply.

Security Redundancy

In designing security for the physical plant and site layout, it is essential to bear in mind one of the most fundamental concepts in our field: defense in depth. Defense in depth (or "layered defense") entails multiple differing security controls protecting the same assets, often with a variety of technological levels and an assortment of the three categories of controls (physical, administrative, and logical/technical).

For a cloud data center to meet sufficient due diligence requirements (and attenuate the likelihood of potential threats and risks) pertaining to physical security, all the basic protective measures must be included, and redundancy should come in the form of layering as opposed to repetition. For instance, layered physical defense does not mean having two or three concentric fence lines at the perimeter; it instead might mean including a guard patrol who monitors the fence line, a video surveillance capability, and electronic monitoring of tampering attempts on the fence. This offers redundancy of protection (in the sense of the single control that is "perimeter security"; other physical security measures are also necessary, of course) as well as resiliency. This particularly challenges human attackers, who will need a variety of tools and techniques to breach the defenses as opposed to just one (in the listed example, a wire cutter). Our goal is to make breaching complicated.

In addition to the perimeter, some other physical security aspects that ought to be included in design include the following:

- Vehicular approach/access, to include driveways that wind and curve and/or include speed bumps as well as bollards, designed to prevent a vehicle from achieving sufficient speed to ram the building

- Guest/visitor access through a controlled entry point, involving formal reception (perhaps a sign-in log, video surveillance, and specific staff tasked with that duty)

- Proper placement of hazardous or vital resources (such as electrical supply, storage, and distribution components, particularly generators and fuel) such that they are not directly located near personnel or in the path of vehicles

- Interior physical access controls, such as badging, keys, combinations, turnstiles, and so on

- Specific physical protections for highly sensitive assets, such as safes and inventory tracking mechanisms (perhaps RFIDs)

- Fire detection and suppression systems

- Sufficient power for all these functions, in the event of a primary power disruption

 Real World Scenario

Rate the Design

Let's review the notional design of a facility in the context of the practices listed in the section "Security Redundancy." Review this diagram of a cloud data center campus and determine if it has sufficient resiliency, redundancy, and security. Consider what you think are both good and bad points.

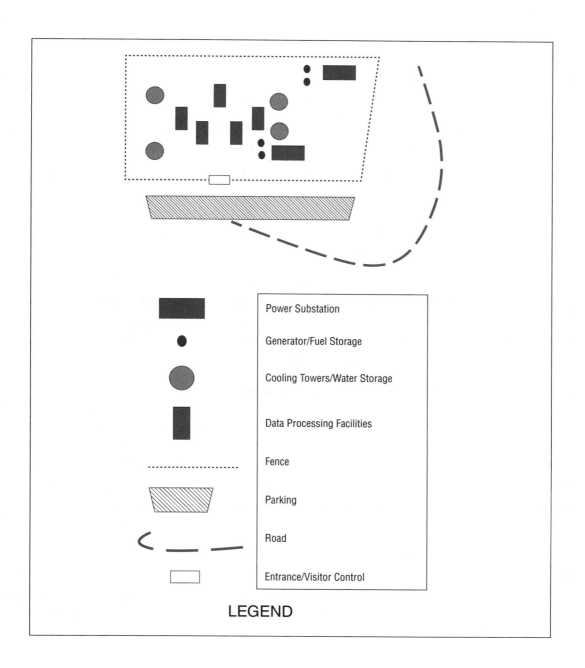

Power Substation

Generator/Fuel Storage

Cooling Towers/Water Storage

Data Processing Facilities

Fence

Parking

Road

Entrance/Visitor Control

LEGEND

What do you think of this facility? Does it feature the proper aspects described in the section "Security Redundancy"?

Here are some of the positive attributes you may have noticed:

- The roadway approach curves to disallow a straight path at the facility.

- There is a centralized entrance for staff and visitors, controlling ingress.

- There seems to be adequate replication of all necessary facilities, including power, water, and data processing.

And here are some questionable aspects:

- One set of generators and fuel storage (the lower set) seems to be too close to some of the other buildings, posing a fire and health hazard.

- We can't explicitly tell from the diagram, but it seems as if there is only one layer of perimeter security—the fence. If possible, it should be augmented with additional, varied layers of security, such as surveillance cameras and security patrols.

- It would be preferable to have the power facilities on the left and right sides of the campus, to provide more separation in the event something happens to the right side.

Holistic Redundancy: The Uptime Institute Tiers

Currently, (ISC)[2] looks to the Uptime Institute (UI) for standards related to data center redundancy in pursuit of continuous operations. The Uptime Institute (https://uptimeinstitute.com) is an advisory organization for matters related to IT service. UI publishes a standard for data center design, and it also certifies data centers for compliance with this standard.

The UI standard is split into four tiers, in ascending durability of the data center. The standard itself is available for download from the UI's website, free of charge. We'll discuss the pertinent specifics in the following sections. (All emphasis in the descriptions of the tiers is added by the author for the purpose of demonstrating the differences between them and not part of the original document.)

Tier 1

A Tier 1 data center is simplistic, with little or no redundancy, and is labeled Basic Site Infrastructure. Tier 1 lists the minimum requirements for a data center, which must include the following:

- Dedicated space for IT systems

- An uninterruptible power supply (UPS) system for line conditioning and backup purposes

- Sufficient cooling systems to serve all critical equipment

- A power generator for extended electrical outages, with at least 12 hours of fuel to run the generator at sufficient load to power the IT systems

Twelve hours is the standard fuel requirement for all four tiers.

Tier 1 data centers also have these features:

- Scheduled maintenance will require systems (including critical systems) to be taken offline.

- Both planned and unplanned maintenance and response activity may take systems (including critical systems) offline.

- Untoward personnel activity (both inadvertent and malicious) will result in downtime.

- Annual maintenance is necessary to safely operate the data center and requires full shutdown (including critical systems). Without this maintenance, the data center is likely to suffer increased outages and disruptions.

If the data center described in Tier 1 is so sensitive to such a wide array of risks, why is it even considered suitable for operation? Who would want to be a customer of such a service? Well, obviously, the cost of running a facility of this type is going to be much less expensive, and that cost savings is most likely reflected in the price the customer will be asked to pay. Also, this type of facility may be appealing to an organization that is only using the cloud service as a backup for its own enterprise and data (perhaps even the organization's own private cloud), and it only needs to be available occasionally and very temporarily. From this perspective, a Tier 1 data center might be suitable as a hot/warm site for the organization, with data uploaded on an infrequent basis (perhaps weekly or monthly), or it might even serve as a cold site, where data is only uploaded at those times when the organization is experiencing an emergency situation and needs to enact contingency operations.

So a Tier 1 data center might be the least expensive (if also the least functional) option for an organization that does not require constant uptime and access to resources and data.

Tier 2

A Tier 2 data center is slightly more robust than Tier 1, and it is named for its defining characteristics: Redundant Site Infrastructure Capacity Components. It features all the attributes of the Tier 1 design, with these additional elements:

- Critical operations do not have to be interrupted for scheduled replacement and maintenance of any of the redundant components; however, there may be downtime for any disconnection of power distribution systems and lines.

- Contrary to Tier 1, where untoward personnel activity *will* cause downtime, in Tier 2 it *may* cause downtime.

- Unplanned failures of components or systems might result in downtime.

With the benefit of rudimentary redundancy, the Tier 2 data center is obviously more suited to cloud operations and is more appealing for that purpose. It may still be more affordable than the higher-tier offerings, but it is now viable as a dependable alternative for continuous use. This may be a good option for small organizations looking to operate in the public cloud environment while still maintaining a relatively low overhead.

Tier 3

The Tier 3 design is known as a Concurrently Maintainable Site Infrastructure. As the name indicates, the facility features both the redundant capacity components of a Tier 2 build and the added benefit of multiple distribution paths (where only a sole path is needed to serve critical operations at any given time). Other characteristics that differentiate Tier 3 from the prior levels include the following:

- There are dual power supplies for all IT systems.

- Critical operations can continue even if any single component or power element is out of service for scheduled maintenance or replacement.

- Unplanned loss of a *component may* cause downtime; the loss of a single *system*, on the other hand, *will* cause downtime. (The implied distinction is that a component is one node in a multinode system; while each system will have redundant components, not all systems are redundant.)

- Planned maintenance (to include scheduled holistic annual maintenance of the facility) will not necessarily result in downtime; however, the risk of downtime may be increased during this activity. This temporary elevated risk does not make the data center lose its Tier 3 rating for the duration.

Obviously, a cloud provider offering a Tier 3 data center is a viable candidate for organizations looking to migrate to the public cloud. Most organizations with regular operational needs might consider a Tier 3 option. Those organizations with specialized needs (perhaps organizations with highly sensitive material, such as governmental agencies or entities that utilize a great deal of intellectual property or large-scale organizations with absolute constant uptime requirements) might instead consider a Tier 4 option, but the Tier 3 should serve the purpose for all others.

Tier 4

The Fault-Tolerant Site Infrastructure is the premium data center offering. As the Uptime Institute repeats in the description of this tier, *each and every* element and system of the facility (whether for IT processing, the physical plant, power distribution, or anything else) has integral redundancy such that critical operations can survive both planned and unplanned downtime at the loss of any component or system. Does this mean a Tier 4 data center is indestructible, with permanent uptime? Of course not. Anyone marketing such an offering should be viewed with suspicion. However, it is the most robust, resilient option available.

In addition to all Tier 3 features, the Tier 4 data center will include these characteristics:

- There is redundancy of both IT and electrical components, where the various multiple components are independent and physically separate from each other.

- Even after the loss of any facility infrastructure element, there will be sufficient power and cooling for critical operations.

- The loss of any single system, component, or distribution element *will not* affect critical operations.

- The facility will feature automatic response capabilities for infrastructure control systems such that the critical operations will not be affected by infrastructure failures.

- Any single loss, event, or personnel activity will not cause downtime of critical operations.

- Scheduled maintenance can be performed without affecting critical operations. However, while one set of assets is in the maintenance state, the data center may be at increased risk of failure due to an event affecting the alternate assets. During this temporary maintenance state, the facility does not lose its Tier 4 rating.

Obviously, a Tier 4 data center should be fit to serve any organization considering cloud migration, regardless of the sensitivity of their information assets or uptime needs. It will likewise be the most expensive selection and will probably be therefore limited to those organizations that have the wherewithal to afford it.

 Real World Scenario

Trusting Redundancy

One particular cloud customer has created a paradigm of utmost trust in the redundancy and resiliency of its network: Netflix.

In 2011, Netflix revealed, via its tech blog (http://techblog.netflix.com), the Simian Army: a set of testing and monitoring applications the company uses to constantly assess its capability to continue service during contingency situations. The use of these tools demonstrates the willingness and foresight of Netflix to actually create hazards in order to refine and improve its service.

The Simian Army is not just a suite of automated alert and response software, although it does include the Doctor Monkey, which performs both functions after searching all of Netflix's resources to find any degradation in performance. The Simian Army includes several programs that confounded computer security professionals because of the bravery required to wield them: the Chaos Monkey and the Chaos Gorilla, specifically. These two programs are not responsive: they are aggressive. They purposefully and randomly shut down elements of the Netflix resource network. Netflix largely runs on the Amazon Web Services public cloud. The Chaos Monkey disables specific production instances, and the Chaos Gorilla shuts down entire Amazon availability zones. The intention is to ensure that all the load-balancing capabilities built into the entire network can weather the failure and continue providing service in a manner that is transparent to customers.

That is beyond bold. It's a move some security professionals might call foolhardy and management at many organizations would deem crazy. Basically, the company is DoSing itself. But it's also brilliant, gutsy, and ultimately necessary: it is quite likely the only way to be absolutely certain that all the planning and design of redundant systems and the automated response controls that manage them are fully functional in real time.

I don't recommend this approach for every organization, but those organizations that want total assurance that their cloud resources are wholly fault tolerant might want to consider it. And Netflix has made that capability available to the world: not only did it announce the existence of the Simian Army on a public website, but in 2014, the company made the Chaos Monkey open source and free for download: `https://github.com/Netflix/security_monkey`.

It's one level of brave to create a methodology as far outside the box as to attack your own resources. It's another to announce to the world that you're using this methodology. What if it goes awry? Wouldn't the failure be compounded by the shame of being caught in your evident hubris?

But it's a champion level of courageousness to publish the toolset of that methodology and let the world play with it, knowing that there will be a subset of users who might try to...well...*monkey* with it, in order to eventually attack you. It's a heroic gamble, that the benefits of a million Chaos Monkeys banging away at systems will be tweaked and refined by the open-source community, and that the goodwill (and improved software) will come back to Netflix like interest on a loan.

This is a very laudable, admirable, and forward-thinking attitude. And I recommend the Netflix Tech Blog for even more, similar content. The blog is written in an approachable, relaxed manner, with a nice blend of technical and managerial information. For readers of this book, especially, the Netflix blog will hold a great deal of interest for its discussion of the company's decision to move into the public cloud, what its approach was, and the pitfalls it faced.

Virtualization Operations

From a cloud provider perspective, virtualization is an absolute necessity. It's the only way to properly manage the cost of hosting multiple customers in a scalable manner and still provide them with near-constant uptime.

Virtualization poses specific risks, many of which have been described in previous chapters. In the next few sections, we'll discuss what a cloud provider should be considering when planning virtualization operations.

Personnel Isolation

Because administrators working for the cloud provider will have physical access to devices that may run instances belonging to several customers in the same field (that is, the cloud customers on the same host may be competitors), the cloud provider has to ensure that any impropriety, conflict of interest, or even perception of conflict of interest doesn't affect the level of service the customers receive. For example, if competing customers are resident on a single host and some contingency forces the administrators to halt one instance or the other in order to maintain the functionality of the device, the administrator should not favor one over the other; preferably, the administrator should make the choice solely on the basis of overall data center performance and operation.

In theory, it is best to mask the nature and details of a customer's business from the administrators. In practice, that might be less than ideal, and it may be impossible to achieve if such knowledge enhances the administrators' ability to meet customers' needs. The Brewer-Nash model, also known as the Chinese Wall model, seeks to ensure that goal. The concept, first posited in a 1989 IEEE paper on the subject, distinguishes access and permissions of administrators based on policy. (You can read the paper at `www.cs.purdue .edu/homes/ninghui/readings/AccessControl/brewer_nash_89.pdf`.) A cloud provider pursuing this end might want to enact such a policy and test it for functionality.

Hypervisor Hardening

Because the hypervisor is a prime target for attackers (controlling the hypervisor might allow access to the data in every instance), the hypervisor should receive all the security attention that would have been shown for a bastion host in the DMZ of a legacy network. The hypervisor should be updated and patched to vendor standards, there should be no default accounts on it, and it should be monitored by automatic sensors as well as continual logging and log review analysis. If the cloud provider has to choose between types of hypervisors, the bare-metal (Type 1) hypervisor is preferable to the hypervisor that runs off the OS (Type 2) because it will offer less attack surface.

Instance Isolation

Each virtual machine (that is, each instance or guest) should be logically isolated from the others with strict logical controls. (They can't be physically isolated, by nature of virtualization and automatic load balancing.) Not only should raw data be prevented from leaking from one instance to another, but all metadata as well. No instance should be able to tell if another instance is even present on the same host, much less what that instance is doing or how long it takes to do it.

Whatever controls are put in place to ensure this isolation should be tested and monitored, both in the sandbox testbed and in the live environment, on a continual basis.

Furthermore, the possibility of guest escape (a user escalating a privilege such that the user can leave the virtual instance and access the host machine itself) should be attenuated as much as possible.

Host Isolation

As with guest escape, the cloud provider should be intrinsically concerned about the possibility of a user on a virtual instance elevating themselves to the point where they can leave the virtual machine, access the host, and reach the network the host is connected to, eventually reaching other host devices or assets on the network.

All hosts must be both physically and logically isolated from one another as much as possible. They will obviously still be connected to the network and so will, in some fashion, all "touch" each other, so those connections should be minimized and secured as much as possible. Moreover, network monitoring should be thorough and detailed, such that any host escape activity would be immediately recognized and response would result.

Storage Operations

In addition to hosts used to run virtualized instances for customer operations, the cloud data center will also include devices used for near-term and long-term storage of both data and instance images.

Clustered Storage and Coupling

Most often, storage devices will be clustered in groups, providing increased performance, flexibility, and reliability. Clustered storage architectures can take one of two types: tightly coupled or loosely coupled.

In the tightly coupled architecture, all the storage devices are directly connected to a shared physical backplane, thus connecting all of them directly (the "tightly" aspect). Each component of the cluster is aware of the others and subscribes to the same policies and rule sets. A tightly coupled cluster is usually confined to more restrictive design parameters, often because the devices might need to be from the same vendor in order to function properly. Although this may be a limiting factor, a tightly coupled architecture will also enhance performance as it scales: the performance of each element is added to the overall performance of the cluster, allowing greater and greater power as it increases in size.

A loosely coupled cluster, on the other hand, will allow for greater flexibility. Each node of the cluster is independent of the others, and new nodes can be added for any purpose or use as needed. They are only logically connected and don't share the same proximate physical framework, so they are only distantly physically connected through communication media (the "loosely" aspect). Performance does not necessarily scale, however, because the nodes don't build on one another. But this might not be an important facet of the storage architecture since storage commands and performance requirements are fairly simple.

Volume vs. Object

Another way of viewing storage options is how the data is stored. Typically, two modes could be used: volume storage and object storage. In volume storage, disk space is apportioned to the customer and is allocated to each of the guest instances the customer uses. The virtualized OS of the guest can then utilize and manipulate the volume as necessary. This is sometimes referred to as *block storage* or *raw disk storage*. Volume/block storage in the cloud is analogous to a mounted drive in a traditional network. In volume/block storage, the user/administrator could install and run programs, or simply impose a filesystem for storing objects. Threats to volume storage include the following:

- Because the volume is simply a drive space, all the traditional data storage threats remain, such as malware, accidental deletion of data, and physical disk failure.

- Moreover, because the data is stored in the cloud, the intermediary threat (a man-in-the-middle attack) exists as data is uploaded and recalled from the cloud and the volume is manipulated by remote users.

In object storage, all data is stored in a filesystem, and customers are given access to the parts of the hierarchy to which they're assigned. This is sometimes referred to as *file storage*. In object storage, the user/administrator is limited to uploading, storing, and manipulating files (objects) as opposed to installing and running programs. Threats to object storage include the following:

- Because object storage does not have a runtime environment, the risk of malware is greatly reduced but may still exist for parasitical viruses, which may infect specific files.

- Loss due to physical disk failure remains.

- The risk of ransomware attacks may also significantly threaten object storage.

Other Storage

There are several other forms of cloud data storage you should be familiar with:

- **Ephemeral Storage:** Temporary resource that is used primarily for processing. Sometimes referred to as *instance store* volumes, ephemeral storage is provided by devices directly connected to a host machine where the virtualized instance runs—somewhat analogous to RAM for the cloud virtual machine. Threats to ephemeral storage: data in ephemeral storage will be lost if the virtual machine instance is shut down or if the physical drive where the instance store resides fails.

- **Long-Term Storage:** Durable data storage capacity, often offered at low cost and large amounts, typically used for archiving/backups. Usually, this type of storage is not suitable for production environments and is not conducive to installing and running programs, but at least some providers offer the capability to run queries and analyze data stored in long-term storage. Threats to long-term storage: insider threat (either users with malicious intent, or administrators at the cloud storage data center); intermediary (man-in-the-middle attack), as the data is uploaded to the cloud; ransomware; vendor lock-in, as the more data a vendor has the more difficult it is to leave that vendor.

- **Content-Delivery Network (CDN):** Typically used for large amounts of data that require time-sensitive communication and low latency, such as multimedia content (games, videos, etc.). Instead of hosting an entire library of content at a single, centralized physical location and distributing content globally, content providers may use a CDN to replicate portions of the data at data centers physically located nearer to users/consumers in order to reduce the potential for delay/disruption and decrease in quality of service. For example, a video content producer in Brussels, with worldwide viewership, may opt to lease services from a CDN service host, replicating copies of popular videos in data centers located in Atlanta, London, Moscow, Beijing, and Bangalore; when users in those locations request those videos, the data is served from their local data center instead of having to travel from Brussels. Threats to CDNs: CDNs may be susceptible to intermediaries, insiders (mainly CDN provider administrators), and potentially malware.

Resiliency

There are two general ways for creating data protection in a cloud storage cluster: RAID (redundant array of independent disks, although originally termed as redundant array of inexpensive disks) and data dispersion. These two ways of creating data protection are very similar and provide a level of resiliency—that is, a reasonable amount of assurance that although the physical and/or logical environment might be partially affected by detrimental occurrences (outages, attacks, and so on), the overall bulk of data will not be lost permanently.

In most RAID configurations, all data is stored across the various disks in a method known as *striping*. This allows data to be recovered in a more efficient manner because if one of the drives fails, the missing data can be filled in by the other drives. In some RAID schemes (there are many, known as RAID 0–10, with different levels of performance, redundancy, and integrity, depending on the owner's needs), parity bits are added to the raw data to aid in recovery after a drive failure.

Data dispersion is a similar technique, where data is sliced into "chunks" (sometimes referred to as "shards") that are encrypted along with parity bits (called *erasure coding* in cloud data dispersion) and then written to various drives in the cloud cluster. The parity bits/erasure coding allow for the recovery of partial data lost (stored on one "drive" or device or storage area) by re-creating the lost data from the remaining data plus the parity bits/erasure code. Data dispersion can be seen as equivalent to creating a RAID array in a cloud environment. This technique is also often referred to as *bit splitting*.

 Secret sharing made short (SSMS) is a method of bit splitting that uses the three phases: encryption, using an information dispersal algorithm, and splitting the encryption key using the secret sharing algorithm. The fragments are signed and distributed to different cloud storage services, making it difficult to decrypt without both arbitrarily chosen data and encryption key fragments.

Data dispersion provides multiple benefits. Depending on the encryption configuration, partial loss of data (say, one component in the storage cluster failing) will not result in total unavailability of the data set; the lost portion can be recovered from the remaining components in the cluster, using the parity bits/erasure coding. Another benefit is greater security from both physical and logical theft: if one device containing dispersed data is taken from the cloud data center, or accessed through unauthorized means, the chunks/shards on that device will not be meaningful or useful to the thief as it will be unreadable out of context with the other chunks/shards and will also be encrypted. This also protects the data of a cloud customer if a device is seized/accessed by regulators/law enforcement for an investigation into another customer—the information of Customer A, if dispersed, is not revealed when the regulator accesses the device looking for Customer B's data.

Physical and Logical Isolation

In this chapter, we've already discussed the need for both physical and logical isolation of personnel, the various virtualized instances, and storage devices in a cluster. The same principles should be applied throughout the cloud data center to include other isolation techniques and technologies. These include restricted physical access to devices, secure interface devices, and restricted logical access to devices.

Restricted Physical Access to Devices

Access to racks in the data center should be limited to those administrators and maintainers who absolutely need to reach the devices in order to perform their job functions. Entry and egress should be controlled, monitored, and logged. Racks should be locked, and keys for each respective rack should have to be checked out only for the duration of use. Likewise, KVMs should have to be checked out by the administrator needing to use them for a specific task and checked in at their return.

Secure KVMs

The human interface devices such as keyboards, video displays, and mice (KVMs) used to access production devices—both processing and storage—should be hardened for security purposes. Secure KVMs differ from their mundane counterparts in that they are designed to deter and detect tampering. They are also, as might be expected, usually quite a bit more expensive.

Secure KVMs should have the following traits:

Secure Data Ports   These reduce the likelihood of data leaking between computers that are connected through the KVM.

Tamper Labels   These provide a clear indication if the unit housing has been breached. They might also be supported by warning lights that alert you when the exterior case is opened.

Fixed Firmware   This cannot be flashed or reprogrammed.

Soldered Circuit Board   Soldering is used instead of adhesive so that the board itself or its chipsets or other components cannot be removed and replaced.

Reduced Buffer   Data is not stored beyond the immediate needs of the device.

Air-Gapped Pushbuttons   When switching between multiple devices connected to the unit, the current connection is physically broken before a new one is made.

Restricted Logical Access to Devices

Where possible, devices should be located on secure subnets, limiting the ability of malicious intruders. (This may be difficult in a cloud environment, where resources are apportioned automatically, often across the entirety of the data center.) Use of USB ports should be severely controlled and eliminated wherever possible. Restrict the potential for any portable media to be carried into or out of the data center undetected.

Cloud Usage

Many new and emerging technologies, such as blockchain, neural networks, and the Internet of Things (IoT), are highly dependent on distributed processing/networking, intense processing, and high-speed connectivity. This makes them ideal for cloud environments.

Other technologies, such as containers, facilitate and further popularize the use of cloud services. Containers are a means, other than or in addition to virtual machines, for running applications in a distributed, heterogeneous IT environment. The container is a package of software necessities (code, bins, libraries, and so on) that can run on any standard OS or platform. An organization using a container can ensure that the organization's applications will perform in a standard way across a nonstandard environment.

Application Testing Methods

In this section, I'll briefly describe some of the methods used for application testing from a rather high-level perspective. Again, readers familiar with the SDLC and its secure implementation should already have some knowledge of this material.

Static application security testing (SAST) is a direct review of the actual source code an application comprises. It is often to referred to as *white-box testing*. Benefits include direct and early assessment of potential flaws, long before the application is even considered for the production environment. Unfortunately, effective SAST requires a great deal of specific knowledge of the particular code as well as expert comprehension of potential negative outcomes. This kind of skillset is usually found in personnel already involved in programming; it's rare that an organization would have this sort of person available for the limited task of software testing. So SAST might often be performed by contract personnel on a finite basis. This introduces an additional potential detriment to the development process: the number of iterations for which they can be tasked might be extremely limited, and certainly expensive. However, application owners want to be sure that applications are *not* being tested by the developers who wrote them. There is too much chance that the developers will miss errors they've made (or else they would not have made them) or that they will be understandably inherently biased toward their own creation. This would pose a conflict of interest and violate the principle of separation of duties. There are also automated tools that can perform code review; however, much like definition-based malware solutions, automated code review tools will only detect known and recognized flaws and vulnerabilities and are not exhaustive.

Dynamic application security testing (DAST), on the other hand, does not pertain to source code. Instead, it reviews outcomes of the application as it is executed in runtime. It is often referred to as black-box testing. DAST often involves a group of users in a test environment, running the application and trying to see whether it performs correctly or will fail under multiple inputs and conditions. This can also be construed as a form of functional testing because the various test inputs can include known good data to determine if known good results are produced. DAST is not nearly as granular as SAST, and something that might have been revealed by expert SAST might be missed in DAST.

Of course, it is possible—and desirable—to perform both kinds of testing on a particular application.

The STRIDE threat model, explained in Chapter 7, is also extremely useful for guiding application testing efforts. Developers and the Quality Assurance/testing team should use the STRIDE approach to help craft test parameters and methods.

Security Operations Center

Most data centers will have a centralized facility for continuous monitoring of network performance and security controls. This is commonly known as the security operations center (or sometimes network operations center or similar terms). Typically, physical access will be limited to security personnel and administrators overseeing live and historic feeds from security devices and agents placed throughout the IT environment. Tools such as DLP, anti-malware, SIEM/SEM/SIM, firewalls, and IDS/IPS will present logs and reports to the security operations center for analysis and real-time response.

For modern IT environments, the security operations center does not have to be physically located inside the data center itself or even on the same campus. A security operations center for an enterprise with many different branches and offices may be located remotely, monitoring at a distance. In fact, in many cases, the security operations and continuous monitoring function might be performed by a contracted third party, a vendor with the tools, knowledge, and personnel for providing security as a core competency.

In a cloud-managed services arrangement, the provider will most likely have a security operations center overseeing the various cloud data centers and underlying infrastructure and, depending on the service and deployment models, the platforms and applications as well. The cloud customer, however, may also have a security operation monitoring its own users/cloud accounts and interactions. There may be some shared responsibility and activity between the provider and customer for detection, reporting, investigation, and response actions. All of these need to be established in the contract.

Continuous Monitoring

The security controls in the IT environment are not durable. A control cannot be purchased, implemented, and then considered complete (and the associated risk the control was intended to address cannot be considered permanently mitigated). Instead, controls must be continually monitored to ensure that they are effective, operating as intended, and addressing the risks or vulnerabilities that they were supposed to mitigate. Moreover, the entire environment must be monitored continually to determine if new or emerging threats or risks are dealt with properly.

Older security paradigms required periodic risk reviews and might deem an IT environment as protected for a certain duration if the review was successful or had no significant findings. Current guidance and industry best standards refute that model, instead stating the preferred approach of continuous monitoring. NIST (in the Risk Management Framework), ISO (in the 27000 series of IT security standards), and the CIS (formerly SANS Top 20 security controls guidance) all make continuous monitoring a central tenet of protecting an IT environment.

Incident Management

When the security operations center detects or receives a report of anomalous or illicit activity, an incident response action might be initiated. Incident response might include the following purposes:

- Minimizing the loss of value/assets
- Continuing service provision (availability)
- Halting increase of the damage

The intended outcome will significantly impact the course of action taken in the response, and it will be different for every industry or organization. For example, a large online retailer that conducts thousands of commercial transactions per hour might be most concerned will availability—continuing the transactions. If the retailer discovers that a piece of malware is skimming money from the retailer so that the retailer is losing hundreds of dollars per hour but the retailer's revenues are hundreds of thousands of dollars per hour, the retailer probably won't want to shut down operations in order to address the malware issue. The retailer may continue allowing the loss to continue for an extended period of time because the impact of shutting down the environment would be much more damaging than the effect of the malware. Another potential outcome might be a form of legal recourse—either a lawsuit or prosecution.

The organization should have an incident response policy and plan. Both the cloud provider and customer will have their own approaches, goals, and methods for incident management. The two parties should coordinate and share these responsibilities and codify this arrangement in the contract.

Moreover, incident response in a managed services arrangement creates additional challenges and risks. For instance, which party can declare an incident unilaterally? Do both parties have to concur that an incident has occurred? If the provider declares an incident, is the provider relieved of the requirement to meet certain SLA performance targets (say, availability) for the duration of the incident? If there are additional costs associated with incident response, such as downtime, personnel tasking, or reporting actions, which party is responsible for absorbing these costs?

The customer will have to consider all these questions (and others) pertinent to incident management when planning cloud migration and selecting a provider.

Knowing Your Cloud

How does a customer verify whether a certain service provider will meet the customer's needs, particular if the customer is in a highly regulated industry or deals with sensitive/regulated information?

There are a great many regulatory schemes globally, for a wide variety of industries and legal frameworks. Many of these legal or contractual constructs offer certification (either by the standard bodies or through the use of approved auditors deemed worthy by them). The customer required to adhere to a given mandate can select from those providers who have obtained the necessary certifications.

For instance, an organization that takes payments via credit card must comply with the Payment Card Industry Data Security Standard (PCI DSS). If that organization is considering cloud migration, the organization needs to find a provider that has likewise obtained PCI DSS certification. If the provider claims to be "PCI DSS compliant," that fact should be included in the contract between customer and provider, and the provider should offer some contractual, binding assurance that the customer will not be found noncompliant because of any deficiency or shortcoming in the managed cloud environment.

Even a customer that is not required to comply with PCI DSS might view a provider that has a PCI DSS certification as more trustworthy and viable than one that does not. The customer might make a choice in providers based on the certifications a provider holds.

Other certifications that customers might consider valuable or noteworthy when selecting cloud providers include the following:

- ISO 27000 series (in particular 27017, which addresses IT security controls in a cloud environment)

- FedRAMP

- CSA STAR

Summary

In this chapter, we've discussed the use of redundancy in the design of cloud data centers and made the reader aware of the Uptime Institute's four tiers for describing and certifying that quality. We also described basic application security methods, including threat modeling and software testing.

Exam Essentials

Understand how redundancy is implemented in the design of the cloud data center.   Be sure to remember that all infrastructure, systems, and components require redundancy, including utilities (power, water, and connectivity), processing capabilities, data storage, personnel, and emergency and contingency services (including paths of egress, power, light, and fuel).

Know the four tiers of data center redundancy published by the Uptime Institute.   While memorizing the aspects of each would be difficult, it is possible to understand the escalation in sophistication of design from Tier 1 to Tier 4 and the basic differences between each.

Understand the differences between SAST and DAST.   Know which is white-box testing, which is black-box testing, which involves review of source code, and which is performed in runtime.

Written Labs

You can find the answers to the written labs in Appendix A.

1. Imagine an application that might be used by an organization hosted in a cloud environment. In one paragraph, describe the purpose and use of this application, including the user base, types of data it processes, and the interface.

2. Using the STRIDE model, analyze potential points of security failure in the application from the first lab. According to Microsoft, it's possible to identify up to 40 points of failure in a two-hour analysis; in 30 minutes, come up with 3.

3. Use one paragraph to describe each potential threat; use an additional paragraph to describe possible security controls that might be applied to attenuate each threat. The controls may be repeated (that is, you can use the same control for more than one threat), but the explanation paragraph of each should apply to each specific threat and therefore cannot just be copied.

Review Questions

You can find the answers to the review questions in Appendix B.

1. What is the lowest tier of data center redundancy, according to the Uptime Institute?

   A. 1

   B. V

   C. C

   D. 4

2. What is the amount of fuel that should be on hand to power generators for backup data center power, in all tiers, according to the Uptime Institute?

   A. 1

   B. 1,000 gallons

   C. Enough to last 12 hours

   D. As much as needed to ensure all systems may be gracefully shut down and data securely stored

3. Who should not be involved in application security testing?

   A. Quality Assurance team members

   B. Testing contractors

   C. User community representatives

   D. Developers of the application

4. Which of the following is part of the STRIDE model?

   A. Repudiation

   B. Redundancy

   C. Resiliency

   D. Rijndael

5. Which of the following is *not* part of the STRIDE model?

   A. Spoofing

   B. Tampering

   C. Resiliency

   D. Information disclosure

6. Which of the following is *not* a feature of SAST?

   A. Source code review

   B. Team-building efforts

   C. White-box testing

   D. Highly skilled, often expensive outside consultants

7. Which of the following is *not* a feature of DAST?

  A. Testing in runtime

  B. User teams performing executable testing

  C. Black-box testing

  D. Binary inspection

8. Which of the following is *not* a feature of a secure KVM component?

  A. Keystroke logging

  B. Sealed exterior case

  C. Soldered chipsets

  D. Push-button selectors

9. What type of redundancy can we expect to find in a data center of any tier?

  A. All operational components

  B. All infrastructure

  C. Emergency egress

  D. Full power capabilities

10. What should be the primary focus of data center redundancy and contingency planning?

  A. Critical path/operations

  B. Health and human safety

  C. Infrastructure supporting the production environment

  D. Power and HVAC

11. Which of the following techniques for ensuring cloud data center storage resiliency uses parity bits and disk striping?

  A. Cloud-bursting

  B. RAID

  C. Data dispersion

  D. SAN

12. Which resiliency technique attenuates the possible loss of functional capabilities during contingency operations?

  A. Cross-training

  B. Metered usage

  C. Proper placement of HVAC temperature measurements tools

  D. Raised floors

13. Which of the following has *not* been attributed as the cause of lost capabilities due to DoS?

   A. Hackers

   B. Construction equipment

   C. Changing regulatory motif

   D. Squirrels

14. If a hospital is considering using a cloud data center, which Uptime Institute Tier should it require?

   A. 2

   B. 4

   C. 8

   D. X

15. What is often a major challenge to getting both redundant power and communications utility connections?

   A. Expense

   B. Carrying medium

   C. Personnel deployment

   D. Location of many data centers

16. Which of the following is generally *not* a high-priority aspect of physical security in the planning and design of a cloud data center facility?

   A. Perimeter

   B. Vehicular approach/traffic

   C. Fire suppression

   D. Elevation of dropped ceilings

17. The Brewer-Nash security model is also known as which of the following?

   A. MAC

   B. The Chinese Wall model

   C. Preventive measures

   D. RBAC

18. Which kind of hypervisor would malicious actors prefer to attack, ostensibly because it offers a greater attack surface?

   A. Cat IV

   B. Type II

   C. Bare metal

   D. Converged

19. Which of the following techniques for ensuring cloud data center storage resiliency uses encrypted chunks of data?

   A. Cloud-bursting

   B. RAID

   C. Data dispersion

   D. SAN

20. Which of the following data center redundancy efforts probably poses the greatest threat to human safety?

   A. Emergency egress

   B. Communications

   C. Generators

   D. Spare components

Chapter

9

Operations Management

THE OBJECTIVE OF THIS CHAPTER IS TO ACQUAINT THE READER WITH THE FOLLOWING CONCEPTS:

✓ **Domain 1: Cloud Concepts, Architecture, and Design**

- 1.1. Understand Cloud Computing Concepts
  - 1.1.2. Cloud Computing Roles
- 1.4. Understand Design Principles of Secure Cloud Computing
  - 1.4.2. Cloud Based Disaster Recovery (DR) and Business Continuity (BC) Planning

✓ **Domain 3: Cloud Platform and Infrastructure Security**

- 3.4. Design and Plan Security Controls
  - 3.4.1. Physical and Environmental Protection
- 3.5. Plan Disaster Recovery (DR) and Business Continuity (BC)
  - 3.5.1. Risks Related to the Cloud Environment
  - 3.5.2. Business Requirements
  - 3.5.3. Business Continuity/Disaster Recovery Strategy
  - 3.5.4. Creation, Implementation, and Testing of the Plan

✓ **Domain 5: Cloud Security Operations**

- 5.3. Manage Physical and Logical Infrastructure for Cloud Environment
  - 5.3.3. Patch Management
  - 5.3.4. Performance and Capacity Monitoring
  - 5.3.5. Hardware Monitoring
- 5.4. Implement Operational Controls and Standards
  - 5.4.1. Change Management
  - 5.4.2. Continuity Management

This chapter covers the essential aspects of operations monitoring, capacity, maintenance, change and configuration management, and BC/DR for cloud data centers.

In other chapters, I often referred to the cloud customer as "your organization" or made other related associations (using *your* or *we* to indicate the cloud customer's perspective in many matters). In this chapter, the focus is almost exclusively on the cloud provider, specifically the provider's data center. I may refer to actions associated with the provider with the same pronouns used for the customer elsewhere (*you*, *your*, or *we*); hopefully, context will prevent any misunderstanding.

In this chapter, we'll discuss the various practices cloud data center operators should use to optimize performance and enhance durability of their infrastructure and systems. This will include coverage of systems monitoring, the configuration and change management program and BC/DR from a vendor perspective.

Monitoring, Capacity, and Maintenance

It's important for data center operators to know how their hardware, software, and network are being utilized and what demand is being placed on all the relevant resources. This information helps data center operators know how to better apportion and allocate all those items in order to fulfill customer needs (and maintain compliance with SLAs).

Monitoring

Software, hardware, and network components need to be evaluated in real time to understand which systems may be nearing capacity and so the organization can respond as quickly as possible when problems arise. This can and should be done with several of the possible tools at the operator's disposal:

OS Logging Most operating systems have integral toolsets for monitoring performance and events. Aside from the security uses mentioned elsewhere in the book, the cloud vendor can set OS logs to alert administrators when usage approaches a level of capacity utilization or performance degradation that may affect SLA parameters. These can include CPU usage, memory usage, disk space (virtual or tangible), and disk I/O timing (an indicator of slow writing/reading to/from the disk).

Hardware Monitoring   As with the OS, many vendors include performance-monitoring tools in common device builds. These can be used to measure such performance indicators as CPU temperature, fan speed, voltages (consumption and throughput), CPU load and clock speed, and drive temperature. Commercial products are also available to collect and supply this data and provide alerts if this functionality is not integral to the devices from the manufacturer.

Network Monitoring   In addition to the OS and the devices themselves, the various network elements need to be monitored. These include not only the hardware and the software, but the distribution facets such as cabling and software-defined networking (SDN) control planes. The provider should ensure that current capacity meets customer needs and increased customer demand to assure that the flexibility and scalability traits of cloud computing are still provided. The provider should also ensure that the network is not overburdened or subjected to unacceptable latency.

As with all log data, the performance monitoring information can be fed into a SEIM, SEM, or SIM system for centralized analysis and review.

In addition to the hardware and software, it is important to monitor ambient conditions within the data center. In particular, temperature and humidity are essential data points for optimizing operations and performance. It's important to capture a realistic portrayal of the temperature within the data center, perhaps by averaging measurements across several thermometric devices located throughout the airflow process. For performance monitoring purposes, our target metrics will be the standards created by Technical Committee 9.9 of the American Society of Heating, Refrigerating and Air-Conditioning Engineers (ASHRAE), published in 2016. ASHRAE offers extremely detailed recommendations for a wide variety of aspects of the data center, including the IT equipment, power supply, and battery backups, all of which can be quite useful to a data center operator or security practitioner. These are available free of charge from the ASHRAE website: `https://tc0909 .ashraetcs.org/documents/ASHRAE_TC0909_Power_White_Paper_22_June_2016_REVISED .pdf`. It's also a generally good read and worth investing some of your time reviewing.

While there are many specific and detailed recommendations, the general ASHRAE recommended ranges for a data center are as follows:

▪ **Temperature:** 64° to 81° F (18° to 27° C)

▪ **Humidity:** Dew point of 42° to 59° F (5.5° to 15° C), relative humidity of 60%

While these ranges give a general notion of the condition of the ambient environment within a data center, the ASHRAE guidance is a lot more detailed regarding specific ranges, based on the type, age, and location of the equipment. The operator should determine which guidance is most applicable to their facility. Moreover, ASHRAE offers this advice solely from a platform-agnostic perspective. Data center operators must also take into account any guidance and recommendations from device manufacturers regarding ambient ranges affecting performance parameters for their specific products.

Effects of Ambient Temperature and Ambient Humidity

What roles do temperature and humidity play, in terms of affecting equipment performance?

An ambient temperature that is too high may allow equipment to overheat. High-capacity electrical components generate a great deal of waste heat, and the devices can be sensitive to conditions that exceed their operating parameters. An ambient temperature that is too low can be a risk to health and human safety; touching bare metal at the freezing point can burn or remove skin; moreover, people working in such conditions would simply be uncomfortable and unhappy, conditions that lead to dissatisfaction, which in turn lead to security risks.

An ambient humidity that is too high can promote corrosion of metallic components as well as mold and other organisms. An ambient humidity that is too low can enhance the possibility of static discharge, which might affect both personnel and equipment as well as increase the potential for fires.

Maintenance

Continual uptime requires maintaining the overall environment constantly. This also includes maintaining individual components both on a scheduled basis and at unscheduled times as necessary. In the following sections, we'll discuss general maintenance matters, updates, upgrades, and patch management.

General Maintenance Concepts

The operational modes of data centers can be perceived as two categories: normal and maintenance mode. Realistically, the data center, taken holistically, will constantly be in maintenance mode, as ongoing maintenance of specific systems and components is necessary for continuous uptime. Therefore, a cloud data center can be expected to be considered in constant normal mode, with various individual systems and devices continually in maintenance mode to ensure constant operations. This is especially true for Tier 3 and 4 data centers, where redundant components, lines, and systems allow for maintenance to occur simultaneously with uninterrupted critical operations.

Let's instead look at systems and devices in terms of the normal and maintenance modes. When a system or device is put into maintenance mode, the data center operator must ensure the following tasks are successful:

All operational instances are removed from the system/device before entering maintenance mode. We don't want to affect any transactions in a customer's production environment. We therefore must migrate any virtualized instances off the specific systems and devices where they might be hosted before we begin maintenance activities.

Prevent all new logins. For the same reason as the previous task, we don't want customers logging into the affected systems and devices.

Ensure logging is continued, and begin enhanced logging. Administrator activities are much more powerful, and therefore rife with risk, than the actions of common users. It is therefore recommended that you log administrator actions at a greater rate and level of detail than those of users. Maintenance mode is an administrative function, so the increased logging is necessary.

Before moving a system or device from maintenance mode back to normal operation, it is important to test that it has all the original functionality necessary for customer purposes, that the maintenance was successful, and that proper documentation of all activity is complete.

Updates

Industry best practice includes ensuring we comply with all vendor guidance regarding specific products. In fact, failing to adhere to vendor specifications can be a sign that the operator has failed in providing necessary due care, whereas documented adherence to vendor instructions can demonstrate due diligence.

In addition to configuration prior to deployment (discussed as part of the section "Change and Configuration Management [CM]" later in this chapter), vendors will issue ongoing maintenance instructions, often in the form of updates. This can be both in the form of application packages for software and firmware installs for hardware. The former can also be in the form of patches, which we'll discuss specifically is a later section.

The update process should be formalized in the operator's governance (as should *all* processes, and they should all spawn from policy). It should include the following elements, at a minimum:

Document how, when, and why the update was initiated. If promulgated by the vendor, annotate the details of the communication, including date, update code or number, explanation, and justification; some of this may be included by reference, such as with a URL to the vendor's page announcing the update instructions.

Move the update through the change management (CM) process. All modifications to the facility should be through the CM methodology and documented as such. Details on the CM process are included later in this chapter, but it should be stressed that sandbox testing be included as part of CM before the update is applied.

1. Put the systems and devices into maintenance mode. Observe the recommendations in the previous section of this chapter.

2. Apply the update to the necessary systems and devices. Annotate the asset inventory to reflect the changes.

3. Verify the update. Run tests on the production environment to ensure all necessary systems and devices have received the update. If any were missed, repeat the installation until it is complete.

4. Validate the modifications. Ensure that the intended results of the update have taken effect and that the updated systems and devices interact appropriately with the rest of the production environment.

5. Return to normal operations. Resume regular business.

Upgrades

In this context, we distinguish updates from upgrades with this purpose: updates are applied to existing systems and components, whereas upgrades are the replacement of older elements with newer ones. The upgrade process should largely map to the one for updates, including formalization in governance, CM methodology, testing, and so forth. Particular attention in upgrading needs to be placed on documenting the changes in the asset inventory, not only adding the new elements but annotating the removal and secure disposal of the old ones. This, of course, means that secure disposal is one element of the upgrade process that is not included in updates.

Patch Management

Patches are a variety of updates most commonly associated with software. We distinguish them here by their frequency: software vendors commonly issue patches both for immediate response to a given need (such as a newfound vulnerability) and for routine purposes (fixing, adding, or enhancing functionality) on a regular basis.

The patch management process must be formalized in much the same manner as updates and upgrades, with its inclusion in policy and so forth. However, patches incur additional risks and challenges, so this discussion is set aside to deal with those specifically. The following subsections relate suggestions and considerations to take into account when managing patches for a cloud data center.

Timing

When a vendor issues a patch, there is a binary risk faced by all those affected: if they fail to apply the patch, they may be seen to be failing in providing due care for those customers utilizing the unpatched products; if the patch is applied in haste, it may adversely affect the production environment, harming the customer's ability to operate. The latter case is especially true when patches are issued in response to a newfound vulnerability and the vendor was rushed to identify the flaw, find and create a solution, publish the fix, and issue the patch. In the rush to deal with the problem (even more especially when the vulnerability is well publicized and garners public attention), the patch may cause other vulnerabilities or affect other systems by reducing some interoperability or interface capability.

It is therefore difficult to know exactly when to apply patches relative to how soon after they were issued. It is contingent upon the operator to make this decision only after weighing the merits of either choice.

In some environments (and with some vendors), it may be desirable to schedule a set patching day/time (per week or per month, for instance) so that it is a regular, anticipated occurrence. In this way, the various participants can coordinate the activity, the change control process can accommodate the required modifications, and specific types of patches can be prioritized and applied in a defined manner.

Of course, sometimes the customer has little to no control of when some patches might take place, particularly with some platform or vendor updates. If the customer knows this might be an issue with a particular vendor or software, they can try to plan ahead about how they might deal with such situations.

> A data center operator may be tempted to allow others in the field to apply the patch first in order to determine its effect and outcome based on the experiences of competitors. The risk in that option is that in the meantime, loss or harm might be caused by or occur via the vulnerability the patch was meant to remediate. This might lend strong support in a lawsuit to recover damages because those customers harmed by the loss can rightly claim that the provider knew of the risk, did not take the steps of due diligence made by others in the field, and allowed harm to come through negligence. This might even support claims for additional or punitive damages. Again, while the tactic may be sound, it carries this additional risk.

Implementation: Automated or Manual

Patches can be applied with mechanized tools or by personnel. There are obvious benefits and risks for both methods. The operator will have to decide which to use on both a general basis (by policy) and for each case when a patch is issued if the circumstances demand. The risks and benefits for each include the following:

Automated   A mechanized approach will allow for much faster delivery to far more targets than a manual approach. Patch tools might also include a reporting function that annotates which targets have received the patch, cross-referenced against the asset inventory, and have an alerting function to inform administrators which targets have been missed. Without a capable human observer, however, the tool might not function thoroughly or properly, the patches might be misapplied, or the reports might be inaccurate or portray an inaccurate picture of completeness.

Manual   Trained and experienced personnel may be more trustworthy than a mechanized tool and might understand when anomalous activity occurs. However, with the vast number of elements that will need to be patched in a cloud data center, the repetitiveness and boredom of the patch process may lead even a seasoned administrator to miss a number of targets. Moreover, the process will be much, much slower than the automated option and may not be as thorough.

Dates

As the patch is pushed throughout the environment, the actual date/time stamp may become an important—and misleading—matter in acquiring and acknowledging receipt. For example, say that an automated tool requires an agent that is installed locally on each target. If certain targets are not running when the patch happens and won't be operating until the next calendar day (according to the internal clock on the target), the local agent may not receive the patch because it may check against the central controller for patches *for the current day.*

This problem can be compounded when patch agents are set to check for patches according to a time specified by the internal clock and different targets have internal clocks set to differing time zones (in the case, say, of customers who are geographically dispersed).

This problem is not limited to automated tools, either. If a manual method is used, the administrators may be applying a patch at a given time/date when not all customers and users have their targets operating, so those targets might not receive the patch, and the administrators might not realize that targets that don't currently appear in scans may need to be patched at some later time/date. Moreover, if patches are being applied manually, the process will necessarily be extended so that administrators can be sure to reach all potential targets as they come online.

All these possibilities are escalated in a cloud arrangement because of the wide use of virtualization. All virtualized instances saved as images and not currently instantiated during patch delivery will be receiving the patch only after they are next booted. This means that the process will endure until all virtual machines have been made live, which could represent a significant amount of time after the decision to implement the patch. The result is a relatively long delay between the time the operator decides to implement the patch and the time of 100 percent completion. This reflects poorly on the process and the operator, especially in the eyes of regulators and courts.

Perhaps the optimum technique is to combine the benefits of each method, using both manual and automated approaches. Manual oversight is valuable in determining applicability of patches and testing patches for suitability in the environment, while automated tools can be used to propagate patches and ensure uniform application.

Regardless of the approach taken, patching (as with all forms of maintenance) should be mentioned in the SLA, and an agreed-upon schedule and threshold of patches is an important contractual consideration.

Change and Configuration Management (CM)

Data center operators, like anyone who owns an IT network, need to develop and maintain a realistic concept of what assets they control, the state of those assets, and explicit information about each asset. This goes beyond (but includes) the asset inventory—the hardware, software, and media they own. It also includes documented records of configuration for all these elements, including versioning, deviations, exceptions, and the rationale for each, as well as a formal process for determining how, when, and why modifications need to be made.

There are two foundational and interrelated processes used to accomplish this effort: change management and configuration management. Configuration management entails documenting the approved settings for systems and software, which helps establish baselines within the organization. Change management is the process used to review, approve, and document any modifications to the environment. In one sense, configuration management is just the first change to a specific system/program; the two practices are linked.

Realistically, in many organizations both sets of functions are accomplished by a single process and body. For the purposes of our discussion of operational functions, I'm going to aggregate them and put them under one label: CM. I'll do this to simplify the information, even though a cloud vendor should probably have the wherewithal and functional and personnel specialization sufficient to provide both as separate activities. The purposes of both are so similar in intent and procedure as to be understood as one concept.

Baselines

CM, regardless of the flavor, begins with baselining, which is a way of taking an accurate account of the desired standard state. For change management, that's a depiction of the network and systems, based on a comprehensive, detailed asset inventory. For configuration management, it's a standard build for all systems, from the settings in the OS to the setup of each application.

The baseline is a general-purpose map of the network and systems, based on the required functionality as well as security. Security controls should be incorporated in the baseline, with a thorough description of each one's purpose, dependencies, and supporting rationale (that is, a statement explaining what we hope to accomplish with each control). It is absolutely essential to include the controls so that we are fully informed about risk management as we consider modifications to the environment through the CM process. If we're changing the control set in any way or adding new systems and functionality to the environment, we need to know if there will be any resultant increased risk and, therefore, if we need to add any compensatory controls to manage the new risk levels.

While creating the baseline, it's helpful to get input from all stakeholders: the IT department, the security office, management, and even users. The baseline should be an excellent reflection of the risk appetite of the organization and provide the optimum balance of security and operational functionality.

Preferably, the baseline should suit the largest population of systems in the organization. If it's going to be used as a template (particularly in configuration management), we'll get the most value from it if it applies to the greatest number of covered systems. However, it may be useful or pragmatic to have a number of baselines that are based on each department's, office's, or project's needs, but it is still essential to ensure that each distinct baseline supports necessary mandates and requirements. It would be inopportune to have an entire department fail a regulatory compliance audit because that department's baseline lost a category of security coverage.

Deviations and Exceptions

It is important to continually test the baselines to determine that all assets are accounted for and to detect anything that differs from the baseline. Any such deviations, intentional or unintentional, authorized or unauthorized, must be documented and reviewed, as deviations pose additional risks/vulnerabilities to the organization. These deviations might be the result of faulty patch management processes, a rogue device set up by a particular office or user, an intrusion by external attackers, or poor versioning and administrative practices.

It is the duty of those personnel who are assigned CM roles to determine the cause and any necessary follow-up activity. (CM roles are discussed in the next section.)

While the baseline serves as the standard against which to compare and validate all systems in the organization, it is best not to use it as an absolute. There will be a significant number of requests for exceptions for particular users, offices, and projects that need functionality not accorded by the general baseline.

Make sure that the baseline is flexible and practical and that the exception request process is timely and responsive to the needs of the organization and its users. A cumbersome, slow exception process will lead to frustrated users and managers, which can, in turn, lead to unauthorized workarounds implemented without the permission of the CM authority.

WARNING An adversarial, unresponsive exception process will undermine security efforts of the organization. Everyone will find a way to perform their job functions, regardless of whether their workarounds are approved or are the most secure means of performing those functions. Uninformed personnel, acting out of desperation, are more likely to make rogue modifications that lack the proper security countermeasures than would the trained, skilled professionals whose job it is to secure the environment. It is much better to compromise the sanctity of the baseline with full cooperation than to mandate that no exceptions will be allowed or to make the process burdensome and complicated for users and offices. Remember: It is the job of security practitioners to support operations, not to hinder those engaged in productivity.

Tracking exceptions and deviations is useful for another essential purpose in addition to ensuring regulatory compliance and security control coverage: if enough exception requests are being made that all ask for the same or similar functionality that deviates from the baseline, *change the baseline*. The baseline is not serving the purpose if it continually needs routine modification for repeated, equivalent requests. Moreover, addressing exception requests takes more time and effort than modifying the baseline to incorporate new, additional security controls to allow for the excepted functionality.

Roles and Process

The CM process (as with all processes) should be formalized in the organization's governance. This policy should include provisions for creating processes and procedures that provide the following:

- Composition of the CM board (CMB, or sometimes CCB, for change control board)
- The process, in detail
- Documentation requirements
- Instructions for requesting exceptions
- Assignment of CM tasks, such as validation scanning, analysis, and deviation notification
- Procedures for addressing deviations, upon detection
- Enforcement measures and responsibility

The CMB should be composed of representatives from all stakeholders within the organization. Recommended representatives include personnel from the IT, security, legal, management, finance and acquisition, and HR departments/offices, in addition to general users. Any other participants that the organization deems useful can certainly be included in the CMB.

The CMB will be responsible for reviewing change and exception requests. The board will determine if the change will enhance functionality and productivity, whether the change is funded, what potential security impacts the change will incur, and what additional measures (in terms of funding, training, security controls, or staffing) might be necessary to make the change successful and reasonable.

The CMB should meet often enough that changes and exception requests are not delayed unduly so that users and departments are not frustrated by the process. However, it should not meet so often that the time set aside for the CMB becomes work; the personnel involved in the CMB all have other primary duties, and participation in the CMB will impact their productivity. In some cases, depending on the organization, the CMB meets on an ad hoc basis, responding only when change and exception requests meet a certain threshold. This can entail some risk, however, as CMB members might lose some familiarity with the process in the interim, and scheduling a meeting of the CMB with so many disparate offices might be awkward if a meeting of the CMB is not a regular, prioritized occurrence. As with much of the material addressed in this book, this is a trade-off of risk and benefit, and the organization should decide accordingly.

The process has two forms: one that will occur once and the other, which is repetitious. The former is the initial baseline effort; the latter is the normal operational mode. A baseline will be created for each type of system in the environment.

The initial process should look something like this (amended as necessary for each organization's individual circumstances):

1. **Full Asset Inventory:** In order to know what is being managed, it's crucial to know what you have. This effort need not be independent of all other similar efforts and may in fact be aided by information pulled from other sources, such as the business impact analysis (BIA). The systems affected by each baseline need to be determined.

2. **Codification of the Baseline:** This should be a formal action, including all members of the CMB (and perhaps more, for the initial effort; each department and project may want to contribute and participate because the baseline will affect all their future work). The baseline should be negotiated in terms of cost-benefit and risk analyses. Again, it is quite reasonable to use existing sources to inform this negotiation, including the organization's risk management framework, enterprise and security architecture, and so on.

3. **Secure Baseline Build:** A version of the baseline, as codified by the CMB, is constructed and stored for later use.

4. **Deployment of New Assets:** When a new asset is acquired (for instance, a new host purchased for use by a new employee), the relevant baseline configuration needs to be installed on that asset, in accordance with CM policy and procedures and CMB guidance.

In the normal operational mode of the organization, the CM process is slightly different:

1. **CMB Meetings:** The CMB meets to review and analyze change and exception requests. The CMB can authorize or disallow requests, and it can require additional effort before authorization. For instance, the CMB can task the security office to perform additional detailed security analysis of the potential impact resulting if the request were authorized, or the CMB might require the requestor to budget additional funding for the request if the CMB determines the request would require supplemental training, administration, and security controls compared to what the requestor initially expected.

2. **CM Testing:** If the CMB authorizes a request, the new modification must be tested before deployment. Usually, such testing should take place in an isolated sandbox network that mimics all the systems, components, infrastructure, traffic, and processing of the production network, without ever touching the production network. Testing should determine whether there is any undue impact on security, interoperability, or functionality expected as a result of the modification.

3. **Deployment:** The modification is made in accordance with appropriate guidance and is reported to the CMB upon completion.

4. **Documentation:** All modifications to the environment are documented and reflected in the asset inventory (and, as necessary, in the baseline).

Secure disposal of an asset is also a modification to the IT environment and therefore needs to be reflected in the asset inventory and reported to the CMB.

Release Management

As a supporting process to change management, release management (RM) is a software engineering process concerned with arranging all required elements to successfully, repeatably, and verifiably release new software versions. The scope of RM includes planning, scheduling, and deploying new software, and it encompasses all environments that code may pass through, including development, QA/testing and staging—everything up to the production environment, at which point the software enters active maintenance. The progression of code and related activities from requirements (often called user stories) to coding, testing, and then to production is known as the pipeline.

RM has grown along with the rise in popularity of Agile software development practices, which aim to deliver functional software more quickly using short development cycles. Waterfall, an older software development methodology, focused heavily on gathering all requirements and delivering them all at once, while Agile focuses on small units of work that can be achieved in a short amount of time, then iterated to deliver additional functionality.

DevOps has also grown as organizations adopt agile. More frequent software releases have driven the need for tighter coordination between engineers developing software, operations staff responsible for maintaining the software, and users who drive the requirements for software. DevOps aims to create cross-functional teams to ensure smoother, more predictable software delivery by encouraging tighter collaboration and more feedback.

While the increased speed of Agile software development has made users happy (no more waiting a year for a new system module to go live), it has created some headaches for security practitioners. There simply isn't time to do many traditional activities like pen testing when new software is going live on a daily or sometimes even hourly basis. To compensate, security practitioners must make use of automation to decrease the time it takes to perform security functions.

Continuous Integration/Continuous Delivery (CI/CD) incorporates heavy use of automation to dramatically shorten the software delivery pipeline. The ultimate goal is to get newly developed software live and running as quickly as possible after an engineer completes their work, sometimes within minutes of code being written. To achieve this, automated testing is used extensively to ensure the newly written code will not introduce bugs into the production environment. Security testing needs to be reevaluated to identify how needed security checks can be integrated with the CI/CD pipeline.

Security automation in CI/CD must include both administrative and technical controls. Examples of administrative controls include checking that new software has a verifiable set of requirements and approvals (i.e., a developer is delivering code that meets a defined user need rather than unwanted functionality) and that all processes have been followed (e.g., a peer review must be conducted). Automated technical controls can include checks such as passing a static code analysis or successful completion of a vulnerability scan run against a live version of the new code in a staging environment.

IT Service Management and Continual Service Improvement

ITIL (formerly the Information Technology Infrastructure Library) comprises a set of practices businesses can use in designing, maintaining, and improving their IT services. This is known as IT service management (ITSM), and the practices can be implemented for any IT function, such as delivering email collaboration capabilities to employees, designing new customer-facing applications, or even the process of migrating from on-prem to cloud infrastructure.

ISO/IEC 20000-1, Information technology — Service management, also defines a set of operational controls and standards that organizations can use to manage IT services. The ISO standard defines a service management system (SMS) designed to support the practice of ITSM, as well as suggested processes, procedures, and organizational capabilities required. Note this is very similar to the approach in ISO 27001, which describes an information security management system (ISMS) and needed support for enabling security. ISO 20000-1 can be used to manage ITSM using a variety of approaches, including ITIL and the ISACA COBIT framework.

The goal of ITSM is to identify user needs, design an IT service that meets those needs, successfully deploy it, then enter a cycle of continuous improvements. Continual service improvement management aims to ensure that IT services provide ongoing business value, and that the services are updated as needed to respond to changing business requirements. Obviously, the shift to cloud computing is a major example of business requirements driving changes to IT services.

Although ITIL was designed in an era when most infrastructure was maintained and used exclusively on-prem, the general principles are quite useful when choosing new or evaluating existing cloud services. Both ITIL and ISO 20000-1 place a heavy emphasis on ensuring that IT services always deliver business value, so these are some key areas/questions to consider for continual service improvement in cloud environments:

- Which type of cloud service model best meets your organization's needs? Has a vendor developed an SaaS platform that can reduce the resources your organization must expend to keep systems up and running?

- Are your users on the move? A more mobile workforce makes secure network design more challenging. Rather than a VPN from your main office to the cloud environment, you may need to provide secure cloud access to users anywhere in the world.

- Do the selected services meet your organization's compliance needs? Expansion into new markets might bring new privacy or security requirements, which will drive changes in the cloud services your organization is using.

- Are your SLA goals being met? SLA metrics should be tied to requirements for the system, and a cloud provider's inability to meet those requirements might necessitate a change of providers.

- Do new cloud services provide cost, time, or resource savings? For example, many cloud PaaS database offerings include automatic data replication and high availability, which removes the need for separate backup/recovery procedures and equipment. Rather than conduct BC/DR exercises yourself, your organization may rely on a provider's SOC 2 Type 2 audit report for assurance of resiliency.

Continual service improvement relies heavily on metrics to identify needed improvements and to measure the effectiveness of any changes implemented. For example, page load time for a web app might be a key metric. Choosing a new distributed cloud web hosting service that significantly reduces page loads delivers an improvement in the user experience for that web app.

Business Continuity and Disaster Recovery (BC/DR)

Business continuity and disaster recovery (BC/DR) has been addressed in other chapters of this book, relative to specific topics. Here, we cover some of the general aspects and approaches, with some additional focus on facility continuity.

There is no total agreement within our industry on the exact definitions of the terms *business continuity, disaster recovery, event,* or even simply *disaster* for that matter. For the purposes of this discussion and to create awareness of the (ISC)² perspective on the matter, I'll use the following explanations:

- *Business continuity efforts* are concerned with maintaining critical operations during any interruption in service, whereas *disaster recovery* efforts are focused on the resumption of operations after an interruption due to disaster. The two are related and in many organizations are rolled into one effort.

- An *event* is any unscheduled adverse impact to the operating environment. An event is distinguished from a *disaster* by the duration of impact. We consider an event's impact to last three days or less; a disaster's impact lasts longer. An event can become a disaster. Causes of either/both can be anthropogenic (caused by humans), natural forces, internal or external, malicious or accidental.

Because they can be so similar, I'll discuss BC/DR efforts together for most of the coverage of the topic and only make distinctions when needed.

Primary Focus

The paramount importance in BC/DR planning and efforts should be health and human safety, as in all security matters. There is no justification for prioritizing any asset to any degree higher than personnel, except in very, very limited cases. These are limited to organizations dealing with national security, and, even in those cases, are likewise limited to situations where human harm and loss of life might only be necessary to prevent greater losses (such as in the protection of assets that might result in vast devastation, such as nuclear, biological, or chemical products).

With that in mind, any BC/DR efforts should prioritize notification and evacuation as well as protection and egress.

Notification should take several redundant and differing forms to ensure widest and most thorough dissemination. Suggestions for possible notification avenues include telephone call tree rosters, website postings, and SMS blasts. Notification should include the organization's personnel, the public, and regulatory and response agencies, depending on who might be affected by the circumstance.

Evacuation, protection, and egress methods will depend on the particular physical layout of the campus and facility. Some aspects that are generally included in addressing these needs include the following:

Getting the People Out   There should be no obstruction or delay of personnel leaving the facility. All doors along the emergency path should fail safe (that is, they can be opened from the inside, allowing egress, even if they are still secure from the outside, preventing ingress). Sufficient lighting should be considered.

Getting the People Out Safely   Sprinkler systems along the egress route should be set to inundate the area and not be restricted due to other considerations (such as property damage). Non-water fire-suppression systems (such as gas) cannot risk human life and must have additional controls (for instance, a last-out switch, which prevents the gas from being released until the final person triggers it on the way out of the affected area). Communicate the emergency plans to all personnel, and train them in execution of the plan.

Designing for Protection   Other architectural, engineering, and local construction code concerns must meet local needs, such as facilities that are built to withstand and resist environment hazards (tornadoes in the Midwestern United States, flooding along the coasts, and so on).

Continuity of Operations

After we've seen to health and human safety concerns, our primary *business* focus should be continuity of critical operations.

To begin with, we have to determine what the organization's critical operations *are*. In a cloud data center, that will usually be dictated by the customer contracts and SLAs. This simplifies delineation of those elements necessary to support critical needs. Other extant sources can be extremely useful in this portion of the effort, most particularly the BIA, which informs us which assets would cause the greatest adverse impact if lost or interrupted. For instance, in a cloud data center, our main focus should be on connectivity, utilities, and processing capacity. These are, therefore, our critical operations. Other ancillary business functions, such as marketing, sales, finance, HR, and so on, might be wholly dismissed or greatly reduced without lasting impact to the organization and can be considered noncritical.

In formulating this inventory of critical assets, it is important to consider all elements that support critical functions, not limited to the hardware and tangible assets, but also specific personnel, software libraries, documentation, fundamental data, and so forth, without which we could not continue critical operations.

The BC/DR Plan

As with all plans, the BC/DR plan should be formalized in and derive from the organization's governance. Policy should dictate roles, terms of the plan, enforcement, and execution.

The plan should include both a general, exhaustive, detailed description of all aspects of BC/DR efforts and also limited, simple, straightforward procedures for enacting the plan and all response activities. Because the two categories of documentation differ so widely in content and purpose, they can often be included in the plan as appendices or attachments and referenced for the purpose of describing how and when each will be used (the detailed content for planning and after-action purposes; the simple procedures for use during the reaction to the event and disaster itself).

The plan should include the following:

A List of the Items from the Asset Inventory Deemed Critical   This should include necessary hardware, software, and media, including versioning data and applicable patches.

The Circumstances Under Which an Event or Disaster Is Declared   Response comes with a cost. It is important to distinguish normal administration functions from event or disaster response because the formal response will obligate resources and affect productivity. Careful attention and explanation should be made for balancing the risks and benefits of overreaction and underreaction in terms of response: too frequently, and productivity will needlessly be adversely affected; too rarely, and response activities may be hindered by delays for the sake of caution.

Who Is Authorized to Make the Declaration   An authority needs to be named (an individual, role, or office) for the purpose of formal declaration of an event or disaster. We want to avoid the possibility of overreaction by allowing just anyone to initiate a formal response (like an emergency brake line in public transit), and we want to ensure that initiation is instigated by someone who is informed, qualified, trained, and responsible for making such a determination.

An authorized party must also formally declare a cessation of BC/DR activity and resumption of normal operations. This should only be done when there is a high degree of assurance that all safety and health hazards have been abated and operating conditions and risks have returned to normal. Resuming standard operations too soon can exacerbate the existing event or disaster or cause a new one.

Essential Points of Contact   This should include the contact information of offices responsible for BC/DR activity and tasks as well as any external entities that may be involved (regulators, law enforcement, corporate authorities, press, vendors, customers, and so on). These should be as specific as possible to reduce difficulty in locating appropriate contacts during an actual response.

Detailed Actions, Tasks, and Activities   Checklists can be quite helpful for BC/DR procedures. Checklists serve several purposes. They describe the specific actions necessary, they can be aligned in order of execution, and they can constitute a record, after the activity is complete, of actions taken, by whom, and when (if each checklist step is annotated with the time and initials of the person completing the action as it occurs). Checklists also serve another fundamental requirement of BC/DR plans used during a response action: they allow for someone to conduct the appropriate actions, even if that person has not had specific training or experience with that plan in that organization. Of course, it is always preferable to have the personnel assigned to BC/DR roles trained and practiced in the specific plan, but, especially during disasters or events, the assigned personnel are not always available.

All these elements can be included by reference. That is, each piece can be split out as an attachment or appendix to the BC/DR policy proper. The basic elements of all policies (explanation and rationale for the policy, enforcement activities, relevant regulations, and so on) can make up the body of the policy, as it will be less subject to continual changing and updating.

Updating the BC/DR policy will be a continual process. Many of the listed elements, as you can see, will be in almost constant flux (the points of contact information, specific personnel assigned particular tasks, the list of the current state of critical assets), so the relevant parts of the plan (the specific appendices and attachments) need to receive updates from the offices that have the pertinent data. For instance, the current state of critical assets might be updated by the CMB, as part of the CM process. The CMB will be in the best position to know all the current versions of systems and components. Often, required CM updates can be detected during regular tests of the plan (see "Testing," later in this chapter).

The BC/DR Kit

There should be a container that holds all the necessary documentation and tools to conduct a proper BC/DR response action. This kit should be secure, durable, and compact. The container may be tangible or virtual. The contents might contain hard-copy versions of the appropriate documentation or electronic copies.

 I recommend that the BC/DR kit exist in both tangible hard-copy and virtual electronic versions, because I am paranoid by habit, nature, and trade.

The kit should have a duplicate in at least one other location, depending on the plan. If the plan calls for reconstitution of critical operations at an off-site location, there should be a mirrored kit in that location. Otherwise, having at least two identical kits on-site, in different locations, aids in reducing the consequences of one being unreachable and destroyed.

The kit should contain the following:

- A current copy of the plan, with all appendices and addenda

- Emergency and backup communication equipment. These can take whatever form suits the purpose, location, and nature of the organization: cell phones, handheld radios, laptop with satellite modem, and so on.

- Copies of all appropriate network and infrastructure diagrams and architecture

- Copies of all requisite software for creating a clean build of the critical systems, if necessary, with media containing appropriate updates and patches for current versioning

- Emergency contact information (not already included in the plan). This might include a full notification list.

- Documentation tools and equipment. Again, these can take many forms: pens and paper, laptop and portable printer, voice recorder, and so on.

- A small amount of emergency essentials (flashlight, water, rations, and so on)

- Fresh batteries sufficient for operating all powered equipment in the kit for at least 24 hours

Obviously, keeping the kit stocked and current requires a level of effort similar to that of maintaining the plan itself (and includes the plan itself, as it is updated).

Relocation

Depending on the nature of the event and disaster and the specifics of the plan, the organization may choose to evacuate and relocate those personnel involved in critical operations to a specified alternate operating location. Prior to the existence of cloud capabilities for the purpose of backing up and restoring data at a secure, off-site location, hot and warm and cold sites were used for this purpose, and a skeleton crew of critical personnel were assigned to travel to the recovery site for the duration of the contingency operations and recovery.

With the advent of ubiquitous availability of cloud backup resources, the relocation site can be anywhere not affected by the event and disaster, as long as it has sufficient facilities for housing the personnel involved and bandwidth sufficient for the purpose. For instance, a hotel outside the area of effect could serve the purpose if it offers broadband capabilities and is additionally useful in that it also fulfills the function of safe lodging for the critical personnel.

If the organization considers relocation for BC/DR purposes, the plan might include these aspects:

- Tasking and activities should include representatives from the HR and finance department, as travel arrangements and payments will be necessary for all personnel involved in the relocation.

- Sufficient support should be provided for relocating dependents and family members of the personnel involved in critical operations for the duration of the response. When a disaster affects a locality, everyone involved will rightfully be concerned with their loved ones first and foremost. If this concern is not alleviated, their morale and focus on the tasks at hand will be diminished. It is better to assume the additional costs related to this option so as to gain the full attention of the personnel involved in the response.

- The distance of the relocation is, like all things related to the practice of security, a balance. You want the relocation site to be far enough away that it is not affected by whatever caused the interruption to standard operations but not so far that the hazard, risk, delay, and expense of travel makes its utility unappealing or infeasible.

- Joint operating agreements and memoranda of understanding can be used to establish cost-effective relocation sites at facilities belonging to other operations in the local area if the event or disaster only affects your organization's campus (in the event of highly localized events and disasters, such as a building fire).

BC/DR Terminology

There are several BC/DR concepts that you need to understand:

MAD (Maximum Allowable Downtime)   How long it would take for an interruption in service to kill an organization, measured in time. For instance, if a company would fail because it had to halt operations for a week, then its MAD is one week. This is also sometimes referred to as maximum tolerable downtime (MTD). Related to this is the mean time to repair (MTTR), which is the average amount of time it takes to repair a damaged system or device that is down.

RTO (Recovery Time Objective)   The BC/DR goal for recovery of operational capability after an interruption in service, measured in time. This does not have to include full operations (recovery); the capability can be limited to critical functions for the duration of the contingency event. The RTO *must* be less than the MAD. For example, a company might have an MAD of one week, while the company's BC/DR plan includes and supports an RTO of six days.

RPO (Recovery Point Objective)   The BC/DR goal for limiting the loss of data from an unplanned event. Confusingly, this is often measured in time. For instance, if an organization is doing full backups every day and is affected by some sort of disaster, that organization's BC/DR plan might include a goal of resuming critical operations at an alternate operating site with the last full backup, which would be an RPO of 24 hours. The recovery point objective for that organization would be the loss of no more than one day's worth of data.

ALE (Annual Loss Expectancy)   Annual loss expectancy (ALE) describes the amount an organization should expect to lose on an annual basis due to any one type of incident. ALE is calculated by multiplying the annual rate of occurrence (ARO) by the single loss expectancy (SLE). The annual rate of occurrence (ARO) is the rate of occurrence of a specific event or security incident one could expect in any given 12-month period. A single loss expectancy (SLE) is the amount of expected damage or loss from any single specific security incident.

Power

Interruptions to the normal power supply often result from events or disasters (or are themselves a reason to declare an event or disaster), so BC/DR plans and activities must take emergency power supply into account.

Near-term emergency power usually takes the form of battery backups, often as uninterruptible power supply (UPS) systems. These can be small units, feeding only particular individual devices or racks, or they can be large, supplying power to entire systems. Failover for these should be close to immediate, with appropriate line conditioning so that transitioning from utility power to UPS does not adversely affect the powered devices in any way. The line conditioner function in UPS often serves as an additional component of normal operations, dampening surges and dips in utility power automatically.

If you ever see an exam question about the expected duration of UPS power, the answer will be, "UPS should last long enough for graceful shutdown of affected systems." Battery backup should only be relied on to provide immediate and near-term power supply. Any power interruption for a longer period should be provided by other systems, such as generators.

Short-term contingency power can be provided by generators. For the cloud data center, sufficient generator power is necessary for all critical systems and infrastructure, including HVAC and emergency lighting as well as fire suppression systems. For the higher-tier centers, redundant power is necessary, duplicating the minimum power required to ensure uninterrupted critical operations.

Generators that supply close to immediate power when utility electricity is interrupted have automatic transfer switches. Transfer switches sense when the utility provision fails, break the connection to the utility, start the generator, and provide generator power to the facility. An automatic transfer switch is *not* a viable replacement for a UPS, and the two should be used in conjunction, not in lieu of each other. Ideally, the generator and transfer switch should be rated to successfully provide sufficient power well within the duration of expected battery life of the UPS. Realistically, generators with transfer switches can be expected to provide power in less than a minute from loss of utility power.

Generators need fuel; this is usually gasoline, diesel, natural gas, or propane. Appropriate storage, supply, and maintenance of fuel should also be described and included in the BC/DR plan. As fuel is flammable, health and human safety concerns must be addressed in the storage and supply designs. For all data centers, the Uptime Institute recommends that a minimum of at least 12 hours of fuel for all generators, powering all critical functions, be available. Resupply of additional fuel should be scheduled and performed within those 12 hours. Supply contracts and appropriate notification information for the supplier should be included in the BC/DR plan and procedure checklists. For BC/DR purposes, the plan should anticipate at least 72 hours of generator operation before other alternatives are available.

Gasoline and diesel spoil, even with conditioning treatments that extend useful fuel life. If your generators use these types of fuel, the plan must also include tasking and contracts for regular resupply and refresh within the spoilage period. Some fuels, such as propane, do not spoil; you may want to consider these when considering backup power alternatives.

All fuel storage should be in secure containers and locations. Fuel and generators should be far removed from the path of vehicles, ideally outside normal traffic areas (with a provision made for secure vehicle access for resupply purposes).

Testing

Much like having backups without trying to restore, or having logs without doing log review and analysis, having a BC/DR plan is close to useless unless it is tested on a regular basis. Because testing the BC/DR will necessarily cause interruption to production, different forms of testing can be utilized for different purposes, adjusting the operational impact while achieving specific goals. You should be familiar with the following testing methods:

Tabletop Testing   The essential participants (those who will take part in actual BC/DR activities and are formally tasked with such responsibilities) work together at a scheduled time (either together in a single room or remotely via some communication capability) to describe how they would perform their tasks in a given BC/DR scenario. This is the InfoSec equivalent of role-playing games, and it has the least impact on production of the testing alternatives.

Dry Run   The organization as a whole takes part in a scenario at a scheduled time, describing their responses during the test and performing some minimal actions (for instance, perhaps running the notification call tree to ensure all contact information is current) but without performing all the actual tasks. This has more impact on productivity than tabletop testing.

Full Test   The entire organization takes part in an unscheduled, unannounced practice scenario, performing their full BC/DR activities. As this could include system failover and facility evacuation, this test is the most useful for detecting shortcomings in the plan, but it has the greatest impact (to the extent it can cause a full, genuine interruption of service) on productivity.

In all forms of testing, it behooves the organization to use moderators. These personnel will act as guides and monitors of the response activity, provide scenario inputs to heighten realism and introduce some element of chaos (to simulate unplanned deviations from the procedures due to potential effects of the event and disaster), and document performance and any plan shortcomings. The moderators should not be tasked with BC/DR response activities for actual situations. Anyone with formal tasking should be a participant in the test. It might be useful to employ external consultants to serve as moderators so that all organizational personnel can take part in the exercise.

Summary

In this chapter, we've reviewed several essential elements of operations management for cloud data centers. We discussed the importance of monitoring system and component performance, performing routine maintenance (to include patching), and certain risks and benefits associated with each. Issues related to environmental conditions such as temperature, humidity, and backup power supply were included. I also detailed specific approaches and methods for BC/DR planning and testing.

Exam Essentials

Understand systems and component monitoring.   Make sure you are familiar with the importance and purpose of monitoring aspects of all infrastructure, hardware, software, and media in the data center, including:

- Temperature
- Humidity
- Event logging

Have a thorough understanding of maintenance strategies and procedures.   These strategies and procedures include maintenance mode versus normal operations, the process for conducting updates and upgrades, and the risks and benefits of manual versus automated patch management.

Know the purpose and general method of change management.   Know the purpose and general method of CM. Understand the composition of the CMB and how it functions.

Understand all aspects of BC/DR strategy, planning, and testing.   Focus on the BC/DR strategy, planning, and testing especially as it pertains to a cloud data center. Know about backup power considerations and methods for testing BC/DR plan efficacy.

Written Labs

You can find the answers to the written labs in Appendix A.

1. Do a web search for power generators suitable for commercial use. Find at least three.

2. Using the ASHRAE standards, determine the suitability of each generator for a cloud data center operating modern IT equipment. The specific load and capacity of the data center can be of your own choosing. Be sure to state any assumptions and simulated input.

3. In a short paper (less than one page), compare and contrast the three generators that you found in your first lab question. Include in your rationale (as a minimum) load capacity, price, and fuel consumption.

Review Questions

You can find the answers in Appendix B.

1. Which form of BC/DR testing has the *most* impact on operations?

    A. Tabletop

    B. Dry run

    C. Full test

    D. Structured test

2. Which form of BC/DR testing has the *least* impact on operations?

    A. Tabletop

    B. Dry run

    C. Full test

    D. Structured test

3. Which characteristic of liquid propane increases its desirability as a fuel for backup generators?

    A. Burn rate

    B. Price

    C. Does not spoil

    D. Flavor

4. How often should the CMB meet?

    A. Whenever regulations dictate

    B. Often enough to address organizational needs and reduce frustration with delay

    C. Every week

    D. Annually

5. Adhering to ASHRAE standards for humidity can reduce the possibility of _____.

    A. Breach

    B. Static discharge

    C. Theft

    D. Inversion

6. A UPS should have enough power to last how long?

    A. 12 hours

    B. 10 minutes

    C. One day

    D. Long enough for graceful shutdown

7. A generator transfer switch should bring backup power online within what timeframe?

   A. 10 seconds

   B. Before the recovery point objective is reached

   C. Before the UPS duration is exceeded

   D. Three days

8. Which characteristic of automated patching makes it attractive?

   A. Cost

   B. Speed

   C. Noise reduction

   D. Capability to recognize problems quickly

9. Which tool can reduce confusion and misunderstanding during a BC/DR response?

   A. Flashlight

   B. Controls matrix

   C. Checklist

   D. Call tree

10. When deciding whether to apply specific updates, it is best to follow _____ in order to demonstrate due care.

   A. Regulations

   B. Vendor guidance

   C. Internal policy

   D. Competitors' actions

11. The CMB should include representations from all of the following offices except: _____.

   A. Regulators

   B. IT department

   C. Security office

   D. Management

12. For performance purposes, OS monitoring should include all of the following except _____.

   A. Disk space

   B. Disk I/O usage

   C. CPU usage

   D. Print spooling

13. Maintenance mode requires all of these actions except_____.

    A. Remove all active production instances

    B. Initiate enhanced security controls

    C. Prevent new logins

    D. Ensure logging continues

14. What is one of the reasons a baseline might be changed?

    A. Numerous change requests

    B. Power fluctuation

    C. To reduce redundancy

    D. Natural disaster

15. In addition to battery backup, a UPS can offer which capability?

    A. Communication redundancy

    B. Line conditioning

    C. Breach alert

    D. Confidentiality

16. Deviations from the baseline should be investigated and _____.

    A. Documented

    B. Enforced

    C. Revealed

    D. Encouraged

17. The baseline should cover which of the following?

    A. As many systems throughout the organization as possible

    B. Data breach alerting and reporting

    C. A process for version control

    D. All regulatory compliance requirements

18. A localized incident or disaster can be addressed in a cost-effective manner by using which of the following?

    A. UPS

    B. Generators

    C. Joint operating agreements

    D. Strict adherence to applicable regulations

19. Generator fuel storage for a cloud data center should last for how long, at a minimum?

   A. 10 minutes

   B. Three days

   C. Indefinitely

   D. 12 hours

20. The BC/DR kit should include all of the following except_____.

   A. Flashlight

   B. Documentation equipment

   C. Fuel for the backup generators

   D. Annotated asset inventory

Chapter
10

Legal and Compliance Part 1

THE OBJECTIVE OF THIS CHAPTER IS TO ACQUAINT THE READER WITH THE FOLLOWING CONCEPTS:

Domain 6, Legal, Risk, and Compliance can be every bit as confusing and difficult to understand as some of the technology discussed throughout this book. International courts and tribunals weigh in on laws and regulations concerning global networking. There is also no shortage of laws, regulations, and standards that require compliance. The combination of all these factors provides a rich arena for discussion.

It is important to remember that the nature of cloud computing lends itself to resource sharing based on demand as opposed to location. Therefore, data centers located around the world store cloud data and run applications from multiple sources simultaneously. This presents challenges with security and privacy issues due to the complexity of local and international laws, regulations, and guidelines. In this chapter, I will attempt to provide a background and review of the important concepts, laws, regulations, and standards so that the CCSP candidate can provide sound advice and guidance when navigating these complex waters.

Legal Requirements and Unique Risks in the Cloud Environment

As one might imagine, the list of US and international laws, regulations, and standards is quite lengthy and complex. The global economy spans multiple continents, many nation-states, and government entities. From the Asia-Pacific region to Australia and New Zealand, the European Union (EU), Eastern Bloc countries, and South America, a wide range of laws, regulations, and rules govern both data privacy and security safeguards. In the following sections, we will begin by exploring some fundamental legal concepts to help the CCSP candidate prepare for working in this complex global environment. To make matters even more concerning, there is no shortage of change and uncertainty.

Legal Concepts

Let's begin our discussion with some basic legal concepts that can be applied both in the United States and internationally. These terms form the foundation of knowledge that allows us to operate cloud activities across international borders with some semblance of consistency and fairness. We'll use US law as a template, but with the caveat that other legal systems may take very different approaches to similar concepts.

There are three general bodies of law in the United States: criminal law, civil law, and administrative law. There is another specific specialized body of law, unique to the military, known as the Uniform Code of Military Justice (UCMJ). If your organization is not involved directly in military work, the UCMJ does not usually affect you, so we won't dwell on that topic, but we'll address the other three. We're also going to examine the concept of intellectual property and the legal protections available for owners of this type of asset.

Criminal Law

Criminal law involves all legal matters where the government is in conflict with any person, group, or organization that violates statutes. Statutes (state and federal) are legislated by lawmakers. They are rules that define conduct prohibited by the government and are designed to provide for the safety and well-being of the public. One example is traffic laws, which when broken result in court appearances, fines, and so on. Other more obvious examples are laws involving robbery, theft, and murder.

Criminal law includes the federal court system and the various state courts. Under criminal law, punishments can include monetary fines, imprisonment, and even death. Enforcement of criminal law is called prosecution. Only the government can conduct law enforcement activity and prosecutions.

For the security practitioner, it is important to keep in mind that privacy violations around the world are in some cases seen as criminal violations. For instance, if certain privacy standards and procedures are not adequately followed—say, in the EU—you can be prosecuted for criminal violations, in addition to whatever damages result from the data breach.

State Laws

State laws are those that we typically think of on a day-to-day basis. Speed limits, state tax laws, the criminal code, and so on are all examples of laws enacted by a state legislature as opposed to those enacted at the national or federal level. Federal laws, however, often supersede state laws, particularly regarding the nature of interstate commerce. For instance, while many states have laws outlining how electronic medical records should be handled, federal legislation is usually more comprehensive and therefore followed. In some cases, such as California, the state law may in fact be more stringent, in which case it is followed.

The United States is divided into 50 member entities that are referred to as *states*, each with its own jurisdictional sovereignty, legislature, and regulatory bodies. Outside of the United States, most other countries use the word *state* as a synonym for *country*, and their member entities are known as *counties*, *jurisdictions*, *zones*, or a variety of other terms. It is important to keep this distinction in mind regarding the meaning of the word *state* when dealing with multiple nations. In the United States alone, there are over 300 various jurisdictions, each with its own capacity for making and enforcing laws or regulations.

Federal Laws

Unlike state laws, federal laws affect the entire country. Generally, issues of jurisdiction and subsequent prosecution are negotiated between law enforcement and courts prior to prosecution of a particular case.

 As of 2005, the US Department of Justice clarified that anyone who "knowingly" violates HIPAA regulations can face fines but also up to one year in jail. Although not a testing requirement, it may be interesting for you to know that the Final Omnibus Rule of March 2013 states that a Tier 3 criminal violation carries a potential 10-year imprisonment penalty. Specifically, it states "if the offense is committed with intent to sell, transfer, or use individually identifiable health information for commercial advantage, personal gain, or malicious harm, be fined not more than $250,000, imprisoned not more than 10 years, or both." See www.law.cornell.edu/uscode/text/42/1320d-6.

Civil Law

Civil law is the body of law, statutes, and so on that deals with personal and community-based law such as marriage and divorce. It is the set of rules that govern private citizens and their disputes. As opposed to criminal law, the parties involved in civil law matters are strictly private entities, including individuals, groups, and organizations.

Typical examples of civil law cases are disputes (in the United States) over property boundaries, contracts, mineral rights, and divorce. Civil cases are called lawsuits or litigation. Punitive measures for civil cases can include restitution of monetary damages or requirement to perform actions (usually in response to a breach-of-contract case, which we'll address later), but not imprisonment or death.

Contracts

A contract is an agreement between parties to engage in some specified activity, usually for mutual benefit. The contract between the cloud customer and cloud provider is a perfect example: in that contract, the cloud customer agrees to give the cloud provider money, and in exchange, the cloud provider agrees to give the cloud customer some services. The contract often includes a finite duration for which the contract is in effect, a list of parties involved, the means for dispute resolution, and the jurisdiction of the contract (a physical place or government, such as "the state of Wisconsin," or "the city of Milwaukee, in the state of Wisconsin, in the United States").

Disputes arise from failure to perform according to activity specified in the contract, which is called a *breach*. In the event of a breach, a party to the contract can sue the others in order to get court-ordered relief in the form of money or other considerations (such as property, or the court forcing the breaching party to perform the activity that both parties agreed to in the first place).

Contract law applies to contractual items the CCSP candidate should be familiar with, such as the following items:

▪ Service-level agreements (SLAs)

▪ Payment Card Industry Data Security Standards (PCI DSS) contracts

A CCSP should be prepared to deal with these types of contracts in a cloud environment and/or with cloud customers. Furthermore, it is important to understand the distinctions regarding consequences and ramifications for violations of such contracts.

> *Common law* is the existing set of rulings and decisions made by courts, informed by cultural mores and legislation. These create *precedents*, which each party will cite in court as a means to sway the court to their own side of a case. In some jurisdictions, the use of precedents is not allowed; the facts and circumstances of each case stand on their own.

Administrative Law

The other body of law is administrative law—laws not created by legislatures but by executive decision and function. Many federal agencies can create, monitor, and enforce their own administrative law. These agencies have their own lawmaking departments, law enforcement personnel, courts, and judges that belong exclusively to them. For instance, federal tax law is administered by the IRS, which creates those laws, investigates and enforces them with IRS agents, and decides outcomes in cases tried by lawyers and adjudicated by judges both in the employ of the IRS.

US Laws

I will now describe and discuss US laws with the largest impact on cloud computing and with which the CCSP should be familiar. While there are emerging state laws that are more stringent and restrictive than federal laws within their jurisdictions, we will focus on US federal laws as they apply to cloud computing. Table 10.1 gives an overview of the most prominent US laws and regulations.

TABLE 10.1 Important US laws and regulations

Name	Purpose	Administrators	Enforcers
The Electronic Communication Privacy Act (ECPA)	Enhance laws restricting the government from putting wiretaps on phone calls, updating them to include electronic communication in the form of data.	*	*

Name	Purpose	Administrators	Enforcers
Graham-Leach-Bliley Act (GLBA)	Allow banks to merge with and own insurance companies. Included in the law were stipulations that customer account information be kept secure and private and that customers be allowed to opt out of any information-sharing arrangements the bank or insurer might engage in.	FDIC, FFIEC	FDIC and DFI
Sarbanes–Oxley Act (SOX)	Increase transparency into publicly traded corporations' financial activities. Includes provisions for securing data and expressly names the traits of confidentiality, integrity, and availability.	SEC	SEC
Health Insurance Portability and Accountability Act (HIPAA)	Protect patient records and data, known as electronic protected health information (ePHI).	DHHS	OCR
Family Educational Rights and Privacy Act (FERPA)	Prevent academic institutions from sharing student data with anyone other than parents of students (up to age 18) or the students (after age 18).	Department of Education	Department of Education (Family Policy Compliance Office)
The Digital Millennium Copyright Act (DMCA)	Update copyright provisions to protect owned data in an Internet-enabled world. Makes cracking of access controls on copyrighted media a crime, and enables copyright holders to require any site on the Internet to remove content that may belong to the copyright holder.	**	**
Clarifying Lawful Overseas Use of Data (CLOUD Act)	Allows US law enforcement and courts to compel American companies to disclose data stored in foreign data centers; designed specifically for cloud computing situations (hence the name).	US federal courts	US federal law enforcement agencies

*The ECPA (and its subordinate parts, including the SCA) prevents the government from surveilling civilians. Ostensibly, the government would also be the entity enforcing and administering this law, and government law enforcement agencies would be the entities most likely to violate the law in the course of their activities. The reader can readily see the issues that might arise from this circular construct.

**The DMCA allows for aggrieved parties to bring civil suits to protect their interests, but it also has a provision that criminalizes a successful breach of access controls on copyrighted material.

You may not have to have a detailed knowledge of each of these laws and regulations, but you should be able to easily identify them and give a brief explanation of what they are about and where they fit into the realm of cloud computing. This chapter will not explore ECPA, FERPA, and DMCA in more detail, but the following sections will take a closer look at HIPAA, GLBA, and SOX.

FedRAMP

Although it isn't a law, it is helpful for you to know about FedRAMP. FedRAMP is a US federal program that mandates a standardized approach to security assessments, authorization, and continuous monitoring of cloud products and services. FedRAMP certification can be quite costly and difficult to achieve but is required for cloud hosting services provided to a US government agency or contractor.

Health Insurance Portability and Accountability Act of 1996 (HIPAA)

The federal Health Insurance Portability and Accountability Act (HIPAA), enacted in 1996, is a set of federal laws governing the handling of electronic protected health information (ePHI). The stated purpose of the law when it was enacted was to make it easier for patients to access their own medical data and move it between medical providers. However, after a decade of changes, it is more about the adoption of national standards for electronic medical transactions and national identifiers for providers, medical insurers, and employers. ePHI can be stored and processed in the cloud but must have adequate security and privacy protections in place.

The Office for Civil Rights (OCR) is the federal enforcement arm of the Department of Health and Human Services (DHHS). They conduct audits, or subcontract to other third-party companies to perform such audits, and are responsible for reporting to DHHS any negative audit findings, policy violations, unreported breaches, and related questionable activity. DHHS then has the authority to impose fines, restrictions, or remedial requirements based on OCR findings.

HIPAA, the Privacy Rule, and the Security Rule

When HIPAA first passed in the 1990s, privacy of patient information was the primary concern. The Internet was still in its infancy and no one had even thought of a data breach of PHI, because it had never happened. The first primary regulation promulgated by the Department of Health and Human Services (DHHS) was the Privacy Rule. It contained language specific to maintaining the privacy of patient information as it was traditionally stored and used, on paper. It was also one of the first regulations in the United States to specifically address privacy.

With the explosion of networking, digital storage, and the Internet came the Security Rule and the Breach Notification Rule, followed by the Health Information Technology for Economic and Clinical Health (HITECH) Act of 2009, which provided financial incentives for medical practices and hospitals to convert paper recordkeeping systems to digital formats. Because data breaches began to happen more and more often, this was an attempt to address issues surrounding this explosion in electronic digital storage of medical information while cloud computing was still in its infancy.

The Security Rule has attempted to address the problems encountered with this explosion of digital patient and medical records information processing and storage. As a result, there are now both a Privacy Rule and a Security Rule associated with HIPAA. For more information, see www.hhs.gov/hipaa/for-professionals.

Gramm-Leach-Bliley Act (GLBA)

The Gramm-Leach-Bliley Act (GLBA), also known as the Financial Services Modernization Act of 1999, was created to allow banks and financial institutions to merge. Lawmakers were wary of customer concerns that this type of consolidation might detract from individual privacy, so GLBA also includes a great many provisions specifying the kinds of protections and controls that financial institutions are required to use for securing customers' account information. For example, it requires all financial institutions to have a written information security plan, and later revisions require that an information security officer be named and given adequate resources in order to implement the plan.

For more information on GLBA, visit www.fdic.gov/regulations/compliance/manual/8/VIII-1.1.pdf.

Sarbanes–Oxley Act (SOX)

At the latter part of the last century, a number of large companies experienced total and unexpected financial collapse because of fraudulent accounting practices, poor audit practices, inadequate financial controls, and poor oversight by governing boards of directors. Some of the companies involved are now a distant memory (Enron, WorldCom, and Adelphia, for example). As a result, in 2002 the Sarbanes–Oxley Act (SOX) was enacted as an attempt to prevent these kinds of poor practices and fraudulent activities from occurring in the future. It applies to all publicly traded corporations in the United States.

The Securities and Exchange Commission (SEC) is the organization responsible for establishing SOX standards and guidelines and conducting audits and imposing subsequent fines should any be required.

If you are interested in learning more about the Sarbanes-Oxley Act, visit www.sec.gov/about/laws/soa2002.pdf.

International Laws

International laws determine how to settle disputes and manage relationships between countries. These include the following:

- Conventions establishing rules expressly recognized by member countries (like the Geneva Convention regarding laws of armed conflict)

- Customs as they are practiced in a country and accepted as law

- General principles of law recognized by civilized nations (such as the right to a trial of some kind if accused)

- Judicial decisions or precedent as it has developed over time in a particular instance

- Trade regulations, including import agreements, tariff structures, and so forth

- Treaties, which can be created to solve a dispute (such as a war) or to create alliances

Laws, Frameworks, and Standards Around the World

Sovereign countries also have their own laws, applicable to their own jurisdictions. The *jurisdiction* is the land and people subject to a specific court or courts. The effects of a country's laws does not cease at its borders, though. If a citizen from another country, or even one of the country's citizens operating outside that country, breaks that country's law, they can still be subject to prosecution and punishment by that country. For instance, a hacker that uses the Internet to attack a target in another country could be subject to that country's computer security laws. The hacker might be extradited (forcibly apprehended in their own country and transported to the country where the law was broken) to face trial. Because there is no global uniformity in how these laws are written and applied, the practitioner is strongly advised to consult with counsel whenever legal matters arise.

It's important to understand the distinctions of laws and principles of various nations because cloud providers and customers might be operating in many different jurisdictions. The cloud is not limited to the borders of any given country.

While many of the legal definitions and principles in the United States apply to other parts of the world, there are some significant differences. The European Union (EU) has for many years taken a much stronger stance on privacy than the United States. In fact, the EU treats personal privacy protections for data in electronic form as a human right, while the United States has no formal, unified personal privacy law. Instead, the United States has certain laws (discussed in the previous sections) that deal with personal privacy for people who engage in activities in specific industries and sectors, such as financial services, medical care, education, and so forth. The EU, on the other hand, is well known for its "opt-in" policies versus the "opt-out" arrangement in the United States. This means that in the EU, generally speaking, in order for someone to access or use an individual's personal data or private information, that individual must first grant their permission, effectively opting in to that specific instance of sharing information. In the United States, the usual statutory model is just the opposite, wherein individuals must notify any party that the individual has shared information with that the data cannot thereafter be shared outside the limits of that initial agreement.

To clarify, let's use the example of a bank account. When a person goes to the bank and opens an account, the bank asks for a set of personal information, such as the person's name, Social Security number, home address, and so on. The person is granting the bank access to that information voluntarily, sharing it with the bank in order to get a bank account. In the United States, the bank is then required (by GLBA) to ask the person if they want to opt out of any additional information-sharing activity. If the person doesn't want the bank to share that data with any other entity (for instance, the bank might sell that information to other businesses), the person must give the bank a written statement declaring that they are opting out. If the person does not opt out, then the bank is free to share that information however they see fit. GLBA requires that the bank ask the person, in writing, in hard copy, if they want to opt out of any data-sharing activity, at least once a year for every year that bank account stays open. In the EU, on the other hand, if a person were to open a bank account, the bank must ask the person if the person would allow the bank to share the person's personal data with any other entity. The bank would not be allowed, by law, to share any of that person's data until and unless the person grants explicit permission to the bank to do so.

Another important concept to consider in dealing with various countries is their approaches to PII. Information that can be used to identify an individual is often referred to in the industry as *personally identifiable information* (PII). It can include the name and address of the individual. In the EU, PII also includes a person's mobile phone number, IP address, and other elements. Although people often voluntarily disclose their PII to a variety of entities, this is done with the expectation that those entities will handle and protect their PII in accordance with their respective countries' regulations. In the EU, the EU GDPR regulates distribution of PII. Many countries use the GDPR as a basic model for their own laws. Table 10.2 provides an overview of various countries and how their laws relate to the GDPR.

TABLE 10.2 Countries and their laws relating to the EU Data Directive and Privacy Regulation

Nation	Federal PII law that complies with the EU Privacy Regulation	Notes
The EU	Yes	The EU comprises 27 member states (countries). The EU treats PII as a human right, with severely stringent protections for individuals.
United States	No	Personal privacy rights are often delineated in industry- and state-specific laws (such as GLBA for financial services and HIPAA for medicine), but there is no overarching federal law ensuring individual personal privacy.

TABLE 10.2   Countries and their laws relating to the EU Data Directive and Privacy Regulation *(continued)*

Nation	Federal PII law that complies with the EU Privacy Regulation	Notes
Australia and New Zealand	Yes	Laws in these countries conform to the EU policies.
Argentina	Yes	Local law is specifically based on the EU guidance.
EFTA	Yes	A four-member body that includes Switzerland, Norway, Iceland, and Lichtenstein. Swiss law, in particular, provides stringent privacy protections, particularly for banking information.
Israel	Yes	
Japan	Yes	
Canada	Yes	The Personal Information Protection and Electronic Documents Act (PIPEDA) conforms to the EU Privacy Regulation.

Israel and Japan won't be discussed in more detail in this chapter, but for exam purposes it is important to remember that they also have personal privacy laws that are accepted by the EU for purposes of compliance with the Privacy Regulation.

The following sections sample some laws in various nations that have developed in response to privacy and data security concerns over the past 30 years. This should give the CCSP candidate a broader view of how the world perceives privacy and in particular some of the legal, regulatory, and operational challenges that come with working in a global environment.

EU General Data Protection Regulation

The EU General Data Protection Regulation (GDPR) is probably the most significant, powerful personal privacy law in the world. This overarching regulation describes the appropriate handling of personal and private information of all EU citizens. Any entity (be it a government agency, private company, or individual) gathering the PII of any citizen of the EU is subject to the GDPR.

The GDPR addresses individual personal privacy by codifying these seven principles:

Notice   The individual must be informed that personal information about them is being gathered or created.

Choice   Every individual can choose whether to disclose their personal information. No entity can gather or create personal information about an individual without that individual's explicit agreement.

Purpose   The individual must be told the specific use the information will be put to. This includes whether the data will be shared with any other entity.

Access   The individual is allowed to get copies of any of their own information held by any entity.

Integrity   The individual must be allowed to correct any of their own information if it is inaccurate.

Security   Any entity holding an individual's personal information is responsible for protecting that information and is ultimately liable for any unauthorized disclosure of that data.

Enforcement   All entities that have any personal data of any EU citizen understand that they are subject to enforcement actions by EU authorities.

This list largely conforms to a set of principles created by the Organisation for Economic Cooperation and Development (OECD). The OECD is a standards organization made up of representatives from many countries, and it publishes policy suggestions. Its standards are *not* legally binding and do not have the effect of a treaty or other law.

> This is an important distinction to be made: although the OECD's principles are not legally binding, the EU's GDPR, which largely conforms to the OECD's principles, *is* legally binding.

In addition to these principles, the GDPR also resulted in a principle unique to the EU: the "right to be forgotten." Under this principle, any individual can notify any entity that has PII for that individual and instruct that entity to delete and destroy all of that individual's PII in that entity's control. This is a very serious and powerful individual right, and compliance can be extremely difficult. Google disputed this principle when it was first proposed, claiming that the company would find it almost impossible to comply. The European Union High Court decided in favor of the right to be forgotten and against Google, and Google had to choose to accept compliance in order to operate in the EU.

Another major provision of the GDPR was to prohibit any entity from collecting the PII of any EU citizen if that entity existed within the jurisdiction of a country that did not have a national law that explicitly supported all the provisions of the GDPR. This meant, for instance, that any company in the United States would not be allowed to do business with EU citizens. The United States does not have a federal law that directly maps to the GDPR.

The Europeans have a dim view of the ability of the United States to ensure the privacy of individuals. The GDPR is a direct reflection of this attitude. And, in all fairness, the Europeans seem quite justified in their opinion, as the US government has proven over a considerable period of time to be willing to collect information on all individuals (including citizens of the United States) without warrants or other legal justification. So the GDPR can be seen as a law that expressly limits US companies.

To allow some US-based companies to operate legitimately inside the EU, the EU created privacy rules designed to outline what American companies must do in order to comply with EU laws. These rules outlined the proper handling of storage and transmission of private information belonging to EU citizens. The program for American compliance with GDPR is called Privacy Shield in the United States.

The Privacy Shield provisions are as follows:

- Any US company that wants to collect EU citizen data must voluntarily agree to comply with the GDPR.

- These companies have to sign up with a federal enforcement entity in the United States that administers the program. For most companies, the Privacy Shield program is administered by the Department of Commerce (DoC). For airlines and shipping companies, the program is administered by the Department of Transportation (DoT).

- The companies have to agree to allow auditing and enforcement by the program administrators. For the DoC, the enforcement arm is the Federal Trade Commission (FTC), and the DoT enforced its own program. Enforcement can include fines assessed for violations.

For more information about Privacy Shield, see www.privacyshield.gov/welcome.

There is one final method that American companies can use if they want to have EU citizen PII and if they don't want to subscribe to Privacy Shield. They can create internal policies called *binding corporate rules* and *standard contractual clauses* that explicitly state full compliance with the GDPR. In this way, the company that chooses to use this method is basically stating their full agreement to be governed by the applicable EU laws. If a company chooses to use this method, however, it must first approach every individual EU country where the company wants to operate and have the government office responsible for oversight and enforcement of the GDPR accept and approve the company's policy.

The GDPR defines roles for entities involved in the collection and creation of PII. It is important for the CCSP candidate to be familiar with these roles and how they apply to the relationship between cloud customers and providers.

Data Subject   The individual to whom the PII refers. A specific human being.

Data Controller   Any entity collecting or creating PII. In the cloud, the data controller is the cloud customer.

Data Processor   Any entity acting on behalf or at the behest of the data controller, performing any manipulation, storage, or transmission of the PII. In the cloud, the data processor is the cloud service provider.

Under the GDPR, the data controller is ultimately responsible for *any* unauthorized disclosure of PII. That includes any malicious or negligent act on the part of the data processor. This is an extremely important point to understand. Legally, the data controller is responsible for all breaches, regardless of fault.

To put this in perspective, let's say a cloud provider, Ostrich Corporation, has two customers, Acme, Inc., and Bravo, LLC, who are competitors. An administrator at Ostrich knowingly and willingly takes some Acme privacy data and sells it to Bravo. For purposes of liability under privacy laws, Acme would *still* be responsible for the breach, even though Acme did nothing wrong. Acme might eventually be able to recover damages from Ostrich (and maybe Bravo) in a civil suit, but the legal liability for the privacy data breach, including any initial legal costs for settling the breach, would be Acme's. Note that this is just for exposure under privacy laws; Ostrich and Bravo might still be prosecuted for the theft of the data, which is a crime.

 Under the GDPR, PII is not limited to electronic data. It also covers any data stored in hard-copy form.

Australian Privacy Act of 1988

The Australian Privacy Act regulates the handling of personal information. It includes details regarding the collection, use, storage, disclosure, access to, and correction of personal information. It consists of fundamental privacy principles covering such issues as these:

- Transparency in the handling of personal information
- The rules on collecting information from solicitation
- Correctness and integrity of collected data

As you can see from the enactment date, Australia has been very proactive in the area of personal privacy rights for decades. It has also become host to a number of global cloud providers, making this law even more important.

Because the Australian Privacy Act meets all the requirements of the EU GDPR, Australian entities are allowed to collect and create PII for EU citizens.

Canada's Personal Information Protection and Electronic Documents Act (PIPEDA)

This Canadian law provides for the protection of personal information collected, used, or disclosed in certain circumstances by providing for the use of electronic means to communicate or record information or transactions. It includes such specifics on filing complaints as how and with whom they are filed and the remedies and enforcements available to the government for redress of such grievances. As you might imagine, Canada has a view of personal privacy more like that of the EU and unlike the United States.

The EU acknowledges PIPEDA as satisfactorily addressing the principles of the GDPR. Therefore, entities in Canada (like those in Australia) can handle EU citizen PII.

Argentina's Personal Data Protection Act

In 2000, Argentina passed the Data Protection Act with the explicit intent of ensuring adherence and compliance with the EU Data Directive (the legal precursor to the GDPR). Because of this, the EU treats entities in Argentina as if they were in the EU and allows them to collect and create PII for EU citizens. Many data centers in Argentina exist that manage services for EU customers.

The EFTA and Switzerland

Switzerland is not technically a member of the EU. Instead, it is a member of a four-nation smaller body known as the European Free Trade Association (EFTA). Swiss law has long been famous for protecting client privacy, specifically to support Switzerland's international banking industry. The EU recognizes EFTA regulation as stringent enough to protect EU citizen data under the GDPR, so Switzerland is ostensibly considered part of the EU in regard to being allowed to process privacy information.

Asia-Pacific Economic Cooperation (APEC) Privacy Framework

The Asia-Pacific Economic Cooperation (APEC) is a regional organization meant to work toward economic growth and cooperation of its member nations. APEC agreements are not legally binding and are followed only with voluntary compliance by those entities that choose to participate.

Where the laws of some other jurisdictions (such as the EU) are meant to provide governmental protections to individual citizens, the APEC intent is to enhance the function of free markets through common adherence to PII protection principles. APEC members understand that consumers will not trust markets if their PII is not protected during participation in those markets. Therefore, APEC principles offer reassurance to consumers as an effort to increase faith in trading practices and thereby ensure mutual benefit for all involved.

APEC framework privacy principles rest on the following core ideas:

▪ Individuals know when their data is used, transmitted, or stored.

▪ Limitations on usage are based on what is known to the individuals.

▪ The entity collecting or creating PII has responsibilities toward maintaining data accuracy and integrity.

Information Security Management Systems (ISMSs)

ISO created the concept of an information security management system (ISMS); a holistic overview of the entire security program within an organization. The ISMS is detailed in ISO 27001.

The ISMS is intended to provide a standardized international model for the development and implementation of policies, procedures, and standards that take into account stakeholder identification and involvement in a top-down approach to addressing and managing risk in an organization. It is built on the premise that information should be adequately secured with practices accepted and recognized by the industry as a whole; it is platform/product agnostic and can be customized for any organization.

ISO 27001 is probably the most well-recognized security program standard globally and will be accepted by many regulators/jurisdictions as meeting due care requirements for reducing liability. However, applying the standard, and being certified as having applied it, is not inexpensive; ISO compliance is a very costly prospect, which may make it unattractive or impossible for small and medium-sized organizations.

For more information, see www.iso.org/iso/iso27001.

The management and oversight of security practices, devices, and tools, as well as business processes such as audit and security functions, constitute what the (ISC)² CCSP Course Outline describes as an "internal information security controls system", which is a holistic program for security controls within an organization. Under the ISO perspective, the ISMS fulfills this purpose.

ISO documents are not free! They can range in price from a hundred or so dollars to several hundred, depending on the specific document, size, age, and so on. And there are literally hundreds of them. This is one of the ways in which the ISO organization generates revenue to continue developing its standards. They are developed primarily by subject matter experts from around the world, who are all volunteers with the exception of the ISO staff. For more information, go to www.iso.org/iso/home.htm.

ISO/IEC 27017:2015

The International Organization for Standardization (ISO) and International Electrotechnical Commission (IEC) created ISO/IEC 27017:2015, a set of standards regarding the guidelines for information security controls applicable to the provision and use of cloud services and cloud service customers. In other words, it provides a set of standards for not only providing cloud services but also for how cloud customer information and privacy should be controlled. Although ISO standards are recognized internationally, they are not law, and they do not reflect regulation by governmental bodies such as the EU. However, in some jurisdictions, some industries are required by law to comply with ISO standards.

ISO/IEC 27018:2019 is also relevant to the CCSP. It focuses specifically on a code of practice and security techniques for processing PII in cloud services.

The Difference between Laws, Regulations, and Standards

So what is the difference between all of these laws, regulations, standards, and frameworks? Laws are legal rules that are created by government entities such as legislatures. Regulations are rules that are created by governmental agencies. Failure to properly follow laws and regulations can result in punitive procedures that can include fines and imprisonment.

Standards dictate a reasonable level of performance; standards can be created by an organization for its own purposes (internal) or come from industry bodies/trade groups (external). An organization can choose to adhere to a standard the organization selects; in some cases, for some industries and jurisdictions, compliance with standards is imposed by law. Following a standard can reduce liability; demonstrating that compliance represents due care.

Laws, regulations, and standards can all impact the information security industry, often in similar or overlapping ways. For example, there are laws, regulations, and standards that all dictate and describe what sorts of data should be considered sensitive and personal information.

Rules related to the handling of sensitive data might come from another source, as well: contractual agreements. For instance, Payment Card Industry (PCI) compliance is wholly voluntary, but it is a requirement for those who choose to participate in credit card processing (namely, merchants who accept credit card payments). Those participants agree to submit to PCI oversight, including audits and review of the participants' adoption and implementation of standards and applicable controls. It's not a law, but it is a framework, complete with enforcers. For more information about the PCI council and the PCI Data Security Standard, go to www.pcisecuritystandards.org.

Regardless of whether you're dealing with laws, regulations, or standards, everyone expects a reasonable degree of transparency—in other words, making things clear for all types of regulators and interested parties, at least to the degree that is expected and possible.

There are descriptions of the differences between laws and contracts at the beginning of this chapter; privacy data can be affected by both laws and contracts. Under a law, your organization has to answer to the government in the event of a PII breach/loss; under a contract, your organization will have to answer to the other party/parties of the contract.

Potential Personal and Data Privacy Issues in the Cloud Environment

Due to the decentralized nature of cloud computing, geographic disparities make personal privacy and data privacy critical issues. In the following sections, we will discuss some of the challenges to protecting and managing personal privacy and data privacy in such a decentralized, dispersed, and global environment.

eDiscovery

Electronic discovery (eDiscovery) refers to the process of identifying and obtaining electronic evidence for either prosecutorial or litigation purposes. Determining which data in a set is pertinent to a specific legal case can be difficult. Regardless of whether information is stored in databases, records, email, or files, identifying and locating applicable data can be quite challenging in the cloud due to the decentralized nature of the technology. Moreover, because cloud computing so often takes the form of a multitenant environment, there is added complication in finding data owned by a specific customer while not intruding on other customers' data that might be located in the same storage volumes, the same drives, or the same machines. Trained professionals certified in the practice of eDiscovery are rare, and most organizations don't have these people in their employ. When faced with eDiscovery activity, an organization would probably best be served by hiring a consultant who is expert and licensed for the purpose. Anyone performing this activity should be extremely familiar with relevant industry standards and guidance, such as ISO 27050 (www.iso.org/standard/63081.html) and CSA guidance (https://cloudsecurityalliance.org/artifacts/csa-security-guidance-domain-3-legal-issues-contracts-and-electronic-discovery/).

It is important for the cloud customer to be familiar with laws, SLAs, and other contractual agreements that can impact the user's ability to conduct eDiscovery should the need arise. This is especially important if international boundaries are crossed in the process.

As demand for eDiscovery capability increases, technology vendors have created products to meet this need. Some cloud providers offer SaaS eDiscovery solutions; cloud-based applications that can perform searches and collection of pertinent data (often in the provider's own cloud data center, for its own customers). There are also host-based tools that can be used to locate applicable information on specific machines (both hardware and virtualized).

Chain of Custody and Nonrepudiation

All evidence needs to be tracked and monitored from the time it is recognized as evidence and acquired for that purpose until the time it is delivered to a court or law enforcement agency. Clear documentation must record which people had access to the evidence, where the evidence was stored, what access controls were placed on the evidence, and what modifications or analysis was performed on the evidence. We call this record and the principles for creating it the *chain of custody*.

Being able to demonstrate a strong chain of custody, where only specific, trusted personnel had access to the material and with no gaps in the timeline or loss of control, is very important for making an argument in court using that evidence. Any discrepancy in the chain of custody introduces doubt as to the disposition and content of the evidence. Although this does not make the evidence inadmissible, it does allow an opportunity for opposing counsel to reduce the power of your narrative. Any doubt regarding a particular piece or set of evidence will make that evidence much weaker.

When creating policies for maintaining a chain of custody or conducting activities requiring the preservation and monitoring of evidence, it is best to get input and guidance from counsel and perhaps even to use specialized consultants who are trained and experienced in this practice area.

The chain of custody provides *nonrepudiation* for the transactions detailed in the evidence. Nonrepudiation means that no party to a transaction can later claim that they did not take part.

Forensic Requirements

Conducting forensic activity in a cloud environment is challenging. The nature of decentralized, off-premises data and its movement, storage, and processing across geopolitical boundaries all lead to a complex and perplexing environment when attempting to gather and analyze forensic data.

The international nature of cloud forensics has created the demand for international standards that are applicable globally. Such standards help establish procedures across borders in an effort to limit the challenges to scientific findings.

ISO has developed a set of global digital forensics standards:

- **ISO/IEC 27037:2012:** Guide for collecting, identifying, and preserving electronic evidence

- **ISO/IEC 27041:2015:** Guide for incident investigations

- **ISO/IEC 27042: 2015:** Guide for digital evidence analysis

- **ISO/IEC 27043:2015:** Incident investigation principles and processes

- **ISO/IEC 27050-1:2016:** Overview and principles for eDiscovery

Conflicting International Legislation

The Internet and cloud facilitate international commerce, allowing individuals and businesses to trade goods and services worldwide. This can lead to legal difficulties because jurisdictions might have conflicting laws for similar activity. For instance, online gambling is against the law in the United States, but is perfectly legal in many other parts of the world; providers offering services to American players may be subject to prosecution in the US (see the "Online Gambling" case study). Cloud service providers may also have to comply with local requirements that differ greatly from the laws within the country where the service is headquartered or be forced to deviate from their own internal policies as well; for example, in order for Google to provide service in China, Google is required to disclose user behavior to the Chinese government, even though it is readily apparent that this reporting might be used to prosecute and persecute users for behavior that is normalized in Google's home country (the US) but illegal in China (Chinese citizens engaged in "dissident" activity or participating in LGBT-oriented activities can face criminal charges).

It is imperative that the CCSP be aware of the various laws affecting their organizations' activities and users in the jurisdictions in which they do business, including the location of cloud data centers, providers, and end users. Contracts with cloud providers must be reviewed in detail for legal impacts in both the provider's and customer's jurisdictions.

Finally, as practitioners in the field of information security, we should all be aware of legal developments that might cause conflicts to arise in our international operations, such as laws that might dictate behavior in one jurisdiction that is illegal in another. (The CLOUD Act requires companies in the US to disclose data to federal law enforcement, even if that data is located outside the US and the disclosure might be against the law in the jurisdiction where the data is located.)

 Real World Scenario

Online Gambling

Sometimes, what is against the law in one jurisdiction is not against the law in another. In those circumstances, extradition can be difficult. If the person's actions are not illegal in their home nation and another nation wants to arrest them and bring them to trial, the home nation might refuse any such requests.

This was the case for David Carruthers, the CEO of a British-based online gambling company. In 2006, Carruthers was arrested by federal agents in the United States while he was changing planes in Dallas, between a flight from the UK and a flight to Costa Rica. The US government charged Carruthers with "racketeering," stemming from the use of his company's services by US citizens engaging in online gambling.

Online gambling, while illegal in the United States, is not illegal in the UK or Costa Rica, nor in many other parts of the world. It would have been difficult for the United States to extradite Carruthers from either the UK or Costa Rica because of this difference in the laws of the various countries, so federal agents waited until he was in the jurisdiction of the United States—the moment his plane touched down.

Carruthers served 33 months in prison.

Cloud Forensic Challenges

The distributed model of cloud computing presents a number of challenges in the area of forensics. Data location, collection mechanisms, and international laws are all factors when dealing with situations involving forensic investigations.

Do you know where your data is to start with? Are some parts of it on-premises or off-premises, and in either case where is the data located? Is it distributed across multiple data centers, and if so, are those data centers across international boundaries? If so, do international laws hinder your abilities to collect forensic information? For example, does the law in a certain country/jurisdiction prevent you from capturing certain types of data (detailed user activity records, for instance)?

Do you have a working relationship with your cloud computing vendors? Do your SLA or other contract elements delineate the rights and responsibilities for data collection and maintenance between the customer and provider? Are you authorized, as a cloud customer, to retrieve forensic data from the cloud data center? What happens if you accidentally collect another customer's data from a multitenant environment? Will your forensic tools be suitable for a virtualized environment? What level of cooperation is necessary on the part of the provider?

Direct and Indirect Identifiers

Privacy information can take many forms. In some jurisdictions, under certain laws, a person's name, birthdate, and home address are considered PII; in other countries/jurisdictions, the person's mobile phone number and IP address are PII as well; this entirely depends on the laws of those jurisdictions. These PII elements are sometimes referred to as *direct identifiers*. Direct identifiers are those data elements that immediately reveal a specific individual.

There are also *indirect identifiers*, which should also be protected. Indirect identifiers are the characteristics and traits of an individual that, when aggregated, could reveal the identity of that person. Each indirect identifier by itself is usually not sensitive, but if enough are collected they may provide sensitive information. For example, if we take a list of indirect identifiers that are not sensitive, such as a man born in Wisconsin and currently living in New Orleans who owns a dog and performs work in the information security field, we might reveal the identity of the author of this book and thus derive sensitive information (an identity) from information elements that are not sensitive (location, birthplace, pets, industry, and so on).

The act of removing identifiers is known as *anonymization*; certain jurisdictions, laws, and standards require the anonymization of data, including both direct and indirect identifiers.

Forensic Data Collection Methodologies

In traditional environments, forensic data collection is performed in a relatively contained environment (the organization's enterprise) with a single owner (the organization itself). The collection process is challenging in a traditional environment; care must be taken to ensure data is modified as little as possible and captured in a manner that is consistent, exacting, and repeatable. Certain techniques, like forensic imaging, are used to reduce the possibility that captured data is not affected while copies are made.

In the cloud environment, the practices and tools used in the traditional environment are not always feasible or useful. There are multiple owners of the resources; depending on the cloud service and deployment models, and the cloud provider or the customer might have possession/ownership and/or administrative rights to certain systems/aspects of the environment. Moreover, the additional concern of third-party data (other cloud customers sharing the same underlying infrastructure) that might be affected by forensic collection complicates the process.

In many situations, forensic collection of cloud data will require the participation/involvement of the cloud provider; the customer will not be able (legally or technically or both) to capture the necessary material in a manner or with the detail required for the satisfaction of a court (where evidence gathered and analyzed forensically often ends up).

The ISO standards mentioned earlier (specifically 27037 and 27042) are excellent guides for collecting, preserving, and analyzing forensic data. However, most cloud customers (and most CCSPs) will not have the skills and tools necessary for defensible evidence collection and analysis readily available. It is highly recommended that cloud customers undertaking a forensic investigation in the cloud enlist the services of forensic professionals certified and licensed to perform those activities.

Audit Processes, Methodologies, and Cloud Adaptations

An audit is a review of an environment in order to determine if that environment is compliant with a standard, law, configuration, or other mandate. The audit process in cloud computing, while very much as in any other environment, does have some unique challenges, which we will explore in more detail.

Virtualization

Cloud computing requires virtualization; virtualization complicates auditing. The auditor is no longer looking at physical devices but software instances or abstractions of devices. Even at the network layer, software-based virtual switches and routers are responsible for moving traffic around the cloud environment. That makes it hard for the auditor to identify all machines in the scope of the audit; the audit is not a simple matter of locating and enumerating tangible devices in a room, as in a traditional environment. At best, the auditor will have access to a management console with which to view the environment. This can at the very least be confusing and difficult for those unaccustomed to cloud computing.

There is also the need to understand the control mechanisms in play in a virtualized cloud environment. Virtualization requires a knowledge base that auditors unfamiliar with cloud technology will find confusing. One example is auditing access to the hypervisor. The auditor can view the accounts of the administrators but may not be able to speak to them as they might reside in a different country.

Scope

Audit *scope* lists which elements, participants, and systems will be included in the audit. Scoping must be performed before the audit begins so that everyone involved (the auditors, the organization being audited, users, etc.) understands the breadth and depth of the audit, how long it may take, and what resources will be utilized/affected.

Defining the scope of an audit in a cloud-computing environment can also present challenges. Are you conducting an audit on the infrastructure of the cloud provider, the platform, or the applications involved? Depending on the service model you are using, audit scope can take many different forms. For instance, if you are simply using the provider as a software as a service (SaaS) vendor, should your audit scope involve the underlying infrastructure? Many vendors provide third-party audits of those services to satisfy this need so that customers' auditors can focus on the higher abstraction levels (that is, the providers' auditors will review the hardware in the data center, and the customers' auditors will review the application and usage).

Additionally, the scope of the audit may or may not be confined to geographical or geopolitical boundaries. The auditor may only be auditing infrastructure as a service (IaaS) within the confines of a certain country. Anything outside these boundaries may be out of scope, depending on the engagement.

Gap Analysis

Once the audit has been complete, the audit results should show both where the organization is currently compliant and where it is not compliant. The gap analysis is a review of the differences, in those areas where the organization is not yet compliant with the given standard/regulation. The purpose of the gap analysis is to aid in determining how to reach the desired end state (full compliance).

Generally, best practices dictate that the auditors do *not* take part in providing specific recommendations on how to close gaps—that auditors do not recommend particular technologies/systems/products for achieving compliance because this may lead to a conflict of interest (where the auditors take part in business functions, diluting the auditors' independence). Moreover, the affected departments within the organization should also not take part in the gap analysis; instead, personnel from outside the target departments should do the review as they are more able to offer unbiased opinion and suggestions.

Restrictions of Audit Scope Statements

If an auditor feels that the organization has not disclosed sufficient information/artifacts/access for the auditor to perform a successful and fair audit, the auditor may issue a "scope limitation" statement or otherwise qualify the audit report/results. This indicates to any recipient of the audit that the auditor did not feel professionally able to render judgement due to the target organization's desire to withhold elements material to the audit.

For example, an auditor is hired to review Ostrich, Inc., for PCI DSS compliance. The management of Ostrich creates an audit scope that does not allow the auditor to review the point-of-sale systems where customer credit cards are presented at the time of purchase. Because PCI DSS requires that cardholder data is protected from the time of collection, the auditor deems, in the auditor's professional opinion, that access to the point-of-sale systems is necessary to determine whether Ostrich is performing the data collection in a secure manner and whether Ostrich is compliant with the standard. When the auditor completes the audit report, the auditor may issue a "qualified opinion," explaining that the report is not sufficient, in the auditor's estimation, to fairly and completely render a sound judgement. The auditor may also issue a "disclaimer of opinion," stating that the audit report is not complete and should not be taken as wholly accurate.

Many popular audit standards and audit bodies, such as the American Institute of Certified Public Accountants (AICPA) Statement on Standards for Attestation Engagements (SSAE) and the International Standard on Assurance Engagements (ISAE) require that auditors note any restrictions on audit scope that may materially impact the quality of the audit.

Policies

Policies provide a voice and expression of the strategic goals and objectives of senior management and play an integral role in forming the security posture of an organization.

Organizational security policies take the form of those intended to reduce exposure and minimize risk of financial and data losses as well as other types of damages such as loss of reputation. Other typical policies include information security policy, data classification and usage policies, acceptable use, and a host of other polices related to software, malware, and so on. In addition, the CCSP should be familiar with disaster recovery and business continuity policies, vendor management or outsourcing policies, and incident response and forensic policies. All these policies are an expression of senior management's strategic goals and objectives with regard to managing and maintaining the risk profile of the organization.

In cloud computing, more emphasis may be placed on policies regarding access controls, data storage and recovery, and so on, where the cloud customer will have some semblance of control; many other policies that were applicable in the traditional IT environment (such as hardware management, personnel access to storage devices, etc.) may not be feasible in a cloud environment as the customer does not have control over those aspects of the cloud. Those, instead, will be in the purview of the cloud provider. However, some policies that an organization may want to dedicate more time and resources to after migrating to the cloud include remote access, password management, encryption, and how duties and responsibilities are separated and managed, especially for administrators.

Different Types of Audit Reports

Internal audits are those performed by employees of an organization. Banks will often have an internal audit department and conduct periodic internal reviews in order to assess operational risks and determine whether employees are following policies. They may also conduct ongoing GLBA audits to ensure that they are meeting all FDIC regulations concerning their information security program.

Here are several of the reasons internal audits are weaker than external audits:

- They tend to get delayed in lieu of activities that meet operational needs.
- The people doing the audits may lack experience.
- There may be pressure to not disclose security issues for fear of retribution (internal political factors).

External audits are performed almost as an audit of internal audits. External audits tend to be more independent because there is greater separation between the auditor and the organization. They also tend to be more thorough, since they typically encompass the entire audit universe as opposed to internal audits of individual departments of the organization.

Auditor Independence

The idea of auditor independence goes back further than SOX legislation, but SOX stringently reinforced that requirement. This has had a very influential effect on auditors and organizations in the United States and somewhat internationally.

It is imperative that the auditors remain utterly objective and not be swayed by either persuasion or vested interest; the auditors must be unbiased and reflect a true and accurate reporting of the target environment/organization. Auditors should not have a financial interest in the outcome of the audit, or in the success of the organization, nor should auditors have personal interactions with client entities if those relationships could influence the auditors or their reports.

AICPA Reports and Standards

The American Institute of Certified Public Accountants (AICPA) represents the accounting and audit professions in the United States. It is a large organization that is responsible for most financial and information security audit practices. It sets the standards, creates the guidelines and frameworks, and sets the bar for service organization audit and reporting practices. The AICPA creates and promulgates the Generally Accepted Accounting Principles (GAAP) and Generally Accepted Auditing Standards (GAAS), which auditors and accountants adhere to in practice.

The current AICPA audit standard, SSAE 18, outlines three families of audit reports: SOC 1, SOC 2, and SOC 3.

These standards, guidelines, and reports serve as the foundation for evaluating the safety and soundness of an organization's control framework and help to determine risk levels of doing business with the organization. They report on the effectiveness of proper separation and segmentation.

As a CCSP, if your organization is considering cloud migration and you have to choose between potential providers, you will almost always have to rely on third-party audit reports as a means to perform your due diligence (demonstrating that you've put forth the effort to choose a trustworthy provider). It is very unlikely that you will be allowed to perform your own audit/site visit/review of the provider's controls as a customer. This is why (ISC)² feels it is important for you to be familiar with the SOC reports and understand what they mean and how they are used.

The first of these reports is called the SOC 1. It is an audit engagement consisting solely of an examination of organizational financial reporting controls. For the purposes of a cloud customer trying to determine the suitability of a cloud provider, the SOC 1 is useless. It doesn't tell us anything about data protections, configuration resiliency, or any other element the customer needs to know. The SOC 1 is instead designed to serve the needs of investors and regulators, the two sets of people interested in the financial well-being of the target. To restate and reinforce: the SOC 1 does not serve an information security or IT security purpose.

SOC 2 reports review controls relevant to security, availability, processing integrity, confidentiality, or privacy. This is the report of most use to cloud customers (to determine the suitability of cloud providers) and IT security practitioners. SOC 2 reports come in Type I and Type II flavors. The SOC 2 Type I report only reviews controls as designed, at a particular moment in time. That is, the audit examines the controls chosen by the target but not how those controls are implemented or how well those controls actually work. For a cloud customer, the SOC 2 Type I is interesting but, again, not too useful.

The SOC 2 Type II, on the other hand, is a truly thorough review of the target's controls, including how they have been implemented and their efficacy, over a period of time (usually several months). The SOC 2 Type II is a goldmine for the cloud customer. It gives the customer a realistic view of the provider's security posture and overall program.

Unfortunately, while the cloud customer will want to see the provider's SOC 2 Type II audit report, the provider may be reluctant to share it, and rightly so. The SOC 2 Type II is so detailed and contains so much information about the actual security controls implemented within the provider's environment that it would be a perfect attack map for a hostile actor. It is quite understandable that the cloud provider would not want to disseminate the SOC 2 Type II.

However, current trends in the industry have created a happy middle ground for the provider and the customer. Many cloud providers are offering the SOC 2 Type II reports to their customers with the stipulation that the customer signs a nondisclosure agreement and that the customer is vetted by the provider for trustworthiness before the provider will release the report. This gives assurances to the customer that the provider's security posture is adequate, and it gives assurances to the provider that their security methods and techniques are not being made available to someone who would want to use that information for malicious ends.

The SOC 3 report, on the other hand, is purely for public consumption and serves only as a seal of approval for public display, without sharing any specific information regarding audit activity, control effectiveness, findings, and so on. It is literally just an attestation from the auditor that the audit has been conducted and that the target has successfully passed the audit. It contains no details and no substance. More cloud providers will be willing to disclose the SOC 3 report than either of the SOC 2 reports because that is what a SOC 3 is designed for. As an accurate reflection of trustworthiness or for due diligence purposes in selecting a provider, it is not a useful or reliable tool.

Summary

As you have seen, the nature of international laws, standards, and regulations make cloud computing complex and at times difficult to comprehend. The International Organization for Standardization (ISO), the International Electrotechnical Commission (IEC), and the Organisation for Economic Cooperation and Development (OECD) have promulgated what have become the de facto standards for information security and privacy for the vast majority of the international community outside the United States. Inside the United States, auditors still work primarily with standards and regulations such as GLBA, PCI-DSS, SSAE18, and HIPAA. Agencies and governmental bodies continually generate these standards and regulations, making a consistent standard difficult to obtain. However, it is the CCSP's responsibility to understand all the challenges these present in order to provide sound advice when working with customers' and vendors' architectural, policy, and management efforts.

Exam Essentials

Have a fundamental understanding of the relevant ISO and ISO/IEC standards, such as ISO 27001.   ISO standards are not laws but are derived from experts all over the world who have come together to develop standards from which to operate. Many countries and coalitions such as the EU base many of their policies on ISO-related standards.

Be familiar with and have a fundamental grasp of US security and privacy standards, regulations, and laws.   This includes contractual and legal compliance regulations, standards, and frameworks such as PCI DSS, HIPAA, SOX, and GLBA. You should know the differences. PCI DSS, for instance, is a contractual standard and not a law. HIPAA, on the other hand, like GLBA, is a federal law, and audits resulting in findings of noncompliance can result in fines, jailtime, and forced interruption of business activity.

Have a clear understanding of issues surrounding and relating to eDiscovery.   This includes forensic evidence, chain of custody, and the challenges facing forensic collection in a cloud environment. Attempting eDiscovery in a cloud environment can be very challenging due to such things as geographical and geopolitical dispersion.

Understand audit processes.   Understand basic audit concepts such as internal versus external audits as well as the differences and the importance of independence in conducting audits. Less reliable internal audits assist internal operations, whereas external audits, being more independent, ferret out more thoroughly sensitive issues that might cause risk to the organization.

Be familiar with the basic definitions of personally identifiable information (PII).   Be familiar with the basic definitions of PII, contractual versus regulated data, country-specific regulations, and the differences between the various kinds of PII. Also, understand the difference between sensitive and nonsensitive PII (using direct and indirect identifiers). In addition, be aware that even though PII may be nonsensitive, when combined with other nonsensitive information, it can become sensitive.

Written Labs

You can find the answer to the written labs in Appendix A.

1. Describe the primary differences between regulations, laws, and standards.
2. What are the HIPAA rules and why are they different?
3. Describe the primary differences between a SOC 1, SOC 2, and SOC 3 report.

Review Questions

You can find the answers to the review questions in Appendix B.

1. What must be collected during the eDiscovery process?

   A. Emails

   B. Anything pertinent to the request

   C. All documentation created during a specific time period

   D. Anything that can provide forensic benefit

2. Legal controls refer to which of the following?

   A. Controls designed to comply with laws and regulations related to the cloud environment

   B. PCI DSS

   C. ISO 27001

   D. NIST 800-53r4

3. Which of the following terms is *not* associated with cloud forensics?

   A. Analysis

   B. eDiscovery

   C. Chain of custody

   D. Plausibility

4. Which of the following is *not* a component of contractual PII?

   A. Scope of processing

   B. Use of subcontractors

   C. Location of data

   D. Value of data

5. Which of the following is a primary component of regulated PII?

   A. Items that *should* be implemented

   B. Mandatory breach reporting

   C. Audit rights of subcontractors

   D. PCI DSS

6. Which of the following is not associated with privacy?

   A. Medical records

   B. Personal hobbies

   C. Birthdate

   D. Participation in a transaction

7. Which of the following is the best advantage of external audits?

    A. Independence

    B. Oversight

    C. Cheaper

    D. Better results

8. Which of the following laws resulted from a lack of independence in audit practices?

    A. HIPAA

    B. GLBA

    C. SOX

    D. ISO 27064

9. Which of the following reports is no longer used?

    A. SAS 70

    B. SSAE 18

    C. SOC 1

    D. SOC 3

10. Which of the following report is most aligned with financial control audits?

    A. SOC 1

    B. SOC 2

    C. SOC 3

    D. SSAE 18

11. Which of the following is the primary purpose of an SOC 3 report?

    A. Absolute assurances

    B. Compliance with PCI/DSS

    C. HIPAA compliance

    D. Seal of approval

12. The Generally Accepted Accounting Principles are created and maintained by which organization?

    A. ISO

    B. ISO/IEC

    C. PCI Council

    D. AICPA

13. Which statute addresses security and privacy matters in the US financial industry?

   A. GLBA

   B. FERPA

   C. SOX

   D. HIPAA

14. Which of the following is *not* an example of a highly regulated environment?

   A. Healthcare

   B. Financial services

   C. Wholesale or distribution

   D. Public companies

15. Which of the following SOC report subtypes represents a point in time?

   A. SOC 2

   B. Type I

   C. Type II

   D. SOC 3

16. Which of the following SOC report subtypes spans a period of time?

   A. SOC 2

   B. SOC 3

   C. SOC 1

   D. Type II

17. The right to be forgotten refers to which of the following?

   A. The right to no longer pay taxes

   B. Erasing criminal history

   C. The right to have all of a data subject's data erased

   D. Masking

18. SOX was enacted because of which of the following?

   A. Poor board oversight

   B. Lack of independent audits

   C. Poor financial controls

   D. All of the above

19. What is a primary component of the Graham-Leach-Bliley Act?

    A. The right to be forgotten

    B. EU Data Directives

    C. The information security program

    D. The right to audit

20. Which of the following are not associated with HIPAA controls?

    A. Administrative controls

    B. Technical controls

    C. Physical controls

    D. Financial controls

Chapter
11

Legal and Compliance Part 2

THE OBJECTIVE OF THIS CHAPTER IS TO ACQUAINT THE READER WITH THE FOLLOWING CONCEPTS:

✓ **Domain 1: Cloud Concepts, Architecture, and Design**

- 1.2. Describe Cloud Reference Architecture
    - 1.2.5. Cloud shared Considerations
- 1.4. Understand Design Principles of Secure Cloud Computing
    - 1.4.3. Cost Benefit Analysis
- 1.5. Evaluate Cloud Service Providers
    - 1.5.1. Verification Against Criteria
    - 1.5.2. System/Subsystem Product Certifications

✓ **Domain 3: Cloud Platform and Infrastructure Security**

- 3.3. Analyze Risks Associated with Cloud Infrastructure
    - 3.3.1. Risk Assessment and Analysis

✓ **Domain 5: Cloud Security Operations**

- 5.4. Implement Operational Controls and Standards
    - 5.4.10. Service Level Management
- 5.6. Manage Communication with Relevant Parties
    - 5.6.1. Vendors
    - 5.6.2. Customers
    - 5.6.3. Partners
    - 5.6.4. Regulators
    - 5.6.5. Other Stakeholders

✓ **Domain 6: Legal, Risk, and Compliance**

- 6.3. Understand Audit Process, Methodologies, and Required Adaptations for a Cloud Environment

  - 6.3.10. Policies

  - 6.3.11. Identification and Involvement of Relevant Stakeholders

  - 6.3.13. Impact of Distributed Information Technology (IT) Model

- 6.4. Understand Implications of Cloud to Enterprise Risk Management

  - 6.4.1. Assess Provider's Risk Management Programs

  - 6.4.3. Regulatory Transparency Requirements

  - 6.4.4. Risk Treatment

  - 6.4.5. Different Risk Frameworks

  - 6.4.6. Metrics for Risk Management

  - 6.4.7. Assessment of Risk Environment

- 6.5. Understand Outsourcing and Cloud Contract Design

  - 6.5.1. Business Requirements

  - 6.5.2. Vendor Management

  - 6.5.3. Contract Management

  - 6.5.4. Supply-Chain Management

In this chapter, we continue our discussion of the legal and compliance challenges in cloud computing. The global, decentralized nature of cloud computing presents numerous issues that we are just now grappling with in our endeavors to protect privacy rights, meet compliance demands, and maintain a secure computing environment.

This chapter will cover effective risk management, risk metrics, and strategies for an effective risk management program. I will round it out with a discussion of outsourcing, contract management, and the all-important service-level agreement (SLA).

The Impact of Diverse Geographical Locations and Legal Jurisdictions

As discussed in Chapter 10, "Legal and Compliance Part 1," the impact of the decentralized, geographically, and geopolitically dispersed model of cloud computing presents numerous challenges, including these:

- Data processing, storage, and computing, each occurring in different geopolitical realms
- Difficulties in assessing data actors
- Difficulties in locating data

A great deal of the difficulty in managing the legal ramifications of cloud computing stems from the design of cloud assets. They are necessarily dispersed, often across municipal, state, and even international borders. Resources are constantly being allocated and reallocated on a moment-to-moment basis. Also, specific control and administration of particular assets can be hard to ascertain and establish.

Some jurisdictions, such as the EU, have rules about the "transparency" of Internet service providers (ISPs), whereby ISPs must refrain from giving preferential pricing or access to any particular customer online or must publicly publish an explanation/specification when they do. So if your organization negotiates a particularly beneficial pricing/service package with a cloud provider that also happens to be an ISP in the EU, the details of this pricing/service might be required, by law, to become public record. You can find the EU law here: https://eur-lex.europa.eu/legal-content/EN/TXT/HTML/?uri=CELEX:32015R2120&rid=2.

It is that transborder aspect that is most troublesome, in terms of allowing the cloud customer to maintain compliance with legal and regulatory mandates. As we discussed in the previous chapter, each jurisdiction can have its own governance, which can vary wildly from jurisdiction to jurisdiction, and jurisdictions can overlap. A city is in a county or other municipality, the latter of which is in a state, which is in a country, and they might all have conflicting guidance and interests. Moreover, legislation and guidance is always in flux, especially in our industry. Lawmakers and standards bodies are constantly trying to catch up to the requirements and questions posed by new technologies and how those technologies are used. And these vagaries of law affect not only the cloud customer, in terms of how the customer must behave and respond to legal action, but also how the cloud provider must perform in response to these same stimuli.

The governance used by both entities—the cloud customer and the cloud provider— must take all of this into account in order to operate reasonably with acknowledgment of legal risks and liabilities in the cloud.

 It is important to not confuse the concepts of "governance" and "corporate governance." Governance refers to the legal and regulatory mandates of regions and countries. Corporate governance is the relationship between shareholders and other stakeholders in the organization versus the senior management of the corporation.

Policies

Policies are one of the foundational elements of a governance and risk management program. They guide the organization, based on standards and guidelines. Policies ensure that the organization is operating within its risk profile. Policies actually define, or are the expression of, the organization's risk tolerance.

Before the organization begins creating its policies, it starts by identifying the stakeholders. This ensures that the right individuals are involved in creating the expression of risk tolerance. These can include the following:

- Business unit leaders
- The board of directors
- Investors
- Regulators

The views, perceptions, and choices of these groups will influence the organization's willingness and ability to accept risk, but most of these stakeholders will not be directly involved in crafting organizational policy. For instance, the regulators won't (or shouldn't) help draft policy, but they enforce the regulations that establish what risks an organization takes and how it takes them. The regulators, ostensibly acting on behalf of lawmakers and in turn working on behalf of the public (because they chose those lawmakers), are expressing the view of the public, vis-à-vis risk, on organizations.

For example, say an organization offered a new product, but the risk of creating that product might result in an employee dying once per month. The organization might be willing to take on that risk if the potential profits were high enough, and the employees might be willing to take on that risk if the pay was high enough. However, regulators might take a dim view of offering such a product at the possible cost of human life, so the risk appetite of the organization would necessarily be limited by regulation.

NOTE   The decision to risk human life is not necessarily unethical or immoral. Deep sea fishing has been one of the most fatal professions in the United States for more than one hundred years, and consumers have not stopped buying seafood en masse out of protest and loathing at the potential human cost of acquiring their meals. People engaged in commercial fishing choose to risk their lives to make very good money and seem to enjoy their work, regulators mandate reasonable safety requirements for the industry, and consumers enjoy seafood.

Once the stakeholder inputs have been adequately identified, the organization can begin building the policies needed in order to operate safely.

Identifying and engaging relevant stakeholders is vital to the success of any cloud computing discussions or projects. But there are also challenges that may need to be overcome in order to effectively engage them.

For instance, policies must be malleable enough to reflect changing business opportunities, requirements, and operations. This may have never been truer than in the example of an organization migrating from a legacy environment to the cloud. Almost assuredly, the organization had policies in place that acknowledged the risks and opportunities of that environment (the legacy, traditional IT environment) and dealt with them accordingly. However, the risks and benefits in the cloud are much different, so the policies must be revisited; the guidance and stakeholder input reexamined; and new policies generated, amended, or appended to the old policies.

The variety and vagaries of multijurisdictional law make the regulatory stakeholders and their input especially complicated for cloud services and management. Instead of one regulatory framework to consider when drafting policy, the organization now must take into account every jurisdiction where the cloud provider might be storing, transmitting, and processing the organization's data as well as every jurisdiction where any of the organization's end customers might reside. This latter part is especially troublesome, because when an organization operates in the cloud, it is assumed that the potential customer base is the web, meaning that the jurisdiction of the organization's customer is the entire planet.

It would be impossible to craft pertinent policy that met the needs and requirements of every jurisdiction in the world. Too many of them inherently conflict with others. So a significant portion of the effort that goes into promulgating policy is determining which jurisdictional mandates are most likely to bear on the organization's operations, where most of the end clientele will reside, where most of the cloud functions will take place, and so forth. It's a cost-benefit analysis of a lesser scale: instead of determining whether the organization has the risk appetite to perform a given function, this part of the effort will be used to determine which laws and regulators will be most likely to impact the organization and which ones should therefore have the most bearing on the organization's policy.

It should go without saying that while subject matter experts (such as the CCSP) will be called on to draft policies related to the organization's operations in the cloud, general counsel will provide an invaluable input when creating all the organization's policies. Attorneys will be the personnel most versed in identifying, understanding, and tailoring documentation to address the multitude of jurisdictional regulation the organization might face.

As mentioned in the preceding paragraphs, subject matter experts will be called on to create particular policies for the organization. These experts might be internal employees and staff of the organization. They might be external consultants hired for the purpose. The policies might be purchased from an existing set that were designed and drafted by experts in that particular area of expertise and then tailored by the organization to meet its own needs. In this regard, the CCSP should expect to be called on to offer input and advice when the organization is formalizing cloud policy.

After the experts have drafted the policy, the policy must be presented to the decision makers: senior management and the board of directors. The subject matter experts may be called on to explain specific aspects of the policy, expound on particular threats and tangible benefits, and explain how these risks are being addressed by the policy. Senior management must understand these draft policies in order to make an informed decision in accepting them (and the risks and benefits they entail) or modifying the policies as they see fit. Ultimately, policy acceptance will involve a senior manager signing the policy document and the board (or other governance body) acknowledging their approval of the policy.

Once the policy has been formally accepted, it must be published and disseminated among those affected by it. Communication in an enterprise environment is challenging in and of itself. Cloud computing makes this communication even more complicated because the IT administration staff may not be local, there might be time zone differences between the provider and customer, and providers could have literally thousands of other customers.

Communication to other business units or departments is vitally important as well. All of the internal and external stakeholders should be kept abreast of any changes or other issues related to policies and operations. Here are some common departments that include internal stakeholders:

- IT
- HR
- Vendor management
- Compliance
- Risk management
- Finance
- Operations

Some things that complicate communication are listed here:

- Disparate administrative workforce
- Time zone differences
- Ignorance of cloud computing models and concepts
- Poor understanding of business drivers
- Poor understanding of the organization's risk appetite

When discussing these matters with stakeholders, remember that in all likelihood they will not have a grasp of the cloud computing concepts held by the CCSP. Therefore, it is in everyone's best interest to take things slowly and to ensure that questions get answered adequately so that everyone is on the same page. It is also the CCSP's job to educate stakeholders about cloud computing risks and benefits so that they are better able to make fact-based decisions as opposed to relying on hearsay and gossip.

Some of the policy elements that the organization will need to appropriately reflect the cloud computing paradigm are as follows:

- Information security policy (ISP)
- Acceptable use policy
- Data classification policy
- Network and Internet security
- Passwords
- Anti-malware policy
- Software security
- Disaster recovery and data backup
- Remote and third-party access
- Segregation of duties
- Incident response plan
- Personnel security
- Identity and access management (IAM) policy
- Legal compliance
- Encryption

There will be times when a cloud provider is unable to meet an organization's internal policy requirements. When that occurs, it is imperative that these deficiencies be taken into account and managed as part of any internal governance process (or this may be the time to find an alternative cloud provider whose service does meet the organization's requirements). This will ensure that any contract elements or SLAs will not violate the organizational policies or place the organization at undue risk outside its tolerance levels.

Implications of the Cloud for Enterprise Risk Management

Cloud computing as it exists today has commoditized compute, storage, and networking services. Enterprise risk management has shifted in response to this change. It is vitally important that both the customer and the provider focus on risk management and the challenges presented with cloud computing. The cloud customer (in the role of data owner) is ultimately responsible for ensuring control effectiveness, but stored data, security, and risk management require a partnership between the customer and provider. Before you explore the detailed discussion of risk management, you need to be familiar with some risk-related terms.

Key Risk Indicators (KRIs)   Key risk indicators are metrics used by an organization to inform management if there is impending negative impact to operations. KRIs typically involve algorithms and ratings systems ascribed to factors selected by analysts and management in order to create an early-warning system for increased risk to the organization.

> KRIs are forward-looking; by contrast key performance indicators (KPIs) help an organization understand risks or events that have already occurred and impacted the business.

Risk Appetite/Tolerance   Risk tolerance and appetite are similar descriptors of how the organization views risk. Senior management dictates the amount of risk an organization is willing to take, generally based on the amount of perceived benefit related to the risk. Regulators and other external factors (such as contracts) may affect the organization's risk appetite as well.

Risk Profiles   The risk profile of the organization is a comprehensive analysis of the possible risks to the organization. The risk profile should include a survey of the various operations the organization is engaged in, public perception of the organization, pending legislation that might affect the organization, the stability of countries where the organization operates, and so forth.

Choices Involved in Managing Risk

An organization always has four choices when faced with risk:

- Risk avoidance
- Risk acceptance
- Risk transference
- Risk mitigation

The following sections will explore each of these options further.

Risk Avoidance

Risk avoidance is not a method for handling risk but a response to the cost-benefit analysis when posed with a specific risk. If an organization is faced with a risk where the potential costs far outweigh the likely benefits, the organization may choose not to engage in the activity that would incur the risk *at all*. This is the only surefire method for eliminating a specific risk: don't conduct the risky activity.

For instance, if the activity is, say, taking a package across the ocean, and the risk includes such potential costs as drowning, soaking the package in seawater and rendering it worthless, losing both the package and the ship, and so on, and the potential benefit is being paid $5 to transport the package, the organization might (rightly) deem the risk not to be worth the reward and choose instead to stay out of the transoceanic delivery business. The organization can then be said to have engaged in risk avoidance.

Risk Acceptance

The direct opposite of risk avoidance is risk acceptance. In examining the potential benefits and risks of a certain activity, if the organization determines that the risks are minimal and the reward is substantial, the organization might choose to accept the risks involved in the endeavor and press on with the activity without any additional consideration.

To use the prior example, if the organization determines that the risks of transporting a package across the ocean are so low as to be negligible (say, if there is a sufficient historical record to indicate that nobody has drowned or lost a ship or package on similar journeys in the past 10 years) and the reward is significant (if the organization is offered $5,000 instead of $5), then the organization make take the job of moving the package without any other consideration. This is risk acceptance.

To use some of the concepts of the prior discussion in this chapter, if the risk of the activity is estimated to be within the organization's *risk appetite*, then the organization might choose risk acceptance.

Risk Transference

Risk transference is a way to handle risk associated with an activity without accepting *all* the risk. With risk transference, the organization finds someone else to incur the potential risk of an endeavor at a fraction of the potential cost the organization would incur if the risk was realized.

Basically, when you think of risk transference, think one word: *insurance*. The organization is going to pay a portion of what the worst outcome would be in order to insulate against the cost of that worst outcome.

Now return to the example from the previous sections: If the organization can buy shipping insurance for the task of delivering the package, then the worst-case scenario (someone drowning, losing the ship, or losing the package, and therefore losing the payment for transporting it) can be offset by a proportional payout from the underwriter. Let's say the organization gets paid $5,000 to ship the package and then buys an insurance policy for $500. The terms of the insurance policy state that failure to deliver the package results in a payout significant enough to mollify the client (the sender of the package) as well as recoup the costs the organization faces in performance (the expenses incurred in performing the activity, such as renting a boat, hiring someone to carry the package, and so on). There might even be an extraordinary payout in the event of an extraordinary risk being realized (the boat is attacked by sharks and everyone on board is eaten along with the package). The reduced profit (reflecting the payment for shipping minus cost of the policy, which is $4,500 instead of the full $5,000) might still be acceptable to the organization because senior management is assured that the risks are being addressed.

Risk Mitigation

The final option in managing risk is risk mitigation, and this is the option that comprises the daily workload of most security practitioners. Risk mitigation is the practice of reducing risk to an acceptable level through the use of controls and countermeasures. That is to say that the organization implements controls in order to bring known risks to within that organization's risk appetite.

Using the same example as in the previous sections, controls that might be implemented to reduce the risk involved with shipping a package across the sea might include putting the package in a watertight container, affixing a tracking device to the package, equipping the ship conveying the package with anticollision sensors, and so on. When the organization has determined that the significant risks have been attenuated sufficiently with the proper controls, then the organization may decide that the business activity—shipping the package—has a sufficient chance of success.

There are two important things to note about risk mitigation:

- It is impossible to remove risk. Never believe anyone who says that something has "zero risk" or that a control offers "100 percent security." Even with all possible controls placed on a business function, there will still remain some level of risk; we call this *residual risk*. If the residual risk that remains *after* controls have been implemented falls within the organization's risk appetite, then the organization might choose to perform that function (that is, accept the risk). If the remaining residual risk exceeds the risk appetite of the organization, the controls are insufficient or the business is just too risky to perform.

- The cost of the controls must be less than the potential benefit of the business process or the process is not profitable or worthwhile. You should never put a $10 lock on a $5 bicycle.

The organization should consider using differing types of controls when choosing to mitigate risk. In the security field, we usually group controls into three general types: physical, technical, and administrative.

Physical controls are controls that limit physical access to assets or that operate in a manner that reduces the impact of a physical event. Examples of physical controls include locks on doors, fire suppression equipment in data centers, fences, and guards.

Technical controls, also referred to as logical controls, are those controls that enhance some facets of the CIA triad, usually operating within a system, often in electronic fashion.

Possible technical controls include encryption mechanisms, access control lists to limit user permissions, and audit trails and logs of system activity.

Administrative controls are those processes and activities (necessarily not physical or technical) that provide some aspect of security. Examples are personnel background checks, scheduled routine log reviews, mandatory vacations, robust and comprehensive security policies and procedures, and designing business processes so that there are no single points of failure and so that proper separation of duties exists.

Combining the types of controls is a good way to provide the organization with some defense in depth (also known as a layered defense); that is, require any malicious actor to overcome not just multiple controls but multiple *kinds* of controls so that more than one skillset would be necessary to access or acquire protected assets. Think of it this way: If we only used locks to protect material and we put locks on external entrances, on internal doors, and on a safe containing sensitive assets, then an intruder would still need only one skillset (lock picking) to acquire that material. Instead, if we combined the use of locks with guard patrols, intrusion sensors, and encryption, then someone who wanted unauthorized access or ownership of sensitive material would not only have to know lock picking, they would have to use subterfuge and stealth as well as decryption to get those assets.

 There is no reason you can't combine some of the various risk management methods, and it's actually a good practice to do so. For instance, an organization can implement risk controls to perform risk mitigation *and* buy insurance to transfer risk *and then* will still have to do risk acceptance when allowing for the residual risk. The only risk management option that can't be combined with the others is risk avoidance, because avoiding the risk means not engaging in that business function, so there is nothing left to mitigate, transfer, or accept.

Risk Management Frameworks

Numerous risk management frameworks exist that are designed to assist the enterprise in developing sound risk management practices and management. However, for the purposes of the CCSP exam, we will only be discussing ISO 31000:2018, NIST SP 800-37, and the European Union Agency for Network and Information Security (ENISA) frameworks.

ISO 31000:2018

ISO 31000:2018 is an international standard that focuses on designing, implementing, and reviewing risk management processes and practices. The standard explains that proper implementation of a risk management process can be used to accomplish the following:

- Create and protect value.
- Integrate organizational procedures.
- Be part of the decision-making process.
- Explicitly address uncertainty.

- Be a systematic, structured, and timely risk management program.

- Ensure the risk management program is based on the best available information.

- Be tailored to the organization's business requirements and actual risks.

- Take human and cultural factors into account.

- Ensure the risk management program is transparent and inclusive.

- Create a risk management program that is dynamic, iterative, and responsive to change.

- Facilitate continual improvement and enhancement of the organization.

For more information please visit www.iso.org/iso/home/standards/iso31000.htm.

NIST SP 800-37 (Guide for Implementing the Risk Management Framework)

NIST SP 800-37 is the Guide for Implementing the Risk Management Framework (RMF). This particular framework is a methodology for handling all organizational risk in a holistic, comprehensive, and continual manner. This RMF supersedes the old "Certification and Accreditation" model of cyclical inspections that have a specific duration (used widely in American military, intelligence, and federal government communities). This RMF relies heavily on the use of automated solutions, risk analysis and assessment, and implementing controls based on those assessments, with continuous monitoring and improvement.

NIST SP 800-37 is a guide organizations can use to implement the RMF. Although NIST standards are developed for use by the federal government, they have begun to be accepted in many non-government organizations as best practices. For instance, companies in the United States may use the NIST model and publications in developing not only their information security program, but also their risk management program and practices. NIST publications and standards have the dual benefit of being widely acknowledged as expert and sensible but also free of charge (all NIST documents are in the public domain). It takes little effort to adopt and adapt the NIST materials from their intended use in the federal space into use in a private sector or nonprofit endeavor.

Keep in mind that these documents are not as accepted in international markets as are ISO/IEC standards. Therefore, if you conduct business outside the United States, you may want to investigate the other standards in more detail. Some overseas companies will not even do business with US companies unless they subscribe to and are certified under ISO standards.

For a free copy of SP 800-37, as well as many other NIST documents, visit https://csrc.nist.gov/publications/detail/sp/800-37/rev-2/final.

European Union Agency for Network and Information Security (ENISA)

You could think of European Union Agency for Network and Information Security (ENISA) as a European counterpart to NIST. It is a standard and model developed in Europe. While it could be considered international because it is accepted throughout Europe, it is not as globally accepted in the way ISO standards are.

ENISA is responsible for producing *Cloud Computing: Benefits, Risks, and Recommendations for Information Security.* This guideline identifies 35 types of risks organizations should consider but goes further by identifying the top eight security risks based on likelihood and impact:

- Loss of governance
- Lock-in
- Isolation failure
- Compliance risk
- Management interface failure
- Data protection
- Malicious insider
- Insecure or incomplete data deletion

For more information about ENISA, please visit www.enisa.europa.eu.

Risk Management Metrics

To understand whether control mechanisms and policies are effective, it is important to identify risk management metrics that will reflect the effectiveness of your program. To do this, you can use what is referred to as a risk scorecard. These cards help you derive some relative value for risk of the activities in which you are engaged. They might, for instance, look something like this:

5. Critical
4. High
3. Moderate
2. Low
1. Minimal

Each of these levels would need to be defined so that risks could be adequately described. For instance, something that is critical (5) might cause irrevocable reputational and financial damage, whereas something that is moderate (3) might only cause some recoverable reputational and financial damage. Some companies even quantify these so there are actual dollar amounts attached to each. For example:

- Critical => $100,000 in damages
- High => $50,000 but < $100,000

Contracts and Service-Level Agreements (SLAs)

The most important documents establishing, defining, and enforcing the relationship between the cloud provider and cloud customer are the contract and the service-level agreement (SLA). The contract describes in detail exactly what both parties' responsibilities are; what services are being contracted; and what provisions are in place for the safety, security, integrity, and availability of those same services. The SLA is the list of defined, specific, numerical metrics that will be used to determine whether the provider is sufficiently meeting the contract terms during each period of performance.

Perhaps the most important relationship between the two documents is that the contract stipulates the penalty imposed on the cloud provider if any metric of the SLA is not met during a certain performance period. For instance, if the period of performance is one month and the SLA contains a metric that states, "Downtime will not exceed five (5) seconds per calendar month," and the cloud provider has six seconds of downtime in December, then the contract should allow the cloud customer to withhold payment for the cost that would otherwise be paid for that month, without any interruption of the continued service that is scheduled for January. This is a penalty imposed on the provider for failing to meet the needs of the customer, a sort of guarantee built into the contract and enforced on a periodic basis.

Let's begin by examining some of the essential components and activities that might be expressed in the contract between a provider and customer:

- Availability
- Performance
- Security and privacy of data
- Logging and reporting
- Data location
- Data format and structure
- Portability
- Identification and problem resolution
- Change management
- Dispute mediation
- Exit strategy options
- Components activity
- Uptime guarantees (the five 9s principle, i.e., 99.999% uptime)
- Penalties (for both consumer and provider)
- Penalty exclusions (instances where penalties are not invoked)
- Suspension of service
- Provider liability
- Data protection requirements
- Disaster recovery
- Security recommendations

As you can see, this assortment of details about services can be quite comprehensive. And if the CCSP or the cloud customer does not complete their due diligence by carefully scrutinizing the details of the contract, both parties could be dissatisfied with the eventual relationship. There are many considerations for what should be in the contract, depending on the needs of the organization.

The SLA, on the other hand, will assign specific numerical values to the performance objectives outlined in the contract. Using a sampling from the list of possible contract elements, the related SLA might include details like this:

- The cloud customer will have full, constant access to the customer's accounts and data at all times, with an allowed exception of service interruption no greater than 24 hours per calendar quarter (where service interruption is the fault of the provider).

- Data moved to or from the provider's resources and control at the defined price will not exceed 40 gigabytes per hour; data movement exceeding this rate will incur additional costs as defined in the standard rate sheet included in the contract.

- Customer service inquiries from the customer to the provider will be addressed via direct email or telephone contact within three hours of transmission.

While both the contract and the SLA may contain numerical values, the SLA will expressly include numerical metrics used to determine that recurring performance goals are met.

It's very important that the customer consider all possible situations and risks associated with the customer's business requirements when crafting and negotiating the contract and SLA. Suppose the provider promises availability that amounts to no more than 24 hours of downtime in any given quarter. But what if the customer is an online retailer who does 30 percent of their annual business the day after Thanksgiving and that is the 24-hour period of an outage? It could devastate the customer's business and yet still meet the terms of the SLA.

It is also important to look at the quality of the items delivered as part of your SLA. For instance, being connected and available is one thing, but if the servers at the other end are sluggish, customer experience may lag. If bandwidth is sluggish or there is jitter, again, consumer experience suffers. So in your SLA you must also adequately address these quality of service (QoS) issues. Here are some more examples:

- Availability
- Outage duration
- Capacity metrics
- Performance metrics
- Storage device metrics
- Server capacity metrics
- Instance startup time metric
- Response time metric
- Completion time metric
- Mean time to switchover
- Storage capability
- Server scalability

The Cloud Security Alliance (CSA) has created an annual report on threats. In 2013 the report was called *The Notorious Nine*, and in 2016 it was named *The Treacherous 12*. It is intended to let people know the nature of prevalent cloud threats, much like the OWASP (Open Web Application Security Project) Top Ten, which is a list of the top ten threats found or exposed in applications across the Internet.

Business Requirements

Before entering into any type of contract for cloud computing services, the organization should evaluate a number of things. First, there should be some compelling reason for engaging the cloud provider. Decisions should be made that assist the business in reaching its long-term goals. Decisions should never be made because they seem attractive or based on what your competitors are doing. You should have sound business reasons for deciding to use a cloud provider and for determining which one to choose.

As part of the due diligence in looking at cloud computing as a viable solution for the business, a few more items should be examined. Perhaps not all business units need to be involved in decision-making. Perhaps some changes will have little or no impact on them, in which case they do not need to be involved. This is called *scoping*, which is used to refer to including only departments or business units impacted by any cloud engagement.

Another important aspect of evaluating cloud computing solution is that of regulatory compliance. It is vital that you investigate what regulators' expectations are with regard to cloud computing solutions and the additional or differing risks that engaging in the cloud solution will bring to the organization.

Lastly, you must look closely at the costs associated with any types of disaster recovery or outage situations and what you are able to withstand. Measurements such as recovery time objective (RTO), recovery point objective (RPO), and maximum allowable downtime (MAD) are critical in making decisions about choosing cloud computing solutions. You must be able to withstand certain amounts of outages based on your risk profile as they are bound to occur at some time. Knowing how to handle them and how your cloud provider will handle them is imperative.

Cloud Contract Design and Management for Outsourcing

It is important that appropriate governance be involved in contract design and management of outsourcing. An in-depth understanding of contracts and contract management is important and is often managed by a specific department in large organizations. It is the CCSP's responsibility to ensure that contract managers understand the details of what they are managing so that the organization does not incur undue risk.

One example of adequate governance is how often contracts are renewed. This can and should be on at least an annual basis (if not sooner, if there are problems). Contracts should also specify how conflicts will be resolved.

Two other vitally important aspects of contracts have to do with the notion of data portability and vendor lock-in. *Vendor lock-in* is getting stuck with a certain provider, generally either as a result of detrimental contract terms or technical limitations. Data portability is the trait customers seek in order to avoid lock-in. *Data portability* is the term used to describe the ease of moving data from one cloud provider to another (or away from the cloud provider and back to a legacy enterprise environment). The greater the portability of the data, the less chance of vendor lock-in.

If you choose to stop doing business with your cloud vendor, what happens to your data? Is it transportable? Can you move it to another provider? Will the data be in some type of universal format so it is usable? Will you have a reasonable amount of time to move your data should conflicts go unresolved? And what will happen to your data once you leave the provider? Have you or they made arrangements for adequate data deletion using such techniques as crypto-shredding? These questions are all important things to consider when managing outsourcing contracts.

Identifying Appropriate Supply Chain and Vendor Management Processes

When discussing supply chain and vendor management in the realm of cloud computing, we are talking about operational aspects that entail risk. For instance, availability could be affected by the entirety of the cloud supply chain:

- Cloud carriers (the ISPs between the cloud customer and the cloud provider)
- Platform providers (the vendors supplying the operating systems used in the cloud service)
- Application providers (the vendors supplying the software used in the cloud service)

These can all be different entities making up the supply chain. Should any one of these become unavailable for some reason or cause problems in accessing resources, the customer faces an outage as well. These are risks associated with supply chain management and must be handled accordingly.

To adequately understand your risk exposure, you must first and foremost understand your SLAs and your provider's abilities to meet the SLA metrics.

Common Criteria Assurance Framework (ISO/IEC 15408-1:2009)

Common Criteria Assurance Framework (ISO/IEC 15408-1:2009) is yet another international standard designed to provide assurances for security claims by vendors. It establishes a universal format for evaluating security functions included in IT products.

The primary goal is to provide customers with assurance that security products they purchase have been thoroughly tested by independent third-party testers and meet the requirements the customer has specified.

One thing to keep in mind is that the Common Criteria certification of the product only verifies that the vendor's claims regarding security functionality are true, *not* whether those security functions are appropriate, meet industry best practices, or will be sufficient for a specific user's/customer's business needs or regulatory compliance. It is also important to note that the configuration of any product must match what was tested for the certification, otherwise the product may not meet the security needs of the organization.

For more information about the Common Criteria and ISO/IEC 15408-1:2009, go to: www.iso.org/iso/catalogue_detail.htm?csnumber=50341.

CSA Security, Trust, and Assurance Registry (STAR)

The CSA STAR program, initiated in 2011, was created in response to market demand for a single consistent framework for evaluating cloud providers. The CSA STAR program was designed to provide an independent level of program assurance for cloud consumers. It is based on three levels of assurance, covers four offerings, and consists of a comprehensive set of cloud-centric control objectives.

The CSA STAR is a registry of security controls provided by popular cloud computing offerings and is designed for users to assess cloud providers, security providers, and advisory and assessment service firms as part of their vendor management due diligence in choosing providers.

The CSA STAR consists of the two following components:

Cloud Controls Matrix (CCM)   A list of security controls and principles appropriate for the cloud environment, cross-referenced to other control frameworks such as COBIT, ISO standards, and NIST pubs. You can download a copy of the current CCM from CSA at https://cloudsecurityalliance.org/artifacts/csa-ccm-v-3-0-1-11-12-2018-FINAL/.

Consensus Assessments Initiative Questionnaire (CAIQ)   A self-assessment performed by cloud providers, detailing their evaluation of the practice areas and control groups they use in providing their services. You can request a copy of the current CAIQ from CSA at https://cloudsecurityalliance.org/download/consensus-assessments-initiative-questionnaire-v3-0-1/. You can also review completed CAIQs and certifications for various cloud providers in the CSA's STAR registry online at https://cloudsecurityalliance.org/star/#_registry.

The CSA STAR program also consists of three levels based on the Open Certification Framework:

Level One: Self-Assessment   Requires the release and publication of due diligence assessments against the CSA's *Consensus Assessment Initiative Questionnaire and/or Cloud Matrix (CCM)*

Level Two: CSA STAR Attestation   Requires the release and publication of available results of an assessment carried out by an independent third party based on CSA CCM and ISO 27001:2013 or an AICPA SOC 2

Level Three: CSA STAR Continuous Monitoring   Requires the release and publication of results of continuous monitoring performed by a certified third party

> There have been several iterations of the CCM, with the most recent and default being CCM v3.0.1, with updates effective November 2018.

Much like the SOC reports discussed in Chapter 10, these levels are representative of varying degrees of compliance with the framework. Involving independent third-party assessors can be quite expensive, and only large providers can usually absorb the cost as they typically also have a large investment in their security infrastructure.

> I highly recommend reviewing the CSA CCM. Not only is understanding it important for study purposes, but it may be useful in many actual IT environments.

Supply Chain Risk

When evaluating supply chain risk, the customer should be thinking of disaster recovery and business continuity: What happens if something goes wrong with one or more of these vendors on which your business depends?

The following supply chain risks are common:

- Financial instability of provider
- Single points of failure
- Data breaches
- Malware infestations
- Data loss

Even more common are natural disasters. What if the data center of your cloud provider is destroyed by an act of nature like the a hurricane or earthquake?

ISO 28000:2007 defines a set of security management requirements, including those that must be applied to all parties within a supply chain. However, ensuring the suitability of each vendor in the supply chain for meeting those requirements and enforcing them up and down the supply chain is the responsibility of the contracting organization. In other words, if you pay someone else to perform a service that in any way might affect your customers, you are obligated to ensure that the entities you've paid are subject to governance equivalent to what you've promised your customers and that your subcontractors are following that governance. ISO 28000:2007 also provides for a certification against certain elements that relate to supply chain risk:

- Security management policy
- Organizational objectives
- Risk management practices
- Documented practices and records
- Supplier relationships
- Roles, responsibilities, and authorities
- Organizational procedures and processes

As the standard grows in popularity with cloud providers, it will in all likelihood be more widely adopted in the future. Much like STAR, ISO certification gives the consumer some level of assurance that the appropriate controls are in place to secure data and privacy.

Manage Communication with Relevant Parties

Both the cloud provider and cloud customers will have to establish durable, resilient lines of communication for business partners along the supply chain for a variety of reasons/purposes. Of particular interest are the following:

- **Vendors and Partners:** Clear communications with vendors is necessary in order to ensure adequate quantities and types of resources/assets are available for operations. This can be especially true for emergency/contingency situations, where the immediacy/availability of resources is crucial (such as fuel for generators, replacement components for damaged systems, and so on).

- **Customers:** *Customers* can mean either individual end users of a product/service or a business that receives products/services in a supply chain. Communication with customers is essential to manage expectations (for instance, alerting customers prior to an interruption of service), maintain brand awareness, and ensure logistic needs are being met. Again, this is particularly true during disaster situations, where delivery may be delayed or interrupted. This might also be required by law, as in those situations involving privacy data, in jurisdictions affected by data breach notification laws.

- **Regulators:** In regulated industries, where a third party determines your ability to conduct business, maintaining communications with regulators is crucial. Regulators should be made aware of any situation where the organization might become non-compliant with pertinent standards or regulation (such as during disasters or in the aftermath of a crime). Regulators should be kept apprised of developments, potential solutions being considered by management, any stopgap measures or compensatory controls used in the interim, and the estimated duration until compliance resumes.

For communications with all parties in the supply chain, secondary and even tertiary communications capabilities are highly recommended, especially for disaster situations. (Don't rely on the telephone to be working during a disaster.)

Summary

In this chapter, we discussed a number of issues dealing with risk and risk management. We examined risk frameworks, contracts, service-level agreements, and certifications that help in assuring cloud customers that sound security practices are in place and that they can rely on their provider.

Exam Essentials

Ensure that you have a good grasp of the models, frameworks, and standards discussed in this chapter.   This includes ISO standards, NIST standards, and ENISA.

Make sure you have a thorough understanding of all the elements of the service-level agreement (SLA).   Understand how SLAs apply to cloud computing.

Be sure to understand the three levels of the CSA Security, Trust, and Assurance Registry (STAR) Open Certification Framework.

Written Labs

You can find the answer to the written labs in Appendix A.

1. Go to the CSA website and read the detailed description of the CSA STAR program at https://cloudsecurityalliance.org/star/. Be sure you understand the three levels in the Open Certification Framework. Then attempt to identify at least three cloud service providers who have met the requirements and write down their names.

2. Name and describe at least two major risk management frameworks.

3. Name at least two important things to look for when reviewing an SLA.

Review Questions

You can find the answers to the review questions in Appendix B.

1. Which is the lowest level of the CSA STAR program?
    A. Continuous monitoring
    B. Self-assessment
    C. Hybridization
    D. Attestation

2. Which of the following is a valid risk management metric?
    A. CSA
    B. KRI
    C. SLA
    D. SOC

3. Which of the following frameworks focuses specifically on design implementation and over-sight of risk management?
    A. ISO 31000:2018
    B. HIPAA
    C. ISO 27017
    D. NIST 800-92

4. Which of the following identifies the top eight security risks based on likelihood and impact?
    A. NIST 800-53
    B. ISO 27000
    C. ENISA
    D. COBIT

5. The CSA STAR program consists of three levels. Which of the following is *not* one of the CSA STAR levels?
    A. Self-assessment
    B. Third-party assessment-based certification
    C. SOC 2 audit certification
    D. Continuous monitoring–based certification

6. Which ISO standard refers to addressing security risks in a supply chain?
    A. ISO 27001
    B. ISO/IEC 28000:2007
    C. ISO 9000
    D. ISO 31000:2018

7. Which of the following is *not* a risk management framework?

    A. NIST SP 800-37

    B. ENISA *Cloud Computing: Benefits, Risks, and Recommendations for Information Security*

    C. Key risk indicators (KRIs)

    D. ISO 31000:2018

8. What is an impossible level of risk?

    A. Condition Alpha

    B. Maximum

    C. Reduced

    D. Zero

9. Which of the following is *not* a part of ENISA's top eight security risks of cloud computing?

    A. Vendor lock-in

    B. Isolation failure

    C. Insecure or incomplete data deletion

    D. Availability

10. Which of the following is a risk management option that halts a business function?

    A. Mitigation

    B. Acceptance

    C. Transference

    D. Avoidance

11. Which of the following best describes a cloud carrier?

    A. A person or entity responsible for making a cloud service available to consumers

    B. The intermediary who provides connectivity and transport of cloud services between cloud providers and cloud consumers

    C. The person or entity responsible for keeping cloud services running for customers

    D. The person or entity responsible for transporting data across the Internet

12. Which of the following methods of addressing risk is most associated with insurance?

    A. Transference

    B. Avoidance

    C. Acceptance

    D. Mitigation

13. Which of the following components is part of what a CCSP should review when looking at contracting with a cloud service provider?

    A. The physical layout of the data center

    B. Background checks for the provider's personnel

    C. Use of subcontractors

    D. Redundant uplink grafts

14. The difference between KPIs and a KRIs is which of the following?

    A. KPIs no longer exist, having been replaced by KRIs.

    B. KRIs no longer exist, having been replaced by KPIs.

    C. KRIs are forward looking, while KPIs are backward looking.

    D. There is no difference between KPIs and KRIs.

15. Which of the following is *not* a way to manage risk?

    A. Enveloping

    B. Mitigating

    C. Accepting

    D. Transferring

16. Which of the following is *not* a risk management framework?

    A. Hex GBL

    B. COBIT

    C. NIST SP 800-37

    D. ISO 31000:2019

17. Which of the following is *not* appropriate to include in an SLA?

    A. The number of user accounts allowed during a specified period

    B. Which personnel are responsible and authorized among both the provider and the customer to declare an emergency and transition the service to contingency operation status

    C. The amount of data allowed to be transmitted and received between the cloud provider and customer

    D. The availability requirements for a given period

18. What is the Cloud Security Alliance Cloud Controls Matrix (CCM)?

    A. An inventory of cloud service security controls that are arranged into separate security domains

    B. An inventory of cloud services security controls that are arranged into a hierarchy of security domains

    C. A set of regulatory requirements for cloud service providers

    D. A set of software development lifecycle requirements for cloud service providers

19. Which of the following is *not* one of the types of controls?

    A. Transitional

    B. Administrative

    C. Technical

    D. Physical

20. Which of the following is *not* an example of an essential internal stakeholder?

    A. IT analyst

    B. IT director

    C. CFO

    D. HR director

Appendix A

Answers to Written Labs

Chapter 1: Architectural Concepts

1. The Cloud Security Alliance website provides a lot of helpful information. Be sure to read the Guidance v4 document and review all of the helpful resources.

2. Answers will vary. Here are some possible responses:
   - The business might be concerned with unauthorized disclosure due to negligence or malice on the part of the cloud provider.
   - The business may be attracted to the dramatic cost savings offered by cloud computing.
   - The business may want to transition from a cumbersome legacy environment into something more flexible and modern.

3. The three cloud computing service models include IaaS, PaaS, and SaaS, and some of their common advantages and disadvantages include (but are not limited to) the following:
   - **IaaS:**
     Advantages: Reduced capital investment; increased redundancy for BC/DR; scalability
     Disadvantages: Reliance on cloud provider for security; responsibility for maintaining OS and apps retained
   - **PaaS:**
     Advantages: Multiple OS platforms to utilize, making it particularly good for testbed and software development purposes; all the advantages of IaaS
     Disadvantages: Reliance on cloud provider for updating OSs; responsibility for maintaining apps retained
   - **SaaS:**
     Advantages: Cloud provider is responsible for all infrastructure, OSs, and apps; all the advantages of PaaS
     Disadvantages: Loss of all administrative control; may not have any insight into security

Chapter 2: Design Requirements

1. The Business Impact Analysis Worksheet is fairly straightforward and easy to use.

2. For this lab, I chose the marketing department, but any department or function can be analyzed.

3. For this lab, I chose the general loss of systems due to any and all possible reasons.

4. My worksheet, still in progress, looks like Figure A.1.

FIGURE A.1 Business impact analysis worksheet

Business X - Fashion Clothing

Ready Business.

Business Impact Analysis Worksheet

Department / Function / Process _____ Marketing _____

Operational & Financial Impacts

Timing / Duration	Operation Impacts	Financial Impact
start of fall line	loss of end customers	up to $20M
>72 hours from trade show	loss of distributors	up to $10M
	loss of market share	Up to $10M

Considerations (customize for your business)

Timing: Identify point in time when interruption would have greater impact (e.g., season, end of month/quarter, etc.)

Duration: Identify the duration of the interruption or point in time when the operational and or financial impact(s) will occur.
- < 1 hour
- >1 hr. < 8 hours
- > 8 hrs. <24 hours
- > 24 hrs. < 72 hrs.
- > 72 hrs.
- > 1 week
- > 1 month

Operational Impacts
- Lost sales and income
- Negative cash flow resulting from delayed sales or income
- Increased expenses (e.g., overtime labor, outsourcing, expediting costs, etc.)
- Regulatory fines
- Contractual penalties or loss of contractual bonuses
- Customer dissatisfaction or defection
- Delay executing business plan or strategic initiative

Financial Impact
Quantify operational impacts in financial terms.

ready.gov/business

Chapter 3: Data Classification

1. The NIST guidelines are helpful and easy to understand. Appendix D.1 provides a handy format that you can use for your devices.

2. Results should look like the example listed in 800-88, D.1:

    Example Statement of Cryptographic Erase Features:

    1. **Make/Model/Version/Media Type:** Acme hard drive model abc12345 version 1+. Media type is Legacy Magnetic media.

    2. **Key Generation:** A DRBG is used as specified in SP 800-90, with validation [number].

    3. **Media Encryption:** Media is encrypted with AES -256 media encryption in Cipher Block Chaining (CBC) mode as described in SP 800-38A. This device is FIPS 140 validated with certificate [number].

    4. **Key Level and Wrapping:** The media encryption key is sanitized directly during cryptographic erasure.

5. **Data Areas Addressed:** The device encrypts all data stored in the LBA-addressable space except for a preboot authentication and variable area and the device logs. Device log data is retained by the device following cryptographic erasure.

6. **Key Lifecycle Management:** As the MEK moves between wrapped, unwrapped, and rewrapped states, the previous instance is sanitized using three inverted overwrite passes.

7. **Key Sanitization Technique:** Three passes with a pattern that is inverted between passes.

8. **Key Escrow or Injection:** The device does not support escrow or injection of the keys at or below the level of the sanitization operation.

9. **Error Condition Handling:** If the storage device encounters a defect in a location where a key is stored, the device attempts to rewrite the location and the cryptographic erasure operation continues, reporting success to the user if the operation is otherwise successful.

10. **Interface Clarity:** The device has an ATA interface and supports the ATA Sanitize Device feature set CRYPTO SCRAMBLE EXT command and a TCG Opal interface with the ability to sanitize the device by cryptographically erasing the contents. Both of these commands apply the functionality described in this statement.

Chapter 4: Cloud Data Security

1. This white paper on preventing data leaks is just one of the many useful resources that ISACA provides. Be sure to explore others when you have the time.

2. An outstanding response would look something like this:

    According to the ISACA white paper on DLP solutions, the following operational risks might be involved in implementing DLP:

    Improperly Set DLP Tools. This is fairly obvious. The data owner must define the rules and categories associated with the organization's data or the DLP solution won't work in the manner intended. In fact, misconfigured DLP tools might actually harm the IT environment by adding extraneous overhead or responding to a significant amount of false positives.

    Improperly Sized Network DLP Module. If the DLP solution isn't correctly scoped for the organization's IT environment, it might miss a significant portion of network traffic, and data that should be prevented from leaving the organization's control might be allowed to go because the tool didn't even inspect it.

    Excessive Reporting and False Positives. See the first item; the rules and characteristics of suspect data have to be properly set by the data owner, and the tool has to understand the rules sufficiently to block only that data that fails instead of blocking legitimate traffic.

    Conflicts with the Traditional Environment. Interoperability will always be a concern for any new tool, including DLP.

Changes in Process of Infrastructure That Affect DLP Ability to Function Properly. The rules and identification capabilities for the DLP solution need to be updated as the environment changes; there is no "one-size-fits-all" DLP mechanism.

Improperly Placed DLP Modules. See the second point; the DLP tool might miss suspect traffic if it's placed in the wrong network location to monitor that traffic.

Undetected Failure of DLP Modules. Like any other toolset, if the DLP mechanisms aren't monitored and maintained properly and failure goes undetected, the organization will end up having a false sense of security.

Improperly Configured Directory Services. The DLP tools can only create an accurate audit chain when there is sufficient traceability in the environment to support that effort.

Chapter 5: Security in the Cloud

1. If possible, be sure to use the cloud providers' actual contracts when you do this. Discrepancies can exist between their marketing materials and contracts, and the contract is what is legally binding in the event of a later problem between you and the cloud provider.

2. Answers will vary. Be sure to record the URLs where you got the materials so you can refer back to them. Also, keep in mind that backup, pricing, and portability needs will vary from organization to organization. There is no one-size-fits-all solution.

Chapter 6: Responsibilities in the Cloud

1. The Cloud Security Alliance's STAR program is widely used. You should be sure to fully understand STAR.

2. This is the questionnaire that registered cloud providers fill out. It includes information on how they handle various aspects of security.

3. This is an important document. It tells you a lot about how a cloud provider provides its services. Take some time to really consider what the information in this document means, particularly in the context of your organization's needs.

4. The Registry lists various cloud providers who have each registered with the CSA.

5. If you have time, it would be a good idea to download several completed questionnaires for different providers and compare them too.

6. Answers will vary. An outstanding response will look like this:

   I chose to review the [name of specific product] from [name of specific provider]. The following three issues came to my attention:

   1. This provider is charging customers for malware and vulnerability scans. These should probably be functions included with the price of the service instead of additional costs.

2. The provider's response about collecting/creating metadata on its customers is vague and leaves room for doubt about what specific information it gathers on customer behavior. It says that the customer owns their virtual machines and that the provider doesn't access or collect the customer's data. Does the provider truly not have any idea how customers are using the service?

3. The provider is securing ecommerce transactions with SSL; it would be better if TLS was used instead.

Chapter 7: Cloud Application Security

1. Answers will vary. An outstanding response would look something like this:

   I use Microsoft's Office 365, an SaaS. The APIs include my browser (Mozilla's Firefox), and any plug-ins necessary to run the various 365 suite of applications; these can include some Java implementations, Microsoft's own specific plug-ins for Firefox (Microsoft Office 2010, Silverlight, and Windows Live Photo Manager), and any other multimedia APIs used for including material in Office work products (possibly including the plug-ins for Adobe Acrobat and the Widevine tools from Google). There may be other plug-ins and add-ons that Firefox uses to manipulate data while 365 is running.

2. The cloud software development lifecycle is extremely similar to other SDLCs. A couple of the major differences to note are the importance of inspecting secure remote access and strong authentication for development of apps that will be used in the cloud.

3. Answers will vary. The cloud application architecture includes many components. These include, but are not limited to, the following: APIs, tenant separation, cryptography, sandboxing, and application virtualization.

4. An identity management provider will be in charge of provisioning, maintaining, and deprovisioning identities on behalf of the cloud customer. This might include providing secure remote access, managing crypto keys, and federation of multiple resource providers.

Chapter 8: Operations Elements

1. Answers will vary. An example might look like this:

   The application I am using as a theoretical sample is a database of information regarding dogs. The primary key will be each dog's RFID chip number, and all other fields will describe characteristics of the dogs, such as weight, color, owner information (including contact data such as email and home address), and so forth. The organization (data owner) is a dog food and toy manufacturer, and it uses this database for targeted marketing to groups of dog owners. The organization's staff (the user base) accesses the database through web portals.

2. STRIDE comprises Spoofing identity, Tampering with data, Repudiation, Information disclosure, Denial of service, and Elevation of privilege. Using this model helps you quickly identify many possible points of failure.

3. Answers will vary. An example:

The database might be subject to these three kinds of threats:

- **Tampering with Data:** SQL injection. A malicious user (either internal or external) might try to enter SQL commands in data fields as a means to corrupt the data or affect the overall system.

- **Controls:** Field validation should be included so that the program can detect SQL commands in data fields and not accept them.

- **Information Disclosure:** Dog owner PII. Because the owners' PII is included in the database (home addresses), the organization should be careful to reduce the likelihood of the PII being disclosed to unauthorized parties, including the organization's employees who do not have a need to know that data.

- **Controls:** Employ masking/obfuscation techniques so that unauthorized users do not see the PII content in those specific fields but instead see blank spaces or Xs.

- **Denial of Service:** DDoS. Because access to the database is via the web, a DDoS attack against the servers could hinder user access to the data.

- **Controls:** Deploy and utilize strong network security tools, such as properly configured routers, firewalls, and IDS/IPS systems, and ensure redundancy of all Internet connections (including DNS nodes).

Chapter 9: Operations Management

1. Answers will vary. Possible choices might include Kohler, Honda, Cummins, Subaru, and Hitachi.

2. Answers will vary. Be sure to compare the specifications for the generators you chose against the hypothetical loads you imagine for your data centers and against the ASHRAE standards.

3. Answers will vary. You should use the listed criteria (load, price, fuel) to justify your choice of preferred generator. The ASHRAE guidance is fairly detailed regarding specific ranges, based on the type, age, and location of the equipment. As you compare the generators, it is important to determine which guidance is most applicable to your facility and take into account any guidance and recommendations from the manufacturers regarding ambient ranges affecting performance parameters for their specific products.

Chapter 10: Legal and Compliance Part 1

1. Laws are dictated by legislatures and enforced by government. Regulations are created by governmental agencies and enforced by government. Standards are prescribed modes for certain types of activity; sources include industry bodies, certifying entities, or internal guidelines within organizations themselves. Contracts can also result in mandates, even if they are entered into voluntarily.

2. HIPAA now includes a number of rules that have been developed to address a range of issues. The two most often referred to are the Privacy Rule and the Security Rule. The Privacy Rule deals with the necessity to protect patient data (PHI), and the Security Rule deals with supporting the CIA triad in a medical organization.

3. The SOC 1 report addresses only financial reporting activity and is of no interest to IT security practitioners. The SOC 2 describes IT security controls and comes in two types, Type 1 and Type 2. Type 1 covers the architecture and control framework design at a point in time, whereas Type 2 is a review of the actual controls as implemented over a period of time. The SOC 3 report is only an attestation that one of the SOC 2 reports has been performed, without any detail.

Chapter 11: Legal and Compliance Part 2

1. The CSA Star program and Open Certification Framework have been widely adopted. While many cloud providers meet their requirements, not all have, so it is still important to confirm this.

2. Answers will vary and might include NIST's 800-37 (Risk Management Framework), COSO, and COBIT.

3. Answers will vary and might include throughput, per-use prices, the customer's business drivers, BC/DR considerations, portability, and more.

Appendix B

Answers to Review Questions

Chapter 1: Architectural Concepts

1. B. Programming as a service is not a common offering; the others are ubiquitous throughout the industry.

2. D. Virtualization allows scalable resource allocation; broadband connections allow users to have remote access from anywhere; encrypted connections allow for secure remote access. Smart hubs aren't widely used in cloud offerings.

3. A. Service-level agreements (SLAs) specify objective measures that define what the cloud provider will deliver to the customer.

4. C. Security is usually not a profit center and is therefore beholden to business drivers; the purpose of security is to support the business.

5. D. Lack of access is an availability issue.

6. B. CASBs don't usually offer BC/DR/COOP services; that's something offered by cloud providers.

7. D. The data on magnetic swipe cards isn't usually encrypted.

8. B. Risks, in general, can be reduced but never eliminated; cloud service, specifically, does not eliminate risk to the cloud customer because the customer retains a great deal of risk after migration.

9. B. Backups are still just as important as ever, regardless of where your primary data and backups are stored.

10. D. The gamer owns the console in their home. The gamer can turn it on and off at their discretion, sell it, or smash it with a hammer. The various members of a community cloud can all share the underlying resources of the community cloud as they choose. In this case, Sony, the game maker, the gamer, and the other players are all members of the community, and all share different underlying components as they choose.

11. B. This is the definition of vendor lock-out.

12. B. This is a nonsense term used as a red herring.

13. C. Under current laws in most jurisdictions, the data owner is responsible for any breaches that result in unauthorized disclosure of PII; this includes breaches caused by contracted parties and outsources services. The data owner is the cloud customer.

14. B. The business impact analysis is designed to ascertain the value of the organization's assets and learn the critical paths and processes.

15. A. Because ownership and usage is restricted to only the one organization, this is a private cloud.

16. B. This is the definition of a public cloud model.

17. D. This is the definition of a community cloud model.

18. B. PaaS allows the cloud customer to install any kind of software, including software to be tested, on an architecture that includes any desired OSs.

19. C. SaaS is the most comprehensive cloud offering, requiring little input and administration on the part of the cloud customer.

20. A. IaaS offers what is basically a hot/warm disaster recovery (DR) site, with hardware, connectivity and utilities, allowing the customer to build out any kind of software configuration (including choosing OSs).

Chapter 2: Design Requirements

1. B. When we gather information about business requirements, we need to do a complete inventory, receive accurate valuation of assets (usually from the owners of those assets), and assess criticality. However, this collection of information does not objectively tell us how useful an asset is.

2. B. The business impact analysis gathers asset valuation information that is beneficial for risk analysis and selection of security controls (it helps avoid putting the $10 lock on the $5 bicycle) in addition to criticality information that helps in BC/DR planning by letting the organization understand which systems, data, and personnel are necessary to continuously maintain. However, it does not aid secure acquisition efforts, since the assets examined by the BIA have already been acquired.

3. D. In IaaS, the service is bare metal, and the customer has to install the OS and the software; the customer is then is responsible for maintaining that OS. In the other models, the provider installs and maintains the OS.

4. C. In PaaS, the provider supplies the hardware, connectivity, and OS; the customer installs and maintains applications. In IaaS, the customer must also install the OS, and in SaaS, the provider supplies and maintains the applications.

5. B. SaaS is the model in which the customer supplies only the data; in the other models, the customer also supplies the OS, the applications, or both.

6. B. The contract codifies the rights and responsibilities of the parties involved upon completion of negotiation. The RMF aids in risk analysis and design of the environment. A memorandum of agreement/understanding (MOA/MOU) is shared between parties for a number of possible reasons. The BIA aids in risk assessment, DC/BR efforts, and selection of security controls by determining the criticality and value of assets.

7. D. Layered defense calls for a diverse approach to security.

8. A. A process is an administrative control; sometimes, the process includes elements of other types of controls (in this case, the access control mechanism might be a technical control, or it might be a physical control), but the process itself is administrative. Keystroke logging is a technical control (or an attack, if done for malicious purposes and not for auditing), door locks are a physical control, and biometric authentication is a technological control. This is a challenging question, so don't be frustrated if you did not get it correct on the first try.

9. A. A firewall is a technological control. The safe and extinguisher are physical controls, and firing someone is an administrative control.

10. D. Fences are physical controls; carpets and ceilings are architectural features, and a door is not necessarily a control: the lock on the door would be a physical security control. Although you might think of a door as a potential answer, the best answer is the fence; the exam will have questions where more than one answer is correct, and the answer that will score you points is the one that is most correct.

11. D. All of these activities should incorporate encryption except for profile formatting, which is a made-up term.

12. A. We don't want to improve default accounts—we want to remove them. All the other options are steps we take to harden devices.

13. B. Updating and patching the system helps harden the system. Encrypting the OS is a distractor. That would make the OS/machine impossible to use. Video cameras are a security control but not one used to harden a device. Background checks are good for vetting personnel but not for hardening devices.

14. A. Homomorphic encryption hopes to achieve that goal; the other options are terms that have almost nothing to do with encryption.

15. B. Senior management decides the risk appetite of the organization. There is no such thing as "reclusion evaluation." Legislative mandates (laws) do not tell an organization which risks are acceptable except in very, very specific industries, and those are outliers. Contracts don't dictate acceptable risk for an organization; the organization should use its risk appetite to guide how it crafts contracts.

16. C. This is the definition of the term *residual*.

17. B. Reversal is not a method for handling risk.

18. D. Although all the other options are ways to harden a mobile device, two-person integrity is a concept that has nothing to do with the topic and, if implemented, would require everyone in your organization to walk around in pairs while using their mobile devices.

19. D. Although the rest of the options are good tactics for securing devices, we can't remove all admin accounts; the device will need to be administered at some point, and that account needs to be there. This question is good practice for the exam, where every word in each question and each answer is important.

20. C. Option C is the definition of risk—and risk is never preventable. It can be obviated, attenuated, reduced, and minimized, but never completely prevented. Any particular, specific risk may be everlasting or transient, but it's not the case that all risks could be described by either of these terms.

Chapter 3: Data Classification

1. **B.** All the others are valid methods of data discovery; user-based is a red herring with no meaning.

2. **C.** All the others might be included in data labels, but we don't usually include data value since it is prone to change frequently and because it might not be information we want to disclose to anyone who does not have need to know.

3. **B.** All the others might be included in data labels, but we don't include delivery vendor, which is nonsense in this context.

4. **D.** All the others might be included in data labels, but multifactor authentication is a procedure used for access control, not a label.

5. **D.** All the others are data analytics methods, but *refractory iterations* is a nonsense term thrown in as a distractor.

6. **B.** The data owner is usually considered the cloud customer in a cloud configuration; the data in question is the customer's information, being processed in the cloud. The cloud provider is only leasing services and hardware to the customer. The cloud access security broker (CASB) only handles access control on behalf of the cloud customer and is not in direct contact with the production data.

7. **C.** In legal terms, when *data processor* is defined, it refers to anyone who stores, handles, moves, or manipulates data on behalf of the data owner or controller. In the cloud computing realm, this is the cloud provider.

8. **B.** Hardware cannot be sanitized by deleting data. Deleting, as an operation, does not erase the data; it simply removes the logical pointers to the data for processing purposes. Burning, deletion, and drilling can all be used to sufficiently destroy the hardware to the point where data becomes irrecoverable.

9. **D.** All the elements except transference need to be addressed in each policy. Transference is not an element of policy.

10. **B.** We don't have physical ownership, control, or even access to the hardware devices holding the data, so physical destruction, including melting, is not an option. Overwriting is a possibility, but it is complicated by the difficulty of locating all the sectors and storage areas that might have contained our data and by the likelihood that constant backups in the cloud increase the chance we'll miss something as it's being overwritten. Crypto-shredding is the only reasonable alternative. Cold fusion is a distractor.

11. **A.** Copyrights are protected tangible expressions of creative works. The other options listed are answers to subsequent questions.

12. **B.** Patents protect processes (as well as inventions, new plant life, and decorative patterns). The other options listed are answers to other questions.

13. D. Confidential sales and marketing materials unique to the organization are trade secrets. The other options listed are answers to other questions.

14. D. Confidential recipes unique to the organization are trade secrets. The other options listed are answers to other questions.

15. C. Logos, symbols, phrases, and color schemes that describe brands are trademarks. The other options listed are answers to other questions.

16. C. The DMCA provision for takedown notices allows copyright holders to demand removal of suspect content from the web, and puts the burden of proof on whoever posted the material; this function has been abused by griefers, trolls, and overzealous content producers. There is no toll exemption in the DMCA. The decryption program prohibition makes DeCSS and other similar programs illegal. *Puppet plasticity* is a nonsense term used for a distractor.

17. B. The US Patent and Trademark Office accepts, reviews and approves applications for new patents. The USDA creates and enforces agriculture regulation. OSHA oversees workplace safety regulations. The SEC regulates publicly traded corporations.

18. C. IRM solutions use all these methods except for dip switch validity, which is a nonsense term.

19. D. The United States does not have a single, overarching personal privacy law; instead, the US often protects personal information by industry (HIPAA, GLBA, FERPA, and so forth). Belgium, like all EU member countries, adheres to the GDPR. Argentina's Personal Data Protection Act cleaves to the EU regulation, as does Japan's Act on the Protection of Personal Information.

20. B. IRM tools should include all the functions listed except for self-destruction, which might hurt someone.

Chapter 4: Cloud Data Security

1. B. *Data discovery* is a term used to describe the process of identifying information according to specific traits or categories. The rest are all methods for obscuring data.

2. D. SIEM is not intended to provide any enhancement of performance; in fact, a SIEM solution may decrease performance because of additional overhead. All the rest are goals of SIEM implementations.

3. B. DLP does not have anything to do with elasticity, which is the capability of the environment to scale up or down according to demand. All the rest are goals of DLP implementations.

4. B. DLP solutions may protect against inadvertent disclosure. Randomization is a technique for obscuring data, not a risk to data. DLP tools will not protect against risks from natural disasters or against impacts due to device failure.

5. A. DLP tools can identify outbound traffic that violates the organization's policies. DLP will not protect against losses due to performance issues or power failures. The DLP solution must be configured according to the organization's policies, so bad policies will attenuate the effectiveness of DLP tools, not the other way around.

6. C. AES is an encryption standard. Link encryption is a method for protecting communications traffic. Using one-time pads is an encryption method.

7. A. DLP tools need to be aware of which information to monitor and what information requires categorization (usually done upon data creation, by the data owners). DLPs can be implemented with or without physical access or presence. USB connectivity has nothing to do with DLP solutions.

8. B. In order to implement tokenization, there will need to be two databases: the database containing the raw, original data and the token database containing tokens that map to original data. Having two-factor authentication is nice, but certainly not required. Encryption keys are not necessary for tokenization. Two-person integrity does not have anything to do with tokenization.

9. D. Data masking does not support authentication in any way. All the others are excellent use cases for data masking.

10. A. DLP can be combined with IRM tools to protect intellectual property; both are designed to deal with data that falls into special categories. SIEMs are used for monitoring event logs, not live data movement. Kerberos is an authentication mechanism. Hypervisors are used for virtualization.

11. A. ITAR is a Department of State program. EAR is a Commerce Department program. Evaluation assurance levels are part of the Common Criteria standard from ISO. Information rights management tools are used for protecting electronic processing of intellectual property.

12. B. EAR is a Commerce Department program. ITAR is a State Department program. Evaluation assurance levels are part of the ISO's Common Criteria standard. Information rights management tools are used for protecting electronic processing of intellectual property.

13. B. Cryptographic keys should not be stored along with the data they secure, regardless of key length. We don't group crypto keys (doing so would violate the principle of secrecy necessary for keys to serve their purpose). Keys should be based on randomized (or pseudo-randomized) generation and not have any dependency.

14. D. We should do all of these except for requiring multifactor authentication. Multifactor authentication might be an element of access control for keys, but it is not specifically an element of key management.

15. A. The physical security of crypto keys is of some concern, but guards or vaults are not always necessary. Two-person integrity might be a good practice for protecting keys. The best answer to this question is option A, because it is always true, whereas the remaining options depend on circumstances.

16. D. All of these things should be considered when creating data archival policies except option D, which is a nonsense term.

17. B. The other options are the names of the phases, but they are out of proper order.

18. B. Cloud access security brokers provide IAM functions. Data loss, leak prevention, and protection are a family of tools used to reduce the possibility of unauthorized disclosure of sensitive information. SIEMs are tools used to collate and manage log data. AES is an encryption standard.

19. C. Databases store data in fields, in a relational motif. Object-based storage stores data as objects in a volume, with labels and metadata. File-based is a cloud storage architecture that manages the data in a hierarchy of files. A CDN stores data in caches of copied content near locations of high demand.

20. D. A CDN stores data in caches of copied content near locations of high demand. Object-based storage stores data as objects in a volume, with labels and metadata. File-based is a cloud storage architecture that manages the data in a hierarchy of files. Databases store data in fields, in a relational motif.

Chapter 5: Security in the Cloud

1. D. Elasticity is the name for the benefit of cloud computing where resources can be apportioned as necessary to meet customer demand. Obfuscation is a technique to hide full raw data sets, either from personnel who do not have need to know or for use in testing. Mobility is not a term pertinent to the CBK.

2. D. This is not a normal configuration and would not likely provide genuine benefit.

3. B. Background checks are controls for attenuating potential threats from internal actors; external threats aren't likely to submit to background checks.

4. B. IRM and DLP are used for increased authentication/access control and egress monitoring, respectively, and would actually decrease portability instead of enhancing it.

5. A. Dual control is not useful for remote access devices because we'd have to assign two people for every device, which would decrease efficiency and productivity. Muddling is a cocktail preparation technique that involves crushing ingredients. Safe harbor is a policy provision that allows for compliance through an alternate method rather than the primary instruction.

6. D. The cloud provider's resellers are a marketing and sales mechanism, not an operational dependency that could affect the security of a cloud customer.

7. A. State notification laws and the loss of proprietary data/intellectual property preexisted the cloud; only the lack of ability to transfer liability is new.

8. A. IaaS entails the cloud customer installing and maintaining the OS, programs, and data; PaaS has the customer installing programs and data; in SaaS, the customer only uploads data. In a community cloud, data and device owners are distributed.

9. C. NIST offers many informative guides and standards but nothing specific to any one organization. The cloud provider will not have prepared an analysis of lock-out/lock-in potential. Open-source providers can offer many useful materials but again, nothing specific to the organization.

10. B. Malware risks and threats are not affected by the terms of the cloud contract.

11. C. DoS/DDoS threats and risks are not unique to the multitenant architecture.

12. B. Hardened perimeter devices are more useful at attenuating the risk of external attack.

13. C. ISP redundancy is a means to control the risk of externalities, not internal threats.

14. D. Scalability is a feature of cloud computing, allowing users to dictate an increase or decrease in service as needed, not a means to counter internal threats.

15. C. Conflict of interest is a threat, not a control.

16. A. One-time pads are a cryptographic tool/method; this has nothing to do with BC/DR. All the other answers are benefits of using cloud computing for BC/DR.

17. C. Cryptographic sanitization is a means of reducing the risks from data remanence, not a way to minimize escalation of privilege.

18. B. Attackers prefer Type 2 hypervisors because the OS offers more attack surface and potential vulnerabilities. There are no Type 3 or 4 hypervisors.

19. B. Vendor lock-in is the result of a lack of portability, for any number of reasons. Masking is a means to hide raw datasets from users who do not have need to know. Closing is a nonsense term in this context.

20. C. Software developers often install backdoors as a means to avoid performing entire workflows when adjusting the programs they're working on; they often leave backdoors behind in production software, inadvertently or intentionally.

Chapter 6: Responsibilities in the Cloud

1. A. In IaaS, the cloud provider only owns the hardware and supplies the utilities. The customer is responsible for the OS, programs, and data. In PaaS and SaaS, the provider also owns the OS. There is no QaaS. That is a red herring.

2. D. While the provider might share any of the other options listed, the provider will not share administration of security controls with the customer.

3. B. The contract between the provider and customer enhances the customer's trust by holding the provider financially liable for negligence or inadequate service (although the customer remains legally liable for all inadvertent disclosures). Statutes, however, largely leave customers liable. The security control matrix is a tool for ensuring compliance with regulations. HIPAA is a statute.

4. D. The SOC 3 is the least detailed, so the provider is not concerned about revealing it. The SOC 1 Types 1 and 2 are about financial reporting, and not relevant. The SOC 2 Type 2 is much more detailed and will most likely be held closely by the provider.

5. B. The SOC 3 is the least detailed, so the provider is not concerned about revealing it. The SOC 1 Types 1 and 2 are about financial reporting and not relevant. The SOC 2 Type 2 is much more detailed and will most likely be held closely by the provider.

6. D. The auditor should be impartial to the success of the target organization; consulting creates a conflict of interest.

7. B. Removing anti-malware agents. Hardening the operating system means making it more secure. Limiting administrator access, closing unused ports, and removing unnecessary services and libraries all have the potential to make an OS more secure. But removing anti-malware agents would actually make the system less secure. If anything, anti-malware agents should be added, not removed, as part of the hardening process.

8. C. Real-time environmental controls will not provide meaningful information and will not enhance trust. All the others will and do.

9. B. The customer does not administer on behalf of the provider. All the rest are possible options.

10. B. SOC 2 deals with the CIA triad. SOC 1 is for financial reporting. SOC 3 is only an attestation by the auditor. There is no SOC 4.

11. C. SOC 2 deals with the CIA triad. SOC 1 is for financial reporting. SOC 3 is only an attestation by the auditor. There is no SOC 4.

12. C. The provider may share audit and performance log data with the customer. The provider will most likely not share A and D since they reveal too much information about the provider's security program. B is already public information and does not enhance trust.

13. A. The customer always owns the data and will therefore always have access to it. The customer will never have administrative access to the provider's security controls, regardless of the model. The customer may or may not have administrative control over user permissions. The customer only has administrative power over the OS in an IaaS model.

14. D. Security is always contingent on business drivers and beholden to operational needs. The virtualization engine does not dictate security controls, and the hypervisor may vary (depending on its type and implementation). The SLAs do not drive security controls; they drive performance goals.

15. B. The customer currently always retains legal liability for data loss, even if the provider was negligent or malicious.

16. A. Knowledge of the physical layout and site controls could be of great use to an attacker, so they are kept extremely confidential. The other options are all red herrings.

17. B. Open-source software is available to the public, and often draws inspection from numerous, disparate reviewers. DBMS is not reviewed more or less than other software. All software in a production environment should be secure. That is not a valid discriminator for answering this question, so option C is not optimum. Proprietary software reviews are limited to the personnel in the employ/under contract of the software developer, which narrows the perspective and necessarily reduces the amount of potential reviewers.

18. D. Firewalls do use rules, behavior analytics, and/or content filtering in order to determine which traffic is allowable. Firewalls ought not use random criteria, because any such limitations would be just as likely to damage protection efforts as enhance them.

19. C. A honeypot is meant to draw in attackers but not divulge anything of value. It should not use raw, production, or sensitive data.

20. C. Vulnerability assessments can only detect known vulnerabilities, using definitions. Some malware is known, as are programming flaws. Zero-day exploits, on the other hand, are necessarily unknown until discovered and exercised by an attacker and will therefore not be detected by vulnerability assessments.

Chapter 7: Cloud Application Security

1. B. The other answers all list aspects of SOAP.

2. B. The other answers are all possible stages used in software development.

3. D. The other answers all include aspects of the STRIDE model.

4. A. SAST involves source code review, often referred to as white-box testing.

5. B. This is the definition of authentication.

6. C. Options A and B are also correct, but C is more general and incorporates them both. D is incorrect because sandboxing does not take place in the production environment.

7. B. Options A and C are also correct, but included in B, making B the best choice. D is incorrect because we don't want unauthorized users gaining access.

8. A. In a trusted third-party model of federation, each member organization outsources the review and approval task to a third party they all trust. This makes the third party the identifier (it issues and manages identities for all users in all organizations in the federation), and the various member organizations are the relying parties (the resource providers that share resources based on approval from the third party).

9. B. Option A is incorrect because it refers to a specific application's security elements, meaning it is about an ANF, not the ONF. C is true, but not as complete as B, making B the better choice. D suggests that the framework contains only "some" of the components, which is why B (which describes "all" components) is better.

10. C. REST and SOAP are two common ways to build APIs. Although SOAP is based on XML, SOAP is more accurate. The other two answers are not used for making APIs.

11. B. Remember, there is a one-to-many ratio of ONF to ANF; each organization has one ONF and many ANFs (one for each application in the organization). Therefore, the ANF is a subset of the ONF.

12. B. Option C is also true, but not as comprehensive as B. A and D are simply not true.

13. B. Option B is a description of the standard; the others are not.

14. D. This is the definition of threat modeling.

15. A. We don't use DAM in place of encryption or masking; DAM augments these options without replacing them. "Reactive or imperative" has no meaning in this context, and is only a distractor.

16. D. WAFs operate at Layer 7 of the OSI model.

17. D. Option D is the best, most general, and most accurate answer.

18. C. The other answers are true of SOAP.

19. C. DAST requires a runtime environment. All tests require money, so A is incorrect. Compartmentalization and inflation have no meaning in this context and are just distractors.

20. B. Physical sandboxing creates a test environment completely isolated from the production environment.

Chapter 8: Operations Elements

1. A. There are four tiers of the Uptime Institute's data center redundancy rating system, with 1 being the lowest and 4 the highest.

2. C. The other answers are distractors.

3. D. The development team should not be involved in direct testing of their own software because they bring personal biases and foreknowledge of the application and also because independent perspective is much more useful. All the other answers may be used as part of the testing team.

4. A. Repudiation is an element of the STRIDE model; the rest of the answers are not.

5. C. Resiliency is not an element of the STRIDE model; all the rest of the answers are.

6. B. Team-building has nothing to do with SAST; all the rest of the answers are characteristics of SAST.

7. D. Binary inspection has nothing to do with DAST, and it is not really a term that means anything in our industry (although it could be interpreted as a type of code review, more related to SAST); all the rest of the answers are characteristics of DAST.

8. A. Keystroke logging is not a characteristic of secure KVM design; in fact, secure KVM components should attenuate the potential for keystroke logging. All the rest of the answers are characteristics of secure KVM components.

9. C. Emergency egress redundancy is the only aspect of data centers that can be expected to be found in data centers of any tier; the rest of the answers list characteristics that can be found only in specific tiers.

10. B. Regardless of the tier level or purpose of any data center, design focus for security should always consider health and human safety paramount.

11. B. Parity bits and disk striping are characteristic of RAID implementations. Cloud-bursting is a feature of scalable cloud hosting. Data dispersion uses parity bits but not disk striping; instead, it uses data chunks and encryption. SAN is a data storage technique but not focused on resiliency.

12. A. Cross-training offers attenuation of lost contingency capabilities by ensuring personnel will be able to perform essential tasks, even if they are not primarily assigned to those positions in a full-time capacity. Metered usage is a benefit for cloud customers associated with ensuring value for payment, but not resiliency. Proper placement of HVAC temperature measurement and raised floors both aid in optimizing component performance but are not practically associated with resiliency. This is a difficult question, and it could be read in ways that would suggest other correct answers.

13. C. Changing regulations should not result in lack of availability. All the other answers have caused DoS outages.

14. B. Tier 4 is the highest in the Uptime Institute standard; it is the only suitable tier for life-critical systems. Tier 2 does not provide sufficient redundancy/resiliency for supporting medical services. There are no Tiers 8 or X. As a test-taking tip, it helps to assume all the hospital's systems will migrate to the cloud unless otherwise stated. There could arguably be hospital systems that are not life-critical which wouldn't require Tier 4, but since that detail is not in the question, the broadest reading is appropriate.

15. D. The location of many data centers—rurally situated, distant from metropolitan areas—may create challenges for finding multiple power utility providers and ISPs as those areas just aren't usually served by multiple vendors. Expense is not usually a concern; economies of scale make costs acceptable as part of the pricing structure. Personnel deployment doesn't usually affect access to either type of connection. The carrying medium has nothing to do with challenges for finding multiple providers and is not even a common industry term.

16. D. The height of dropped ceilings is not a security concern, except in action movies. The rest of the answers are all aspects of physical security that should be taken into account when planning and designing a data center.

17. B. The Brewer-Nash model is also known as the Chinese Wall model.

18. B. Type II hypervisors run via the OS on the host machine; this makes them attractive to attackers because both the machine and the OS offer potential attack vectors. *Cat IV* and *converged* are not terms associated with hypervisors. Bare-metal hypervisors (Type I) are less preferable to attackers because they offer less attack surface.

19. C. Data dispersion uses parity bits, data chunks, and encryption. Parity bits and disk striping are characteristic of RAID implementations. Cloud-bursting is a feature of scalable cloud hosting. SAN is a data storage technique but not focused on resiliency.

20. C. Generators require fuel, and fuel is flammable. All the other answers do not represent an appreciable threat to human safety.

Chapter 9: Operations Management

1. C. The full test will involve every asset in the organization, including all personnel. The others will have lesser impact, except for D, which is a red herring.

2. A. The tabletop testing involves only essential personnel and none of the production assets. The others will have greater impact, except for D, which is a red herring.

3. C. Liquid propane does not spoil, which obviates necessity for continually refreshing and restocking it and might make it more cost-effective. The burn rate has nothing to do with its suitability, unless it has some direct bearing on the particular generator the data center owner has chosen. The various relative prices of fuel fluctuate. Flavor is a distractor in this question and means nothing.

4. B. Frustrated employees and managers can increase risk to the organization by implementing their own, unapproved modifications to the environment. The particular interval changes from organization to organization.

5. B. A data center with less than optimum humidity can have a higher static electricity discharge rate. Humidity has no bearing on breaches or theft, and inversion is a nonsense term used as a distractor.

6. D. The UPS is intended to last only long enough to save production data currently being processed. The exact quantity of time will depend on many variables and will differ from one data center to the next.

7. C. Generator power should be online before battery backups fail. The specific amount of time will vary between data centers.

8. B. Automated patching is much faster and more efficient than manual patching. It is, however, not necessarily any less expensive than manual patching. Manual patching is overseen by administrators, who will recognize problems faster than automated tools. Noise reduction is not a factor in patch management at all.

9. C. Checklists serve as a reliable guide for BC/DR activity and should be straightforward enough to use that someone not already an expert or trained in BC/DR response could ostensibly accomplish the necessary tasks. Flashlights and call trees are certainly useful during BC/DR actions, but not for the purpose of reducing confusion and misunderstanding. Control matrices are not useful during BC/DR actions.

10. B. A data center that doesn't follow vendor guidance might be seen as failing to provide due care. Regulations, internal policy, and the actions of competitors might all inform the decision to perform an update and patch, but these don't necessarily bear directly on due care. This is a difficult, nuanced question, and all the answers are good, but option B is the best.

11. A. Regulators are not involved in an organization's CMB; all the rest are.

12. D. Print spooling is not a metric for system performance; all the rest are.

13. B. While the other answers are all steps in moving from normal operations to maintenance mode, we do not necessarily initiate any enhanced security controls.

14. A. If the CMB is receiving numerous change requests to the point where the amount of requests would drop by modifying the baseline, then that is a good reason to change the baseline. None of the other reasons should involve the baseline at all.

15. B. A UPS can provide line conditioning, adjusting power so that it is optimized for the devices it serves and smoothing any power fluctuations; it does not offer any of the other listed functions.

16. A. All deviations from the baseline should be documented, including details of the investigation and outcome. We do not enforce or encourage deviations. Presumably, we would already be aware of the deviation, so "revealed" is not a reasonable answer.

17. A. The more systems that are included in the baseline, the more cost-effective and scalable the baseline is. The baseline does not deal with breaches or version control; those are the provinces of the security office and CMB, respectively. Regulatory compliance might (and usually will) go beyond the baseline and involve systems, processes, and personnel that are not subject to the baseline.

18. C. Joint operating agreements can provide nearby relocation sites so that a disruption limited to the organization's own facility and campus can be addressed at a different facility and campus. UPS systems and generators are not limited to serving needs for localized causes. Regulations do not promote cost savings and are not often the immediate concern during BC/DR activities.

19. D. The Uptime Institute dictates 12 hours of generator fuel for all cloud data center tiers.

20. C. The BC/DR kit is intended to be compact, and generator fuel is too cumbersome to include with the kit. All the other items should be included.

Chapter 10: Legal and Compliance Part 1

1. B. eDiscovery must collect and produce any data pertinent to the legal request that initiated the process.

2. A. Legal controls are those controls that are designed to comply with laws and regulations, whether they be local or international.

3. D. Plausibility, here, is a distractor and not specifically relevant to cloud forensics.

4. D. The value of data itself has nothing to do with it being considered a part of contractual PII even though the data may have value.

5. B. Mandatory breach reporting is the best example of regulated PII components. The rest are generally considered components of contractual PII.

6. B. Personal hobbies are not an element of privacy laws/contracts anywhere in the world (yet).

7. A. The primary advantage of external audits based on the choices given would be that of independence. External audits are typically more independent and therefore lead to more trustworthy results.

8. C. SOX was passed primarily to address the issues of audit independence, poor board oversight, and transparency of findings.

9. A. The SAS 70 was a report used in the past primarily for financial reporting and was oftentimes misused in the service provider context. The SSAE 18 standard and subsequent SOC reports are its successors.

10. A. The SOC 1 report focuses primarily on controls associated with financial services. While IT controls are certainly part of most accounting systems today, the focus is on the controls around those financial systems.

11. D. The SOC 3 report is more of an attestation than a full evaluation of controls associated with a service provider.

12. D. The AICPA is the organization responsible for generating and maintaining what are known as the Generally Accepted Accounting Principles in the United States.

13. A. GLBA deals with financial security and privacy. FERPA deals with data protection in the academic industry, HIPAA in the medical industry. SOX is a distractor here.

14. C. Wholesalers or distributors are generally not regulated, although the products they sell may be.

15. B. A SOC Type I report reviews a specific point in time as opposed to a report of effectiveness over a period of time.

16. D. A SOC Type II report reviews a period of time as opposed to a specific point in time.

17. C. The right to be forgotten is about the individual's right to have data removed from a provider at any time per their request. It is being tried in the EU at the moment but does not yet apply here in the United States.

18. D. Options A, B, and C are reasons leading up to the creation and passage of SOX.

19. C. The most important aspect of GLBA was the creation of a formal information security program.

20. D. Financial controls are not addressed by HIPAA.

Chapter 11: Legal and Compliance Part 2

1. **B.** The lowest level is Level 1, which is self-assessment. Level 2 is an external third-party attestation, and Level 3 is a continuous-monitoring program. Hybridization does not exist as part of the CSA STAR program.

2. **B.** KRI stands for key risk indicator. KRIs help the organization identify and recognize changes to risk.

3. **A.** ISO 31000:2018 specifically focuses on design implementation and management. HIPAA refers to health care regulations, NIST 800-92 is about log management, and ISO 27017 is about cloud-specific security controls.

4. **C.** ENISA specifically identifies the top eight security risks based on likelihood and impact.

5. **C.** The SOC 2 report is not a part of the CSA Star program. It is a totally different audit reporting standard developed by the AICPA.

6. **B.** ISO/IEC 28000:2007 specifically applies to security controls in supply chains. The others address other matters.

7. **C.** Key risk indicators are useful, but they are not a framework. ISO 31000:2018 is an international standard that focuses on designing, implementing, and reviewing risk management processes and practices. NIST SP 800-37 is the Guide for Implementing the Risk Management Framework (RMF), a methodology for handling all organizational risk in a holistic, comprehensive, and continual manner. The European Union Agency for Network and Information Security (ENISA) *Cloud Computing: Benefits, Risks, and Recommendations for Information Security* identifies the top eight cloud security risks.

8. **D.** There is no such thing as zero risk. All the other answers are distractors.

9. **D.** ENISA's top eight security risks of cloud computing do not include availability, even though it is certainly a risk that could be realized.

10. **D.** Avoidance halts the business process, mitigation entails using controls to reduce risk, acceptance involves taking on the risk, and transference usually involves insurance.

11. **B.** A cloud carrier is the intermediary who provides connectivity and transport of cloud services between cloud providers and cloud customers.

12. **A.** Transference usually involves insurance. Avoidance halts the business process, acceptance involves taking on the risk, and mitigation entails using controls to reduce risk.

13. **C.** The use of subcontractors can add risk to the supply chain and should be considered; determining how much you can trust the provider's management of their vendors and suppliers (including subcontractors) is important. Conversely, the customer is not likely to be allowed to review the physical design of the data center (or, indeed, even know the exact location of the data center) or the personnel security specifics for the provider's staff. *Redundant uplink grafts* is a nonsense term used as a distractor.

14. C. Key risk indicators (KRIs) try to predict future risk, while key performance indicators (KPIs) examine events that have already happened. The other answers are just distractors.

15. A. *Enveloping* is a nonsense term, unrelated to risk management. The rest are valid ways to manage risk.

16. A. Hex GBL is a reference to a computer part in Terry Pratchett's fictional Discworld universe. The rest are risk management frameworks.

17. B. Roles and responsibilities should be included in the contract, not the SLA; a good method to determine whether something might belong in the SLA at all is figuring out whether a numerical value is associated with it—in this case, the element involves names and offices (roles), not numerical values, so it's immediately recognizable as something that isn't appropriate for the SLA. Options A, C, D are explicitly defined by exact numbers that describe recurring events/circumstances and are just the sort of elements that belong in the SLA.

18. A. The CSA CCM is an inventory of cloud service security controls that are arranged into separate security domains, not a hierarchy.

19. A. *Transitional* is not a term we associate with types of controls; the rest are.

20. A. An IT analyst is generally not high enough of a position to be able to provide quality information to other stakeholders. However, the IT director would be in such a position, as would the others.

Index

Note to the Reader: Throughout this index **boldfaced** page numbers indicate primary discussions of a topic. *Italicized* page numbers indicate illustrations.

C

Comprehensive Online Learning Environment

Register to gain one year of FREE access to the online interactive learning environment and test bank to help you study for your (ISC)² CCSP certification exam—included with your purchase of this book!

The online test bank includes the following:

- **Assessment Test** to help you focus your study to specific objectives
- **Chapter Tests** to reinforce what you've learned
- **Practice Exams** to test your knowledge of the material
- **Digital Flashcards** to reinforce your learning and provide last-minute test prep before the exam
- **Searchable Glossary** to define the key terms you'll need to know for the exam

Register and Access the Online Test Bank

To register your book and get access to the online test bank, follow these steps:

1. Go to bit.ly/SybexTest.
2. Select your book from the list.
3. Complete the required registration information, including answering the security verification to prove book ownership. You will be emailed a pin code.
4. Follow the directions in the email or go to www.wiley.com/go/sybextestprep.
5. Enter the pin code you received and click the "Activate PIN" button.
6. On the Create an Account or Login page, enter your username and password, and click Login. A "Thank you for activating your PIN!" message will appear. If you don't have an account already, create a new account.
7. Click the "Go to My Account" button to add your new book to the My Products page.

Do you need more practice? Check out CCSP *Official (ISC)² Practice Tests, 2nd Edition* (ISBN: 978-1-119-60349-8, available February 2020). With nearly 1000 additional questions spread across the domains and two additional practice exams, it's a great way to build your confidence and readiness for exam day.